Forensic Linguistics

John Olsson

Forensic Linguistics

*An introduction to Language,
Crime and the Law*

John Olsson

continuum
LONDON • NEW YORK

Continuum
The Tower Building, 11 York Road, London SE1 7NX
15 East 26th Steet, New York, NY 10010

First published 2004 by Continuum.
Reprinted 2004
© John Olsson 2004

British Library Cataloguing-in-Publication Data
A catalogue record for this book is available from the British Library.

Library of Congress Cataloguing-in-Publication Data
A catalogue record for this book is available from the Library of Congress.

ISBN 0–8264–6108–5 (hardback)
ISBN 0–8264–6109–3 (paperback)

Typeset by RefineCatch Ltd, Bungay, Suffolk
Printed and bound in Great Britain by
Antony Rowe Ltd, Chippenham, Wilts

CONTENTS

DEDICATION

For Jean

ACKNOWLEDGEMENTS

There are several people I would like to thank for their assistance in making this book possible. In fact, that is not quite true: there are not several people, but a great many, starting with my grandparents, parents, aunts and uncles and teachers. However, such a list would be far too long, so I will have to confine myself to those of more recent provenance. Firstly, I am indebted to Dr June Luchjenbroers of Bangor University, Wales, whose patient editing in the first instance helped to make the forensic texts themselves even more central to the book.

Secondly, I would like to place on record my thanks to Professor Malcolm Coulthard and to Mr Tim Johns, my former supervisors at the University of Birmingham, both of whom encouraged me to devote more time to discourse analysis and technical writing.

For specialised help in the preparation of this book, I am deeply indebted to:

- Mr Derek Painter, former head of mathematics at Llanfair Caereinion High School, Powys, Wales, and now its deputy head teacher, who read the sections on statistics and made many helpful suggestions. I hope I have implemented all of these – but if any errors remain, they are entirely my own. Mr Painter has also kindly given of his valuable time to several other forensic projects involving the synergies of computation;
- Professor Robert Hagiwara, of the University of Manitoba, who – with very little time to do so – read the phonetics chapter and gave important technical and other advice for its improvement.

I think it is important to mention Nebraska Wesleyan University, where I teach the world's first online course in forensic linguistics. NWU is a true liberal arts college in the best mid-west tradition because it is also a very forward looking university – being not only the first school in the world to teach forensic linguistics online, but also the first to include forensic linguistics as part of a postgraduate forensic science course.

Finally, my special thanks go to Anthony Haynes, Jenny Lovel, Sylvia Marson and Benn Linfield, and everyone else at Continuum for working so hard to bring this project to fruition.

John Olsson

CHARTS, FIGURES, TABLES, TEXTS, FORENSIC TEXTS AND EXERCISES

Charts

Figures

Tables

Texts

Forensic texts

Exercises

INTRODUCTION

WHAT IS FORENSIC LINGUISTICS?

Forensic linguistics is an application of linguistics. Perhaps then we should begin by asking what linguistics is. Linguistics is the scientific study of language. There are many branches within linguistics, and the linguist might specialize in anything from language acquisition to grammar, language and society or – as in the present case – language, crime and the law.

In addition, linguists look at how the individual's use of language changes through the course of life, language universals – the elements shared by all languages, the structure of language sounds, language and society, and of course the subject of this book – language, crime and the law.

Language is the most advanced means of communication known to us, and its use is absolutely central to our existence. In the past few decades, the study of language and languages has greatly increased at centres of higher learning throughout the world. This has had massive benefits to both the science itself, and to students worldwide: whereas previously, linguistics inhabited its very own ivory tower within academia, it has in this time become less and less concerned with abstract theory and more concerned with the application of knowledge to everyday issues. One area that has greatly benefited from this approach is the interface between language and crime. In 1968, when Jan Svartvik analysed the statements of Timothy John Evans – hanged for the murder of his wife and baby, and posthumously pardoned – he coined the term *forensic linguistics* but for years little happened in the field. In time, however, it became evident that linguists could be of service to the law by helping those who had been treated unjustly by it, and in the early 1990s Malcolm Coulthard began to analyse other police statements. One of these was the text attributed to Derek Bentley, also hanged in the 1950s and – thanks largely to Coulthard – later pardoned.

In the interim, forensic linguistics has grown exponentially, both in the number of people with an interest in practising it and in the number of disciplines and sub-disciplines within its ambit, some of which are listed in Table 1.1.

In this book we will be discussing most of the above areas of forensic linguistics, except for language rights, courtroom discourse, and legal interpreting and translation. This is not because I view these areas as less interesting or important, but rather because they require a different approach from those areas that I will be dealing with.

Table 1.1 *Disciplines of forensic linguistics*

Category	Description
Authorship identification	Identifying authors of texts
Mode identification	Ascertaining whether a text was produced by speech, writing or some combination of both (e.g. part written, part dictated)
Legal interpreting and translation	Interpreting and translating in the courtroom, *viva* interpreting for police and defendants/witnesses; translating statements and other legal documents – issues of accuracy and fairness, the role of interpreters, their licensing, 'control', etc.
Transcribing verbal statements	In some legal systems statements are audio/video recorded and require transcription for courtroom use – issues of completeness and bias
The language and discourse of courtrooms	A study of the relationship between courtroom participants and the language they use – issues of power, prejudice, culture clashes, etc.
Language rights	These include: the language rights of minority groups in cultures dominated by other languages or other dialects of the same language, the linguistic rights of those without language, and the oppressiveness of bureaucratic language. Note that some of the other areas mentioned here are also concerned (sometimes indirectly) with language rights, e.g. interpreting, transcription of statements, courtroom discourse, etc.
Statement analysis	Analysing witness statements for their veracity
Forensic phonetics	Analysis of audio material for speaker identification and other purposes; voice line-ups

Textual status	Analysing texts and auditory material for their genuineness, e.g. genuine *vs* hoax emergency calls, genuine *vs* simulated suicide/ransom notes, etc.; assessing risk from text

FORENSIC LINGUISTICS: AN UMBRELLA SCIENCE FOR MANY FIELDS OF STUDY

A forensic linguist is sometimes a general practitioner, and sometimes a specialist in any of a number of sub-areas within the science. For example, if you are a Shakespeare scholar, questions of authorship might interest you. If your interest is in phonetics, then voice identification may appeal. A conversational analyst might be interested in the detection of emergency hoax calls, while a dictation specialist may wish to analyse text for mode (speech, dictation, writing). Someone with a background in psychology, however, could be interested in discovering what it is that separates genuine from simulated text. A specialist in a foreign language, on the other hand, may be required to analyse English-language forensic text produced by speakers of that foreign language. A police officer with an interest in forensic linguistics could seek to study the question of veracity in language. A judge might take an interest in courtroom language. A rehabililated offender could study the language of prison life. A doctor might investigate the use of language and crime in the medical context. Child language experts might study how children respond to questions from adults, what their answers mean and their reliability as witnesses. Specialists in reading and interpreting handwritten manuscripts could investigate forensic textual criticism.

As the reader can see, there are few if any boundaries, but perhaps we should make this discussion more concrete by looking closely at the many different types of forensic text which the linguist encounters in forensic work.

TYPES OF FORENSIC TEXT

Any text or item of spoken language is potentially a forensic text. If a text is somehow implicated in a legal or criminal context then it is a forensic text. A parking ticket could become a forensic text, a will, a letter, a book, an essay, a contract, a health department letter, a thesis – almost anything.

In practice, however, forensic linguists have mostly confined their attention to a small number of text types, some of which are included in the Forensic Text Appendix in this book.

Thus, the Appendix contains, among others, a forged will and a statement alleging sexual assault. There is a letter from a pipe bomber attempting to rationalize his crimes and a complaint about the practice of verballing.[1] We have a young mother claiming that she was carjacked and her children kidnapped and in another text the same woman appealing at a press conference for the safe return of her children. Finally, in another text we see this woman admitting to having killed her children.

There is a stalker text from John Hinckley – the man who attempted to kill President Reagan – addressed to a film star. There is the well-known police statement wrongly attributed to Derek Bentley and there are several other defendant and witness statements. There are a number of emergency calls to a fire department – several of which are hoax and the ransom note from Carlos the Jackal demanding safe passage out of Austria for himself and his hostages. There are also several other ransom demands, including that for the Enigma machine stolen from Bletchley Park in England. There are the Gilfoyle 'confession' and 'suicide' letters, as well as examples of smear, hate, trick, terror and incitement mail. Several confessions will be found among the texts, including that of a Serbian truck driver who transported bodies for the authorities during the Kosovo conflict. You will find a pair of texts plagiarized by two medical students, and an excerpt from the Unabomber's text. There are the apparently forced confessions of the three westerners in the Saudi terror case, and the ransom note in the JonBénet Ramsey murder case, as well as the ransom note in the Lindbergh kidnap and murder. There are several death row final statements; a number of the seventeenth-century Salem confessions; a 'suicide' note faked for literary purposes (this is not strictly speaking a forensic text, but is of interest to forensic linguists for comparison purposes). Finally, there are several attested suicide notes including that of author Virginia Woolf and several elderly patients in hospital who were unwilling to burden their relatives with their illnesses, and miscellaneous other texts. Many of these texts are disputed; quite a few are attested. There are *no* invented examples. What is not included? I have tried to think of everything, but have become aware of several text types that could have been included. For example, Internet scams and hoaxes, e-mail threats, e-mail communications which include computer viruses, etc. And, if this were an audio book, I would have included examples of disputed spoken language.

However, despite these gaps I hope that the reader will be able to judge from the above that the types of text encountered by forensic linguists are many and varied, and are thus of great importance as linguistic objects of study. Of course they also have importance for their social, legal and criminal provenance.

Those interested in developing their knowledge of forensic linguistics come to the discipline at a very interesting time. The science is young and new; nothing is yet cast in stone. Universities around the world are beginning to offer programmes in the field. Law enforcement agencies are beginning to see the importance of forensic linguistics. Within the science itself, many new developments are in the air. The discipline's main journal, *Forensic Linguistics*, has now been established for some years, but continues to be fresh and exciting in its approach. The whole area is ripe with debate and argument, and there is a healthy interest in new techniques and methods, although most universities have yet to commit major resources to research. At the time of writing, several books are newly published or are about to be published. There is a second major title in the field by Gerald McMenamin, another work edited by John Gibbon. There is Malcolm Coulthard's long-awaited study of the field, while many other major practitioners and researchers in this science are also continuing to contribute. The website www.thetext.co.uk will continue to list and review books and journals in this field.

WHO SHOULD USE THIS BOOK

This book is intended for students of forensic linguistics at undergraduate and postgraduate levels. It can be used on its own or in conjunction with other titles in the field. As indicated above, the book is also intended for non-specialists, such as law enforcement officers, legal professionals at all levels – from the newly qualified solicitor to the senior barrister, the magistrate to the judge. Psychologists and sociologists will also find the title of interest, particularly those who already have an interest in language. I have also received many e-mails from forensic chemists, fingerprint experts and even handwriting analysts who have been keen to learn about forensic linguistics. Nebraska Wesleyan University now include a course in Forensic Linguistics as part of their Masters of Forensic Science degree. Therefore, it is evident that experts in all forensic disciplines will be able to find this book useful.

HOW TO USE THIS BOOK

The first six chapters of the book are devoted to authorship, which is a major topic in forensic linguistics, but other areas such as statement analysis and plagiarism have not been neglected. It is suggested that you work through the authorship section thoroughly before going on to the other areas of forensic linguistics. You should do all the exercises given (see Appendix A, for my comments on the exercises from a forensic linguistic perspective). Additionally, thoroughly familiarize yourself with the relevant texts in the Appendix. As mentioned above, the book contains significantly more forensic texts than any other book published to date. There is also a forensic linguistic website at www.thetext.co.uk. You should consider authorship to be one of the cornerstones of forensic linguistics. A grasp of authorship will enable you to progress to the other areas of the discipline. The university lecturer or college instructor using this book could consider going through a chapter a week in the first instance and then perhaps return to study areas of particular interest to the group at a later date. I believe this is a book that can be studied at many levels: while it is possible to gloss over the details and go for the broad picture in the first instance, sections can also be looked at in minute detail.

ABOUT THE AUTHOR

John Olsson spent a number of years in the 1970s as an interpreter for the Metropolitan Police in London, after which he studied psychology at degree level. A stint in business was followed by two post-graduate degrees in linguistics at Bangor, Wales and Birmingham, England. His M.Phil. dissertation was a statistical and qualitative analysis of the Derek Bentley text. He is frequently consulted by solicitors and law enforcement agencies requiring opinions on forensic texts, and operates an Internet consultancy service. He also runs online forensic linguistics courses for private individuals, law enforcement agencies and universities at www.the text.co.uk. He is an adjunct professor at Nebraska Wesleyan University in the Masters of Forensic Science program.

CHAPTER 1

Previous authorship studies

BIBLICAL AUTHORSHIP DISPUTES

Authorship controversies do not seem to have existed prior to the eighteenth century, quite possibly because up until then books had not been so widely distributed, and the Cartesian concept of individuality and the individual ownership of ideas had yet to receive general acceptance. As is generally accepted the earliest-known controversy related to the authorship of the Bible, and was voiced by a German priest, H. B. Witter, who in 1711 pointed out that the different names for divinity in the Pentateuch could indicate that several authors had contributed to it. Jean Astruc, a French medical doctor arrived at a similar conclusion later in the century, while J. G. Eichhorn, a Lutheran professor at the University of Jena, reached this view about 100 years after Witter (Eichhorn, 1812). Interest among scholars in biblical authorship questions intensified with the rise of Darwinism and related theories and continues to the present day.

SHAKESPEARIAN AUTHORSHIP DISPUTES

Some time after Witter but before Eichhorn, according to Olivia Hill (Hill, online) the earliest reference to the Shakespeare controversy occurred. In 1785 the Reverend James Wilmot wrote that Bacon was the real author of the Shakespeare plays, but did not publish his ideas, as he had no appetite for contention. For this reason the controversy did not really surface until James Corton Cowell first presented it to his local philosophical society in Ipswich, England in 1805. However, it was not until almost half a century later that the interest in authorship questions began to be pursued scientifically.

EARLY SCIENTIFIC AND STATISTICAL APPROACHES

Among those who expressed an early interest was Augustus de Morgan, the first Professor of Mathematics at University College, London. In 1851 he wrote a letter to his friend the Rev. Heald at Cambridge, suggesting that Heald, who had expressed an interest in the question of the authorship of biblical letters attributed to St Paul, should:

> count a large number of words in Herodotus, say all of the first book, and count all the letters; divide the second number by the first, giving the average number of letters per word in that book. Do the same in the second book. I

should expect a very close approximation. If Book 1 gave 5.624 letters per word, it would not surprise me if Book 2 gave 5.619. But I should not wonder if the same result applied to two books of Thuycidides gave, say 5.713 and 5.728. That is to say I should expect the slight difference between one writer and the other to be well maintained against each other, and very well agreeing with themselves. If this fact were established, then, if St Paul's Epistles which began with . . . gave 5.428 and the Hebrews gave 5.516 for example [implying a difference of just below 2 per cent as evidence of a difference in authorship], I should feel quite sure that the Greek of the Hebrews (passing no verdict on whether or not Paul wrote in Hebrew and others translated) was not from the pen of Paul . . .

(De Morgan, 1882: 215–16)

Although De Morgan appears to have been the first to express these ideas, it is not known whether he studied the topic in any greater depth than this. Then, thirty years later, a professor of physics and mechanics at Ohio State University, T. C. Mendenhall, published his thoughts on authorship of text, primarily using word-length average as a marker (Mendenhall, 1887). He published a second article some years later (Mendenhall, 1901), but does not appear to have taken any further interest in the subject of statistical measurement of authorship.

LATER STATISTICAL STUDIES

Udney Yule – the well-known Cambridge theoretical statistician – had been interested in the statistics of what we now term genetic engineering and the work of Mendel in particular before becoming interested in authorship questions. He saw *mean sentence length* (Udney Yule, 1938, 1944) as a viable marker. However, neither his approach, nor that of any of the other scientists of the time, resulted in anything remotely resembling the ability to 'fingerprint' authors, although each of the values suggested – e.g. average word length, average sentence length, etc. – has proved useful in different kinds of language testing. Other statisticians have since shown great interest in authorship attribution, including the analysis by Mosteller and Wallace (1964) of the Federalist papers, and Kenny (1982). However, one of the disadvantages with pure statisticians approaching this issue is that generally they do not bring any knowledge of language with them to the problem. If Yule, for example, had been a linguist, he would have been aware that there are significant differences between sentence length in speech from that of writing. To be more precise, it is probably the case that mean sentence length reduces as formality increases. Sentence length, just like any other measure, is therefore dependent on genre and register as much (if not more) than it is dependent on the individual writer/speaker. This is a basic error that many non-linguists have fallen into repeatedly, even though these elementary facts about language have been known for decades e.g. de Vito since the 1960s. This is not to say that statisticians should not have input into these questions. On the contrary, I am sure that collaborations between linguists and statisticians can prove very fruitful.

THE ERA OF COMPUTATIONAL LINGUISTICS

From the mid-1980s onwards, powerful computers became more widely available and the science of *computational linguistics* began to emerge. The field is really a partnership between computational studies and linguistics.

In computational linguistics the goal of authorship research is essentially that of finding authorship algorithms. For some computational linguists it is axiomatic that individual style can be attributed to the level of precision we associate with the science of fingerprinting. This is a position which I refute utterly, and discuss in more detail in this and following chapters.

For example, Ephratt (Ephratt, online) says that 'each specific text carries the fingerprints of its creator'. His belief in algorithms stems from his observation that text uses all possible linguistic domains, from semantics to phonology. Each domain offers, according to this author, choices. The longer the text, the greater the number of choices. The text is an end product of choices. That is why, according to Ephratt, each text carries its author's 'fingerprint'. However, Ephratt does not offer any scientific evidence of author 'fingerprinting'. Many claims of linguistic 'fingerprinting' have been made, but not one – to my certain knowledge – has offered scientific evidence of any quality. The flaws in Ephratt's approach are not uncommon, and centre primarily around the question of choice. We may have choice with regard to some lexical items, some of the time, but our ability to choose in language is generally exaggerated. The more formal the context, the less choice there usually is, and even in informal situations it is not the case that choice is necessarily as wide as Ephratt and others suggest.

Moreover, the anomaly (and even irony) of *choice* as a factor of authorial stability does not appear to have occurred to some analysts: put simply, if we have choice, what is there to stop us exercising it? Why would we limit ourselves? The idea of choice is in strong contrast to those who believe that authors have habits.

There appears to be a belief among some who favour a computational linguistic approach that all aspects of language can be reduced to mathematics, for example Nilo *et al.* (1999) favour the application of principal component analysis to authorship studies. However, the mathematics of this method is almost alien to most linguists, as indeed are most kinds of factor analysis.

Not only are some of the mathematical methods in use quite abstruse, but often the results cannot be applied to forensic work, because in general computational linguistics tends to take the easy way out – failing to show an interest in authorship problems except where there are large amounts of data.

Among those working in a computer/literary tradition, J. F. Burrows favours a multivariate approach to authorship (a type of statistical method of which factor analysis is one among several sub-types). So far he has confined his work to long literary texts, such as those by Jane Austen. Usually the excerpts he looks at have a minimum length of 2,000 words (Hoover D.L.), Burrows (1987).

Computational linguistics is really a 'curious relationship between the twin disciplines of computer-assisted classification and literary description based on empirical measures' according to Craig (Craig, online), who questions the value of computational studies as an aid to understanding works of literature. Since the techniques favoured by computational linguistics do not take into account the specific problems of texts in forensic cases – i.e. too few texts which are invariably too short – computational linguistics usually has very little application to authorship attribution questions. The importance of developing authorship attribution methodologies for short texts is critical, and computational linguistics does not so far appear to have addressed this question at all. Some statistical methods in use in forensic linguistics are discussed at different stages in the book, including in this section.

Here is a typical example of an authorship attribution method, which actually demands large corpora of long texts (between 17,000 and 50,000 words) although it claims to work on 'short' texts. Stamatos et al. (Stamatos, online) claim that their method of authorship attribution relies exclusively on a set of style markers. They claim that other methods which use lexical measures require long texts and large corpora. This is a fairly typical approach to authorship by many non-forensic linguists. In forensic work we often find texts of fewer than 300 words and most texts are fewer than 700 words long. Stamatos et al.'s method requires at least a dozen author candidates and in some cases forty or fifty texts per author. They claim their method is successful 87 per cent of the time. However, for a test to be of value in forensic work it should be successful better than 95 or even 99.5 per cent of the time, otherwise its usefulness in the provision of court evidence is highly limited. Students of forensic linguistics need to be aware that this is a discipline which is driven by the requirements of legal evidence.

Because there seems to be some misunderstanding about the requirements of forensic corpora, it is perhaps worth reiterating that many forensic inquiries present too little data to justify a full-scale statistical study. Often there are no more than two candidates, as few as three attested texts, and perhaps no more than one or two questioned texts. This is why most methods described as authorship detection do not work in the forensic context.

AUTHORSHIP AND THE BIRTH OF FORENSIC LINGUISTICS

Almost simultaneous with the rise in computational hardware – but conceptually quite separate – the discipline of forensic linguistics came into being with the publication by Svartvik of his classic study into the altered police statements in the *Evans* case (Svartvik, 1968) some fifteen years after Timothy John Evans had been hanged. John Christie had murdered a succession of women at his home in 10 Rillington Place, west London, and had duped Evans into believing he, Evans, was partly responsible for the death of his own wife and child, which had actually taken place at Christie's hands. Evans had gone to his uncle's home in Merthyr Tydfil, south Wales, but after a short period he had handed himself into the police and confessed to having killed his wife. Two statements were given at Merthyr Tydfil and two at Notting Hill police station, London, where Evans was taken on the day following his arrest. In his analysis, Svartvik demonstrated the presence of two very different registers in Evans's statements. However, this case was not an authorship study as such: its importance lies in Svartvik's pioneering technique in analysing textual alteration, and his name for the new science, *forensic linguistics*.

Some years later, Coulthard (1994) undertook a groundbreaking linguistic study of the alleged statement of Derek Bentley who, like Evans, had been hanged in the 1950s. Coulthard's analysis of this statement was a major factor in Bentley's posthumous pardon, but whereas Svartvik's investigation was primarily a descriptive statistical study, Coulthard's is more of a general linguistic analysis. Coulthard refers to his approach as *forensic discourse analysis*, but it can also be seen as a combination of insights from different linguistic fields including speech act theory, corpus linguistics, register, and even psycholinguistics.

MORTON: QSUM ANALYSIS

In marked contrast to Coulthard's approach to forensic linguistics, Morton has proposed the analysis of text using the Qsum or Cusum (abbreviation for cumulative sum) method (Michaelson and Morton, 1990). Morton's method is interesting because Morton himself admits to having no idea why Qsum works. Although a biblical scholar of some reputation, Morton makes no claims to any linguistic knowledge. However, he does make high claims for his method, the chief of which is that Qsum always works, even on short texts. According to Morton, speakers' habits do not vary significantly, and there is no difference between speech and writing in terms of an individual's habits.

The assumption behind Cusum analysis is that, in using language, each speaker exhibits a set of unique habits, and that these habits form statistically identifiable patterns in the text. One such habit, according to Michaelson and Morton (*ibid.*), is the number of two- and three-letter words in a sentence. Another is vowel-initial words. To carry out a Qsum test on habits such as the use of vowel-initial words and two–three-letter words, you would first identify all occurrences of each type of word in the text, and then plot their distribution in each sentence. You would compare the qsum distribution for these habits with the average sentence length for the text. These two sets of values should track each other. Certainly this does seem, from Chart 1, to be the case. According to Michaelson and Morton (1990) and Farringdon (1996), any altered section of the text would exhibit a different pattern than the rest of the text.

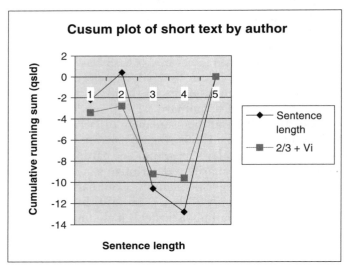

Chart 1 *A Cusum plot of an earlier version of the preceding two paragraphs (see endnotes)*

In fact this is exactly what Chart 2 seems, at first, to show: text from another author was inserted after sentence 2. Looking at Chart 2, we do seem to see some discrepancy between the values of the two reference points between sentences 3–5, which does indeed appear to be larger than

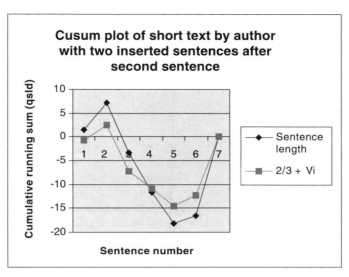

Chart 2 *A Cusum plot of the same text as the previous chart, but with an inserted section*

the differences seen elsewhere in the two plots. However, the key question is this: just exactly what constitutes a discrepancy? How do we judge when we have a good fit? Clearly, interpretation of such results will tend to be subjective. Schils and de Haan (1995) expressed other concerns about Cusum, namely that there is 'considerable intra-author variation', which would preclude a reliable basis for inter-author discrimination, while Sanford *et al.* (1994) found that the Cusum technique was 'based on assumptions which are at best of limited reliability, and are most likely completely false'. Canter and Chester (1997) conducted a detailed evaluation of a revised Cusum technique and found that 'the weighted Cusum technique does not reliably discriminate between single- and multiple-authored texts'. Methods which claim to be infallible, and those which blatantly run counter to linguistic knowledge and experience should be treated with scepticism. The Cusum technique falls into both of these categories. In the next section I am going to take a brief look at statistics – at

Exercise 1.1

It has sometimes been suggested that Morton's linking of words of two and three letters in a sentence with sentence length is not accidental, in other words that there is a correspondence between numbers of short words and sentence length. Collect together about ten texts (but do not use any of the forensic texts in Appendix B)[2] and see if you can give a demonstration for or against this proposition.

least a more conventional use of statistics in forensic linguistics than that discussed in this section. In the meantime consider the following question.

HOW DO WE USE STATISTICS IN FORENSIC LINGUISTICS?

In forensic linguistics we use statistics to measure *probability*. Actually all sciences base their results on probability. No science 'proves' or attempts to prove anything. In the following paragraphs I am going to simplify the demonstration considerably, just for ease of understanding. Please go away and consume several textbooks on the subject of statistics, and even consult a statistician. If you are really dedicated to understanding forensic linguistics, you can do no better than enrolling yourself in a course of statistics. The level of statistical knowledge usually found in the forensic linguistics community currently is fairly low. You might like to try to help overcome this situation!

The first step in your inquiry is to gather evidence, in the case of forensic linguistics this means the texts relevant to an inquiry. So, if we want to discover who wrote a particular letter (or other text) we gather texts from our chief suspect and several other possible suspects, people whose backgrounds, professions and levels of education are all fairly similar to each other. Let us assume we have three suspects, A, B and C, each of whom submits three questioned texts. These are in addition to the three questioned texts, Q, in the inquiry.

We then apply a test[3] to each text, with the following results:

Text 1.1		Results of a hypothetical authorship test			
		A	B	C	Q
	1	30.9	35.3	41.2	36.7
	2	31.1	36.6	40.7	34.9
	3	30.4	35.6	39.8	35.8
Mean		**30.80**	**35.83**	**40.57**	**35.80**

From the first row across the table we see that there are three candidates, A, B and C, with a set of texts, 'Q', i.e. Questioned.[4] A, B and C have each submitted three texts, labelled in the first column 1, 2 and 3. When the test is applied, A averages 30.8, B averages 35.83 and C averages 40.57. The Q texts average 35.8. Of course B *appears* the closest, but we cannot make an attribution just on what *appears* to be the case. Rather, we have to submit every set of texts to a comparison with every other set of texts. Thus we have to compare A with Q, B with Q and C with Q, and even A with B, B with C and A with C. We do this with the following, highly specific question in mind: 'What is the probability that A and Q are the same author?'; '. . . that B and Q are the same author . . .?', etc. Here are the results of the above test:

Text 1.2	Probability of authorship across a given candidature
A–Q	0.005
B–Q	0.962
C–Q	0.002
A–B	0.001
A–C	0.000
B–C	0.001

From the above test we see that the probability of A and Q being of the same authorship is 0.005, in other words 5/1,000. This is pretty low. If I told you the chance of your horse winning was 1/1,000, would you bet? I doubt it. Going through all of the other possibilities we note they are all similarly low, except for B. B appears pretty high: a probability of 962 out of a thousand, in other words a 96.2 per cent probability. Generally in statistics we accept the result of a test if it has a probability of over 95 per cent, in other words more than 19 chances out of 20, although this is not always high enough for forensic purposes. Incidentally, the type of statistical test used to compare two sets of texts (or two of anything, in fact) is called a *t test*. You will need to remember this term, and study its meaning and use in books on the subject of statistics.

So, to recap:

- A probability of 0.005 is 5/1,000. This is low.
- It is written $p < 0.05$ (i.e. less than 5 per cent), or $p < 0.01$ (less than 1 per cent).**
- A probability of 96 is 96 out of a hundred. This is high.
- It is written $p > 0.95$, (i.e. more than 95 per cent).

** Note: all the candidates except **B** were $p < 0.01$ (i.e. less than 1 per cent) – see next section.

QUANTITATIVE AUTHORSHIP ATTRIBUTION: CHASKI AND THE X^2

In a blind trial of four women writers, Chaski (2001: 10) found that in a frequency count of a set of verbal features, three of the possible candidates demonstrated $p < 0.05$ with regard to the authorship of Q, the questioned text. This appeared encouraging because, as it turned out, none of these three candidates was the author of Q. Conversely, the actual author (designated Author No. 016) demonstrated $p = 0.23$. In other words it would seem that the probability of the actual author being the author was 23 per cent, according to one interpretation of Chaski's results. For Chaski both sets of results seem to have been a triumph: in her article she appears pleased that her non-authors showed less than 5/100 chances of being the author, while the actual author (as it turned out) showed 23/100 chances of being the author. However, as Grant and Baker (2001) point out, $p = 0.23$ is not high enough to make an attribution. Indeed, in our own earlier example, we only admitted one author – B: B demonstrated $p = 0.96$. All that can be said about Chaski's study is that Author No. 016 (the actual author) cannot be discounted as the writer of the questioned text. But, since the other authors were not below 0.01, then it is not possible to discount any of them as the questioned author. In other words, regrettably, Chaski's test proves nothing. Evidently, she requires a more powerful test.

In using the X^2 (pron: 'ki squared') statistic Chaski (2001) dismisses qualitative or descriptive data as having any application to forensic linguistics, and sets out to demonstrate that text can and must be evaluated empirically. As Chaski phrases it, linguists have a responsibility to 'create . . . theoretically sound hypotheses, test these hypotheses and perform the empirical evaluation of our own methods' (Chaski, 2001: 2). However, as noted above, Chaski's results do not measure up to her claims of being scientific, and moreover there are many in the social science community who would take issue with her claim that non-quantitative results do not constitute scientific methodology. On the positive side, Chaski is one of the few linguists who is realistic about text length as it applies to forensic work, and so this makes her study an important milestone in the application of statistics to forensic work.

McMENAMIN: FORENSIC STYLISTICS

McMenamin (1993) describes a number of authorship attribution cases. One involved attributing authorship of a questioned diary in a homicide inquiry. McMenamin entered the known and questioned texts into a database, and then formulated a series of categories under which to make comparisons between the known and questioned texts. These included the overall design of pages, punctuation, orthography, etc., in addition to lexico-grammatical features. With characteristic attention to detail he even included notes on categories such as *Expressions of Cleaning And Grooming*.

McMenamin then took each category and listed the similarities and dissimilarities between the known and questioned texts, finally making a convincing attribution of the questioned text to its author.

In the 'Mrs Brown'[5] case McMenamin looked for the style of 'a single individual and a set of identifying characteristics found in her language' (McMenamin, 1993: 3). What is distinctive about McMenamin's approach is that he does not make a full comparison between the candidates, and then make a judgment between them. He studies the material, makes a preliminary attribution, and then seeks to find evidence in favour of his preliminary findings, basing his attribution on whether he does in fact find the necessary evidence.

The first of McMenamin's categories in the Brown case was *Format of Page Arrangement*, a category I have sometimes found useful in attribution work, especially where texts are entered in word processors or are produced on typewriters.

McMenamin's next category is *Punctuation*. He successfully demonstrates that the known author uses the same types of punctuation, in similar proportions, to those found in the questioned text. This, too, is a technique I have found useful in a number of inquiries. It seems that in many cases inter-author variation is significantly higher than intra-author variation.

Misspellings is another category found to be of importance by McMenamin in his Mrs Brown inquiry as many of the spellings of this author seem to be quite idiosyncratic. There are several other categories including one termed 'profanity'. Referring to the questioned texts and the known texts of Mrs 'Brown' he relays the information that the known texts of Mrs 'Brown' and the questioned texts share 17/26 items of profanity in common. For McMenamin this seems to be very convincing evidence. He says: 'It is extremely unlikely that this close lexical match in profanity could be due to chance coincidence between different known and questioned authors' (McMenamin, 1993: 9). I am quite sure that McMenamin is absolutely right in this point, and in fact the odd spellings of some of the profanity terms are very distinctive. There are very close matches between the known and questioned texts: nobody would dispute that.

However, not all courts would accept McMenamin's methodology, and some might consider phrases like 'extremely unlikely' not to have any scientific meaning. This issue is specifically dealt with in Chapter 3.

But those who would dismiss McMenamin's method of attribution, should look closely at the requirements of evidence under the 'Daubert' rules. In fact McMenamin's method meets three out of the four 'Daubertian' conditions:

- the use of the technique is widespread and is considered to be reliable;
- the technique has been subjected to peer review;
- there is general acceptance in the relevant scientific community.

Arguably, McMenamin's method also has the merit of being repeatable[6]: we could find these and similar categories in other texts, and we could differentiate authors on the basis of such categories, and in fact I have done so on a number of occasions. I have to admit I like McMenamin's method. His style of writing is clear and unambiguous. His presentation of results is simple and straightforward. However, there is also great depth to his observations.

HÄNLEIN: AUTHOR RECOGNITION

Heike Hänlein's (1998) study evaluates the styles of several journalists writing freelance for *Time* magazine. From the outset Hänlein makes clear[7] that her aim is to achieve a method of authorship recognition, rather than attribution or identification. According to Hänlein, an identification task is one where the author is not known, whereas recognition involves highlighting those characteristics of an author which we can distinguish as different from other authors. Hänlein makes some valuable points about the focus of authorship studies having moved from canonical works of literature to language encounters and texts of all types – not excluding documents as diverse as Australian land treaties between white settlers and aboriginal peoples, police statements and copyright claims. Taking us through different views of style from classical times onwards, Hänlein then considers style in terms of a person's character (Plato); style in terms of a set of prescriptions (*ars rhetorica*). Later she views style as the 'dress of thought' (a quote often attributed only to Samuel Johnson (1779) but which is also found in Richardson's *Clarissa* (1747): 'for what are words but the body and dress of thought?').

In antiquity *ars rhetorica* contained five parts (which are self-explanatory): *inventio, disposito, memoria, elocutio, pronunciatio*. However, Pierre de la Ramée (also known as Peter Ramus) proposed that *inventio, disposito* and *memoria* were part of logic, not of rhetoric: *ars rhetorica* was reduced to *elocutio* and *pronunciatio* and finally to the notion of figure of speech. It did not matter what was said, only how it was said. The relationship between text and context was lost. As Sandblom has said:

> Ramus[8] reducerade sin definition av retorik i Rhetorica till enbart orna-mentering eller tillämpningen av troper. Detta innebar att retorik enbart handlade om hur man sade saker och inte vad man sade.
>
> (Sandblom, 1997, Sandblom, online)

Probably, we owe the rescue of *ars rhetorica* to Francis Bacon, who advocated a plain style of writing. He in turn had borrowed much from Thomas More and Erasmus. 'Dressing' thought had always implied concealment of feeling, but this notion became obsolete in the new romantic age. In fact, new genres such as private letters, could not have surfaced under those conditions. Style came to be considered as a set of features or characteristics which were 'natural to the writer' (George Puttenham, cited in Hänlein, 1998: 26).

Close reading

More recently the notion of close reading (following the New Criticism movement) became popular: in close reading the sole focus is on the text, not on the writer's biography or personal psychology. Style began to be perceived as a property of all types of text, not just literary ones: stylistics, therefore, is the study of style in text, whatever the text type, with the word 'text' here including both oral and written forms, as has been made clear in earlier chapters.

For Hänlein, style is essentially choice, but sometimes 'situational constraints . . . impose restrictions on the freedom of choice' (Hänlein, 1999: 28). For example, in some contexts *companion* is more appropriate than *friend*, while on other occasions *mate* might be more suitable than either.[9]

Choices in language, according to Hänlein, happen on various levels, including syntax, lexis and semantics and style emerges as 'a consistent pattern of choices . . . made by the individual writer' (Hänlein, *ibid.*: 30). If a choice is recurrent it is seen as an individual style marker. Following Leech and Short's (1981, cited in Hänlein, *ibid.*: 30) observations about occasional deviating choices, Hänlein also uses the Leech–Short term *internal deviation*.

However, Hänlein maintains we should not allow notions of internal deviation to obscure the writer's linguistic fingerprint: 'In individual style, all style markers come together to form a stylistic profile . . . [and] profiles will be used to trace what is called a "stylistic fingerprint"' (Hänlein, *ibid.*: 30).

Stylistic profiling

Hänlein cites Crystal (1991) in further support of the notion of the linguistic fingerprint: 'there is an immediate, intuitive plausibility about the idea of a "stylistic profile", and the possibility of devising a single procedure for explicating the notion of stylistic identity ought to be explored'.

To enable the analyst to test the significance of features Hänlein notes that it is essential to have a reference corpus. The reference corpus should be appropriate in terms of 'genre, period, dialect, field of discourse, medium, attitude (formality/informality) and/or authorship' (Rygiel, 1989, cited in Hänlein, *ibid.*: 33).

Register

The term *register* is of key importance in this discussion: not only is it necessary for the reference corpus to contain texts from a similar register (field – topic; mode – spoken, written, etc.; tenor – relations, formality), but it is also important that the analyst be aware of the effect that extra-linguistic variables can have on the form of language of a given text. In this regard the linguist needs to take into account the text type under analysis, since some text types lend themselves to the expression of individual style whereas others are highly conventional, preconceived even, leaving little or no room for individual style. Thus, according to Hänlein, text type may be viewed as a set of rules which provide a 'primary spectrum' of choices. This spectrum may be termed a style scenario, abbreviated S. The key question for the analyst is this: is the text a manifestation of individual style *in vitro* – that is to say unhindered by any restriction whatsoever; or is the text a manifestation of individual style, minus S? Of course we would probably conclude that it is somewhere between the two. However, if in a given corpus little deviation from S was found, it would be necessary to conclude that the corpus in question tended to be productive of a rather 'stereotypical, regulatory text type' rather than texts which were 'free form' in nature.

Turning to the question of perception of style Hänlein notes that readers' past experiences may influence their perception of a writer's style, just as an individual's perception of the world can influence their use of language. Thus, if we are previously sensitized to a given linguistic feature, even a low occurrence of such a feature in a text under study may yield the impression of it being much more prominent than it actually is. Following from this, it is clear, at least for Hänlein, that style is a manifestation of mind. We cannot convey anything neutrally: whatever we say is coloured and clouded by our view of it. We can even simulate an attitude, invent an entire world, or create a whole universe – the way in which we do this is, at some level, a manifestation of how the writer's mind 'works'. More mundanely even at the topic choice level there is room for individual style. Writers write about problems and situations which concern them and which may be totally different from those of concern to other authors. It would be trivially easy to provide a passable imitation of someone else's style, using their lexis, organization of ideas, etc.

Intuitive and statistical methods

Hänlein sees the task of authorship attribution as a combination of intuitive and statistical methods. To her, topic choice can be significant in distinguishing one author from another: 'Subject matter is seen as a stylistic feature by many stylisticians' (Hänlein, *ibid.*: 93).

Having discussed subject matter in some depth, Hänlein then highlights three key approaches in her search for style markers: word-frequency lists, keywords and proper nouns. Each of these lexical sub-categories has its advantages in distinguishing one author from another, particularly in those cases where there is no restriction of topic.

Locution, illocution, perlocution

This is also known as – 'what I say, what I mean, what you think I mean'. Realizing to some extent the limitations of authorship recognition methods which rely on authors making choices at a more or less conscious level (within the parameters of genre and topic), Hänlein then goes on to talk about the pragmatics of essay writing. Drawing parallels with speech act theory, she cites the three-pronged nature of utterances: locution, illocution and perlocution. First she assigns a 'superordinate illocutionary point' to each essay, and she then describes by what moves authors carry out their pragmatic intentions. Hänlein herself admits that this could be considered questionable, mainly because there may be more than one illocutionary point to each essay.

A perhaps slightly controversial part of Hänlein's thesis is to do with the relationship between content, choice and motivation. The object of the pragmatic study is to discover the communicative goal. While it is accepted that most heavyweight magazine essays (for example, of the *Time* variety) have clear-cut superordinate illocutionary points, e.g. a call to peace, a plea for conservatism, the care of the environment, etc., it is also seen that most *Time* essays have fairly routine ways of reaching these goals – providing one keeps the terms of reference broad enough. Thus, for example, most essays are probably argumentative, with persuasion (as Hänlein notes) being the most common illocutionary device. To carry out this point various strategies (found throughout the text type) are employed, for example 'comparison, exemplification, generalization, analogy, personal opinion, scientific support' (Hänlein, *ibid.*: 117). What is not clear is exactly how Hänlein has uncovered each writer's pragmatic goals (and their methods of reaching them) as a practical, measurable objective in an authorship recognition study. More importantly, how can this process be replicated in future studies?

Even though some of the main pragmatic goal headings are given, for example:

- type of beginning – recent event, past event, autobiographical;
- personal opinions;
- *pros* and *cons*;
- predictions, etc.

Nevertheless, the process is a long and intricate one and, in my view, not at all easy to replicate. Moreover, so many of the pragmatic goals are open to subjective interpretation, as to render the exercise a very partial one. If, for example, we find a particular author's political opinions widely different from our own, what is to stop us using labels of description to reflect this? We should recall that readers are no more neutral than writers.

Having outlined the broad pragmatic goals, Hänlein then proceeds to describe one characteristic which sets each author in the corpus apart from the others: this characteristic is, initially, found by intuition. She then attempts to justify her choice by measurement. This is an interesting part of Hänlein's thesis, and she is very exacting and thorough in her exposition of this concept.

If I have been circumlocutory in arriving at this point it is only to emphasize the difficulties of testing Hänlein's method in a real-world authorship inquiry.

For one thing, each of the essays in Hänlein's corpus is approximately 2,000 words in length, each author has contributed several essays, and the authors themselves come from different backgrounds, are of different age groups and have different interests. Contrast this with the Gilfoyle corpus (see Chapter 5) where texts are on average only 150–300 words in length, where there are only two candidates, each presenting homogeneity in terms of age, background, dialect and even – to some extent – topic. When we look at the kind of texts under consideration by Hänlein and, by contrast, those found in a real authorship inquiry we see that, however thorough Hänlein's method, very little of it is applicable to forensic work.

However, it did strike me that two related areas of interest to Hänlein – keywords and high-frequency words – could prove useful in forensic work. An example of this is explored in Chapter 5.

Insofar as Hänlein is concerned with author recognition rather than identification, I do believe the technique of analysing keyword and high-frequency word distribution is useful. It certainly seems possible when we consider the Gilfoyle texts. However, it is limited by register and sub-corpus considerations. By this I mean that the keywords of one set of texts will in all probability not transfer to another set of texts in, say a different genre and, of course, register. In other words, we cannot automatically consider a keyword or high-frequency word found in a particular author's work to constitute an authorship marker; the occurrence of such a word is dependent on text and context. It is not necessarily related to an author's 'style'.

So, despite some of the apparent successes of authorship recognition, we should be in no doubt that recognition on its own has limited applicability in forensic work.

You cannot go before a judge and jury and say: 'I have looked at the texts in this case and I believe that Mr X is responsible for them because I *recognize* his style'. To be fair, Hänlein does not intend this to be an application of her work.

However, recognition can be useful in investigative work, for example if the police are in the middle of an important investigation it may be very useful to them to know that a questioned text demonstrates aspects of a particular person's writing style.

Such information might help them: (a) to make appropriate inquiries relating to other aspects of the crime under investigation; and (b) to know what kind of questions to ask a suspect. In cases involving ransom demands it might be useful in helping police to assess the nature and scale of a stated threat.

CHAPTER CONCLUSION

In this chapter I have given a very brief outline of some current authorship studies, including a description of methodology where appropriate. However, even a brief visit to the Internet, or to your university or faculty library, will show you that there are literally thousands of references to this topic, and that my choice is of necessity very limited, perhaps narrowly reflecting those areas I have found to be of interest in my own day-to-day forensic researches. One thing, however, is certain and that is that the debate as to what constitutes a scientific approach will continue. This science is only in its infancy, and is still capable of being shaped and influenced in major ways. There is, therefore, an exciting opportunity awaiting today's students to be involved in the genesis of a whole new approach to linguistic evidence.

SUGGESTIONS FOR FURTHER READING

Gibbons, J. (ed.) (1994) *Language and the Law*, London: Longman, Introduction by editor.

Hänlein, H. (1998) *Studies in Authorship Recognition: A Corpus-based Approach*, Frankfurt: Peter Lang, European University Studies, Chapters 1 to 3.

McMenamin, Gerald R. (1993) *Forensic Stylistics*, Amsterdam: Elsevier.

CHAPTER 2

Individuals and language use

In this brief chapter I will consider some of the arguments relating to the notion of the linguistic fingerprint, or individual style. First, I will consider the prerequisites for style, mainly to do with acquisition, education and culture. Then I will look at style itself, what it is, its relationship to genre, and its status as a psychological construct. Finally, I will consider the question of individual style from a practical point of view, as applied to forensic linguistics.

THE MYTH OF THE LINGUISTIC FINGERPRINT

The *linguistic fingerprint* is a notion put forward by some scholars that each human being uses language differently, and that this difference between people can be observed just as easily and surely as a fingerprint. According to this view, the linguistic fingerprint is the collection of markers, which stamps a speaker/writer as unique. However, although the linguistic fingerprint is a powerful concept with great attractions for law enforcement and other agencies worldwide, there is so far little hard evidence to support the notion. This is why I refer to its existence as a myth: the proof of its existence is notable for its absence.

Despite this, there are nevertheless innumerable references to a 'linguistic fingerprint' e.g. Lancashire (Lancashire, online) writes that 'Many theorists of literary style from Buffon to Barthes postulate that style is dictated by the subconscious and forms the "genetic" fingerprint of a writer's work'. Similarly, Pennebaker (1999) claims that using 'new behavior/language sampling technology for field research', he and his group will 'reconstruct a person's "linguistic fingerprint"' from his or her daily interactions and relate it to a variety of self-reported personality characteristics, situational variables and physiological markers. Finally, Bax (Bax, online) refers to an undergraduate course which would 'describe aspects of their [Johnson, Boswell, etc.] language use (e.g. grammatical variation, idiosyncratic spelling systems, vocabulary) in an attempt to discover what could be called their "linguistic fingerprint"'.

As the reader will see from the above, the notion that individuals have a linguistic fingerprint is now widely disseminated in paper journals and across the Internet. Unfortunately there are even some branches of academia invoking these as yet unproven ideas, as well as the usual commercial interest.

The difficulty I have with these claims is simple: nobody has yet demonstrated the existence of such a thing as a linguistic fingerprint: how then can people write about it in this unexamined, regurgitated way, as though it were a fact of forensic life?

31

Perhaps it is this word 'forensic' that is responsible. The very fact that it collocates so regularly with words like *expert* and *science* means that it cannot but raise expectations. In our minds we associate it with the ability to single out the perpetrator from the crowd to a high degree of precision, and so when we put *forensic* next to *linguistics* as in the title of this book we are effectively saying *forensic linguistics* is a genuine science just like *forensic chemistry, forensic toxicology,* and so on. Of course, insofar as a *science* is a field of endeavour in which we seek to obtain reliable, even predictable results, by the application of a methodology, then forensic linguistics is a science. However, we should avoid giving the impression that it can unfailingly – or even nearly unfailingly – provide precise identification about individuals from small samples of speech or text. In the next several sections I will demonstrate why, in my view, the notion of linguistic fingerprint is essentially flawed.

LANGUAGE ACQUISITION

Language is an acquired property, not an inherited one. It is not like an individual's fingerprints or DNA. Moreover, language is acquired, not all at once, but in stages. Individuals continue acquiring language throughout their lives, although the core development is generally complete by 30 months or so (Radford, 1990). The reverse of acquisition and development is atrophy: language is not only acquired, it is also lost. At no time in an individual's life is language 'fixed'. In that case, if language is not a fixed property, how is style to be measured? Aside from the variation exhibited by the individual, how often does an individual's use of language change, and to what extent? What makes it change? Of course this is aside from diachronic change in language generally (see Lightfoot, 1979).

UNIVERSAL EDUCATION AND LINGUISTIC HOMOGENEITY

Several hundred years ago we may have been able to distinguish most individuals from each other through their use of language, because in those days dialectal variation was significantly greater than now. There was little standardization.[10] Those who were able to write, frequently invented their own spelling and grammar rules. However, with the advent of universal education, mass Internet access and cheap travel, those who speak the same language have started to use language more like each other in the way they speak and write than at any previous time. For example, aside from apparently minor lexical differences which are not always easily observed, and a few orthographic variations, there is frequently little to distinguish writers from different English-speaking countries from each other. We do not readily know if the writer is Caribbean, Canadian, South African, Australian, British, etc. unless perhaps specific cultural issues are being dealt with.

Moreover, frequent linguistic intercourse across cultural and national boundaries has a homogenizing effect on language: we become like each other in the way we use language in order to communicate better. Nowadays, we are all of us virtually using a language product which is being handed down by the combined forces of dictionary makers, pulp fiction writers, schools, universities, the media, and – not least – the political establishment (each with its fair share of prescriptivists). If the decline in the number of languages being spoken across the world is anything to go by, we may observe that linguistic uniformity is in direct proportion to the degree of mass human intercourse. As Crystal notes: 'In the 19th century, there were more than 1,000 Indian languages in Brazil, many spoken in small, isolated villages in the rain forest; today there are a mere 200, most of which have never been written down or recorded' (Crystal, online). In Africa, the United Nations estimate that more than half of the 1,400 indigenous languages are either in decline or under threat. This is due largely to the influence of English and other colonial languages. In other parts of the world, other major languages, such as Russian and Chinese have probably contributed to similar linguistic decimation in their own countries. Standardization within a language, and the decline in the number of languages worldwide is part of the same process of linguistic homogenization facing us at this time, and may contribute to *reducing* linguistic individuality. There is little room, then, for believing that humans use language idiosyncratically. Finally, it should be said that the difficulties in distinguishing one author/speaker from another are increasing, not diminishing. Technology is not solving the problem of distinguishing authors from each other, it is making the task more difficult: as the availability of information explodes exponentially, writers have access to more and more information, and in many cases are free to plagiarize from each other, almost with impunity.[11]

Section conclusion

In this section I have tried to outline my reasons against the notion of style being an individual property. The reasons I have put forward relate to acquisition, culture and education, as well as internationalization and globalization. In the next section I will discuss *style* in more detail, what it is, and its possible role in authorship questions.

TOWARDS A THEORY OF STYLE

Style must be one of the most widely abused words in forensic and literary linguistics. To some it is a way of using language, a set of mannerisms which fulfil a certain formal or defined communicative need. To others it is an individual's marked way of using language habitually, something which is special to that individual, also called *idiolect*, although idiolect is also taken to mean the language of an individual as opposed to the language of a society, i.e. *sociolect* Bilgrami (1993: 66–73). Properly speaking, idiolect refers to speech, but has come to include all forms of language. Idiolect and sociolect are – as I have argued in previous sections – not mutually exclusive: your idiolect is 'part of' your sociolect. Your sociolect changes as your idiolect changes. There is, in fact, a mutual dependency between the two.

There are two diametrically opposed views on style: (a) it is, as suggested above, a collection of markers consciously chosen by a speaker; (b) it is a set of unconscious habits not normally observed by the author, but which – once uncovered by the linguist – can also be observed and measured.

These two opposing views place the linguist in something of a difficulty: if on the one hand the set of markers used by the speaker can be observed, then the speaker can alter them and anyone else can imitate them. Thus, if a style can be imitated by anyone, its potential for remaining unique is surely reduced.

On the other hand if the speaker's habits are unconscious, then we are in difficulty because we do not know whether the set of 'unconscious' markers differs from author to author, or whether it is a fixed set across all authors. This is similar to the habits–choices debate. According to Morton, 1990 (see Chapter 1), language idiosyncrasy comes about because we each have a set of (unconscious) habits, while according to Ephratt (Ephratt, online – see Chapter 1), linguistic individuality exists because we as writers/speakers exercise linguistic choice.

If the set of markers differs from author to author, then it is impossible to know in advance what to look for, and – since each individual (according to this view) would be different – the researcher would be able to decide arbitrarily what to test for. This could produce subjective results. Conversely, if the set of style markers were fixed across all authors, this would imply some kind of predetermined relationship between language and the individual. This would lead us to wonder how such a relationship could be acquired, and to ask what there is about *style* to enable it to be fixed.

GENRE AND STYLE

Genre is a type of text arising from a specific set of communicative requirements. On the one hand, it can be taken in the narrow sense to refer to the work of a community of language users to whom text contributions are a kind of badge of membership (Swales, 1990). This is in addition to its use in the broad sense, e.g. crime genres, romance genres, the private letter genre, etc.

Whichever definition of genre we use, though, it is impossible to avoid the realization that there is a conflict between the notions of style and genre. I write in an identifiable style: but what happens when I write in a different genre? How do I get to write in that genre, if it is a badge of membership? Something, surely must change within me as a writer. Each genre has its own demands, one may almost say its own 'style'. Faced with this 'style' the style of the individual will not remain intact. In that case it is logical to doubt whether style is a property of the individual. It may in reality be a property of the genre. That is the essence of the conflict between style and genre.

We may consider a kind of compromise to the above, namely that style may be partly conscious and partly unconscious. So, while some features could be within our control, others may not be. Similarly, it may be the case that yet other aspects of style relate to or stem from the genre rather than the individual. In other words that in reality *style* – the way an individual uses language – is a complex, fluid interaction of the individual, language and society. In that case, it is certainly not a fixed property, and so cannot be used as a means of identification. This returns us, in a sense, to square one.

Whichever view of *style* we take, it seems certain that style is not a primitive; it is a multifaceted construct which appears to be beyond the complete control of the individual and is at least in part dependent on genre and context. It is important to realize that language is not a personal possession. We use it in common with all other speakers of the same language as ourselves. It is, essentially, the property of its community of its users, or rather of the communities of its users. It is a social property, not an individual one.

Exercise 2.1

Write a brochure outlining what forensic linguistics is. Aim it at two distinctive audiences. First, prospective students with a linguistics background: tell them what forensic linguistics is and why you think they should study it. Second, members of the legal profession: tell them what you believe the limitations of authorship studies to be. Research the views of other linguists, lawyers, etc., on the Internet.

THE 'LINGUISTIC FINGERPRINT': A PRACTICAL APPROACH

At the practical level in forensic linguistics, there is probably little need in most authorship investigations to think in terms of unique style. It is simply not necessary. Rather, when conducting an investigation, the emphasis should probably be upon these questions.

1 How was the text created?

2 Was there more than one author?

3 Are there sections of the text which are stylistically different from each other?

CHAPTER CONCLUSION

The intention of this chapter has been to pose background questions relating to the existence of a unique language style in each individual. The concept of uniqueness and the individual is dear to the human psyche. We are indoctrinated from an early age in the belief that we are each unique. This is meant also to imply that we are all 'special', 'wonderful', etc. In fact our belief in our uniqueness is part of the western creed. It is reinforced by such observations as the uniqueness of the individual's fingerprints, the individual's DNA, and the apparent uniqueness of other kinds of biometric data. Somehow we have the same expectation when it comes to language: we expect that the language of the individual should be unique, we want to believe that we each use language uniquely, that it is part of our individuality. It is surely no accident that one of the most frequent collocates of the word *unique* is in fact *style*, according to *Cobuild English Collocations* (1995).

However, the evidence to support the belief that individuals possess a unique style of language needs careful examination, and we should be aware of the pitfalls, especially in an age of mass standardization in education. As both language and education become more regulated in industrial societies across the globe, individuality in language use may be more and more difficult to detect. It could turn out that the most practical option for the forensic linguist is to look for ways of distinguishing individuals from each other rather than attempting to establish the uniqueness of each individual.

SUGGESTIONS FOR FURTHER READING

Hänlein, H. (1998) *Studies in Authorship Recognition: A Corpus-based Approach*, Frankfurt: Peter Lang, European University Studies, Chapters 4 and 5.

Swales, J. M. (1990) *Genre Analysis, Cambridge Applied Linguistics*, Cambridge: Cambridge University Press, Chapter 3.

CHAPTER 3

Evidence in court

This chapter is divided into two sections. In the first section, I offer a brief description of how courts in a number of countries view expert evidence (legal requirements across the globe). Moving from the general to the specific, I then consider to what degree forensic linguistic evidence is acceptable to courts in their efforts to try criminal and civil cases. I attempt to compensate for the abstractness of this approach by looking at an actual authorship inquiry. Although the particular case I will be referring to has never come to court, I will outline the difficulties involved in using the linguistic evidence from this type of case in a legal forum.

LEGAL REQUIREMENTS ACROSS THE GLOBE

The United States

In the USA until fairly recently, evidence of a scientific or technical nature had to pass the Frye test. This was a fairly simple test: providing a method had acceptance from the scientific community it could be held to be valid in a court of law. In recent years, however, this standard was shown to be flawed after it was demonstrated that the use of hypnosis to reactivate memory could result in false-memory syndrome. The fact was that although the use of hypnosis had 'acceptance from the scientific community' it still produced a false result: it was time for the legal standard to be revised. This occurred in the now famous case *Daubert* v. *Merrell Dow Pharmaceuticals*. In this case a group of mothers asserted that their ingestion of Benedictin, a prescription drug, had caused their children to be born with defects.

According to the expert witness, the method used by the defendants to claim that the drug was harmful had not received general acceptance from the scientific community, thus failing the Frye test.

Because the petitioners' expert testimony failed the Frye test, their evidence was ruled inadmissible. Later, the Court of Appeal overturned the Federal Court's ruling. However, the Supreme Court of the United States vacated the judgment, ruling that there were other criteria than 'general acceptability' for the admission of expert testimony, including:

- *Knowledge and stature*: The expert must have sufficient knowledge of the subject area ('knowledge skill, experience, training or education'). Additionally, the expert must have stature in the academic or other peer community;

- *Testing*: The technique must be empirically tested. It must be falsifiable and refutable;

41

- *Peer review*: The technique must have been subjected to peer review and publication;
- *Scientific method*: The expert must be able to demonstrate the known error rate;
- *'Straightforwardness'*: The technique must be able to be explained with sufficient clarity and simplicity so that a court and jury can understand its plain meaning.

Collectively these criteria have come to be known as the 'Daubert' criteria, or just 'Daubert'. Note that, in essence, Daubert is nothing more than an interpretation by a particular court of existing rules of evidence, in this case Rule 702, 'Testimony by Experts', which states that:

> If scientific, technical, or other specialized knowledge will assist the trier of fact to understand the evidence or to determine a fact in issue, a witness qualified as an expert by knowledge, skill, experience, training, or education, may testify thereto in the form of an opinion or otherwise, if (1) the testimony is based upon sufficient facts or data, (2) the testimony is the product of reliable principles and methods, and (3) the witness has applied the principles and methods reliably to the facts of the case.

In the United States it is now becoming common for courts to demand evidence which passes the 'Daubert test'. However, a worrying development is the range of interpretations, which can be placed on 'Daubert', in particular the insistence that error rates must be known. The related topics of confidence limits and error rates are more appropriate to a discussion on statistics, but in essence what this part of Daubert is demanding is nothing less than that any technique used by an expert witness must give its results using inferential rather than descriptive statistics.

However, many forensic disciplines (according to O'Connor)[12] fail the Daubert test. These include ballistics, forensic phonetics, forensic anthropology, child abuse accommodation syndrome, etc. On the other hand, polygraph (lie detector) analysis, previously inadmissible under the Frye test, is now acceptable to many courts under Daubert.

But, as Paul Roberts of the University of Nottingham School of Law points out, criteria such as error rates and falsifiability 'make good sense when applied to the traditional realms of scientific endeavour: physics, chemistry, biology . . . but how should one apply . . . Daubert . . . to less demonstrable forms of inquiry, such as psychiatry or psychology or the proliferating human and social sciences, which may now be presented as "social framework evidence . . . ?" '.

Fortunately, in the US, case law exerts a strong influence, and not all courts have been inclined to read Daubert completely literally. Roberts cites *Kumho Tire Co v. Carmichael*, in which the 11th Circuit Court judges ruled that the expert testimony of a tyre specialist was admissible, even though it was based on specialist knowledge and opinion, and not on a falsifiable technique with a known error rate. Specifically, the judges said: 'whether Daubert's specific factors are, or are not, reasonable measures of reliability in a particular case is a matter that the law grants the trial judge broad latitude to determine', (judgment given, March 1999).

Australia

In Australia, the situation is somewhat different from the USA. Prior to a revision of the Australian expert witness guidelines in 1998, the task of the expert witness had in fact been described in 1997 by Gordon Samuels, a former president of the Australian Court of Appeal as one of furnishing 'basic scientific or technical data', and 'to present inferences and conclusions from the facts which the judge or jury, for lack of specialised knowledge, cannot draw themselves'.

The emphasis in Australian law has now been placed on the requirement to be relevant and reliable (the relevance and reliability rule). Expert witnesses are not required to provide the kinds of scientific evidence required under a strict interpretation of Daubert, rather they are obliged to qualify their findings (where they believe there may be incomplete or inaccurate evidence), and they must give reasons for their opinions. This implies, of course, that Australian law does not exclude experts from giving their opinions. However, as is the case in several countries, lawyers are reluctant to accept linguistic evidence because many believe themselves to have adequate linguistic knowledge to form their own opinions. Many do not see the study of language as a separate, technical subject.

England and Wales

In the early 1990s Lord Woolf was appointed to oversee a wide-ranging reform of the civil court system in England and Wales. There was growing concern among legal professionals that the law was becoming inaccessible to members of the public. One of Woolf's main concerns was the contribution of expert evidence to the quality of justice. Woolf contended that the use of experts could contribute significantly to a case's costs and therefore deter individuals from seeking legal redress. Among other reforms, Lord Woolf has proposed the appointment of a single expert for both parties – a controversial concept and one which is anathema to many solicitors and barristers who have grown up with the traditional adversarial system. In those cases where the parties are unable to agree on an expert, Woolf proposed that the court itself should make the appointment. In essence, Woolf's aim was to give courts wide-ranging discretionary powers in the matter of experts: 'the calling of expert evidence should be under the complete control of the court'. According to Woolf, the use of experts should be 'economical' and the issues between experts – where there is more than one expert (which, given Woolf's adherence to the notion of single experts is far from certain) – should be narrowed 'as early as possible'. Woolf has not gone so far as to propose scientific standards of evidence, such as were put forward in Daubert. It is worth noting that Lord Woolf's reforms were made relative to the civil justice system. However, there is no suggestion that these principles, or at least some version of them, will not also apply to criminal cases in the future. Many Commonwealth countries have based their legal system on that of England and Wales, and so similarities can be found with regard to expert witness evidence almost across the globe.

Canada

In Canada the determination as to whether an expert witness should be called was formulated as early as 1931,[13] with the memorable juridical phrase: 'the subject matter of the inquiry must be such that ordinary people are unlikely to form a correct judgment about it, if unassisted by persons with special knowledge'.

More recently, this observation was added to with the injunction that expert evidence must be both helpful to the court in its role as 'trier of fact' and relevant.[14] Several important guidelines for experts were formulated in *Perricone* v. *Baldassarra*:

> Expert evidence presented to the court should be, and should be seen to be, the independent product of the expert uninfluenced as to form or content by the exigencies of litigation. An expert should provide independent assistance to the court by objective unbiased opinion in relation to matters within his or her expertise. An expert witness should never assume a role of advocate. An expert should state the facts or assumptions on which the opinion is based and should not omit to consider material facts which detract from that opinion. An expert should make it clear when a particular question or issue falls outside of the expert's expertise. If an expert's opinion is not properly researched because insufficient data is available, this must be stated with an indication that the opinion is no more than a provisional one.

Crucially, Canadian courts demand that experts are unbiased, and may not act as advocates: expert evidence may be ignored insofar as it attempts to bypass this rule of impartiality. As regards Daubert, the Canadian expert witness newsletter Economica[15] notes that scientific criteria can be applied to subject areas which do not constitute pure science 'with some modifications'. So although, for example, some techniques do not have a known error rate, yet the fact that they may have been subjected to 'peer review and publication' will constitute an acceptable criterion. Canadian courts have wide latitude as to what constitutes acceptable scientific practice.

France,[16] Germany (inquisitorial system)

In France, Germany and other countries which follow an inquisitorial legal system (as opposed to an adversarial system, such as the USA and the UK) experts are appointed by the court, not by the parties to a case. The investigation is carried out by a judge or panel of judges. Lawyers acting for each side submit questions the judge may ask the witness. The rather restrictive rules of evidence found in Anglo-Saxon systems do not apply: in the inquisitorial system evidence is much more freely evaluated. Several other countries use an inquisitorial system. These are mostly western European countries.

Other countries

In the Philippines, the rules of evidence with reference to expert witnesses state that 'The opinion of a witness regarding a question of science, art or trade, when he is skilled therein, may be received in evidence'.

FORENSIC LINGUISTICS AND LEGAL STANDARDS OF EVIDENCE

Courts generally attempt to deal in facts, but ultimately science does not deal in facts, it deals in probability. Daubert may have been the first piece of official evidence machinery to recognize this, which is in itself a major step forward. However, it seems that the social sciences and the 'hard' sciences are different from each other with regard to the ways in which they are able to demonstrate refutability.

The aim of any scientific procedure is to be able to draw an inference which can be applied more generally than the narrow frame of reference of the original observation. Minimally, science is observation, but the optimum is inference, i.e. discovery of a principle.

Kerlinger defines scientific research as the 'systematic, controlled, empirical, and critical investigation of hypothetical propositions about the presumed relations among natural phenomena' (Kerlinger, 1973: 11). For *natural* phenomena here, we can substitute – with no loss of meaning – *social* and *behavioural* phenomena, as indeed Lewin *et al.* (2001: 25) have in their recent major work on expository discourse.

The general idea is that we need to observe before we can describe, and we must first describe before we can formulate our research hypothesis and eventually draw any necessary inferences or explain the phenomena we have observed.

What is popularly called the 'scientific method' – which involves the testing of a null hypothesis in order to assert or verify a research one, is

45

really just one interpretation of the notion of 'scientific method', or one way of carrying it out.

In advancing the most radical view of scientific methodology since Bacon, Popper proposed that progress in science comes about largely through a process of deduction and falsification. This was in direct contradiction to the earlier belief which proposed that humans learn through induction. For Popper – like Kerlinger – prior experience was everything, as witness his lifelong formula:

$$P_n - TS - EE - P_{n+1}$$

which can be translated as follows: on being confronted with a problem (P_n) we attempt a trial solution (TS). Later we modify this, mainly by error elimination (EE) which then produces a revised appraisal of P_n, now P_{n+1}.

The Baconian idea of learning through induction was rejected by Popper, because he believed that we learn only through experience. Inductive thinking is, according to Popper and his disciples, counter-intuitive to this idea of learning through experience. For Popper it is creativity which produces ideas. We prove things by attempting to disprove them. Failure to 'disprove' simply means success in demonstrating. This is the essence of experimentation. If I can disprove my own theory it becomes more believable, since no matter how many times I observe something I cannot draw an absolute principle from it. This is essentially the problem posed by Scottish philosopher David Hume in the eighteenth century. Even though I cannot draw an absolute principle from my observations – because an exception can always occur – I can nevertheless propose a principle, no matter how tentative. I can suggest that – for example in 19 cases out of 20 – my observations are valid, or 99/100 or 999/1,000. In other words I can set a confidence limit, the inverse of which is the error rate (i.e. 1/20, 1/100 or 1/1,000).

The notion of verifiability through falsifiability is an excellent one, but we should not be too carried away by its romanticism. In reality we do not disprove our idea to prove it – we simply set up a null hypothesis, in the hope of being able to reject it. For example, supposing I believed that men earn more than women do, and I wished to conduct some research to demonstrate this. I begin with a hypothesis: 'men earn more than women'. This is my research hypothesis, but if I were to follow the 'scientific method' along Popperian lines, I would not start out with such an assertion. Rather, I would begin by hypothesizing that there was no difference between the sexes with respect to earnings, i.e. I would hypothesize a null difference. I would then hope that my research would allow me to reject this null hypothesis. Note that this would not enable me to assert that there was actually a difference between what men and women earn, but rather that the hypothesis that there was no difference, should be rejected. This is what is meant by rejecting the null hypothesis. This is how scientists have interpreted Popper's method: by rejecting the null hypothesis in order to be able to assert the research hypothesis.

However, what we really want to know is **not** whether we can destroy our own theory, but how sound our theory is. How often is it likely to be the case that an exception will be thrown?

In recent years it has become very fashionable for exponents of quantitative research and qualitative research to deride each other's respective practices. Chaski cites the *Van Wyk* case in which the court ruled that there was a 'lack of scientific reliability . . . [in] forensic stylistics' (Chaski, 2001: 2). As observed in Chapter 1, Chaski is critical of linguists who use non-quantitative methods, which she claims are unscientific. However, Chaski herself falls into several errors in this. First, we cannot really speak of the 'Daubert standard', as though it were an inviolable, unalterable set of performance conditions which must apply, at all costs to all types of scientific data. Daubert is simply an interpretation of the rules of evidence. It has the status of setting a legal precedent, but it is not set in stone. The important item is the body of law upon which Daubert depends, namely the Federal Rules of Evidence. In the *Kumho Tire* appeal Daubert was seen to be applied – not because the method adopted by the tyre (tire) expert did not use the standard null hypothesis method, but because the tyre expert based his view on knowledge and opinion and did not offer any means of assessing the reliability of his method. Anyone who thinks this was automatically a good result for forensic linguistics, or for the social sciences generally, should – however – pause for thought. There are innumerable instances where we use judgement and opinion, rather than 'more' scientific methods to evaluate data, and there are some situations where, in reality, we cannot (and perhaps should not) use anything other than judgement and opinion.

Chaski apparently has a horror of 'junk science', and this is to be commended, but as discussed in Chapter 1, it is not the case that non-quantitative methods are, *ipso facto*, not scientific.

The point is that different sciences reach conclusions differently, though all have the same overall goal, namely the discovery of principles through observation, experimentation and hypothesis. Data can be gathered and evaluated in many ways. It need not be numerical, and even if it is numerical the means of evaluating it need not be statistical.

Thus, use of the null hypothesis to verify a research hypothesis is not the only possible way of applying a scientific method, though it is the principal one at this time. It should not be the case that our method is unscientific just because we are unable to propose, and then reject the null hypothesis, which is – as far as I am aware – the only true 'technical' way of setting the error rate of a procedure. Moreover, the term 'error rate' should not be taken as an inviolable statement about the number of times our procedure fails, since that is something which can only be estimated and never actually proven. In this respect Daubert is quite wrong to imply that an error rate can be known, or is derived from the data. The term 'error rate' should be taken in its strict technical sense, namely to demonstrate only that we ourselves have imposed a boundary of, say 0.05 or 0.01

as the maximum degree to which it is probable that our result will have been arrived at through non-random means. It is not necessarily the case that judges always understand this point, and all non-statisticians should consult the standard texts on these topics.

In the future, courts will need to consider Daubert carefully, and look at its applicability with regard to the social sciences. Because forensic texts are on the whole very short, there are very particular sampling problems attached to the task of authorship attribution. In addition, it is certainly the case that there is more than one possible scientific method and courts need to recognize this.

Exercise 3.1

As an exercise in research, and to develop your own awareness of handling forensic issues, research 'Daubert' and 'Frye' on the Internet (or in your faculty library). Look at case histories, and read the judgments given. Ask yourself whether either of these applications of the Federal Rules of Evidence is satisfactory to forensic linguistics. Read what other linguists have had to say on this question. Do you feel lawyers and judges understand what forensic linguistics is?

SUGGESTIONS FOR FURTHER READING

Daubert:
http://www.daubertontheweb.com/
http://supct.law.cornell.edu:8080/supct/html/92–102.ZS.html
Gibbons, J. (ed.) (1994) *Language and the Law*, London: Longman, Part 1.

CHAPTER 4

An authorship inquiry

In the last chapter we briefly discussed some aspects of evidence acceptability in the court environment. In particular the difficulties of giving linguistic evidence were outlined, especially when compared to the kinds of evidence offered by the so-called hard sciences. In this chapter I want to make this discussion concrete by demonstrating how I approached a particular authorship attribution case some years ago. As the reader will appreciate, I have deliberately chosen a case which did not lend itself to analysis by 'the scientific method', as described in the previous chapter. This case became known as the *Dog Club Treasurer* case, and is described below.

DESCRIPTIVE ATTRIBUTION: THE *DOG CLUB TREASURER* CASE

In the *Dog Club Treasurer* case, the president and other senior committee members of a mid-west dog club had received a series of vicious anonymous letters. Since the texts included details of club management and policy, and an apparent intimacy with virtually all of the committee members it seemed that the writer was probably a member of the committee, or someone who had the full cooperation of a member of the committee in writing the offensive texts. What is useful about this case from the point of view of the student is that it gives us the opportunity of demonstrating distinctive style in a fairly simple and transparent manner. After examination of the texts a number of potential authorship markers were identified. These were as follows:

- grammar, orthography and metaphor;
- punctuation;
- capitalization;
- layout and text management: method of dating; indentation of first paragraphs; farewell salutation.

Grammar, orthography and metaphor

There were several important distinguishing features in this category which connected one of the candidates, the treasurer of the dog club, and the questioned 'hate mail' texts. These included writing 'apologize' as 'apologies'; confusion between the past and present participles – '*been* brought into question' for '*being* brought into question', and confusion (or misspelling) of particle for adverb – 'to' for 'too'.

Punctuation

There were several punctuation features in common across the known and unknown texts, including the use of a comma instead of a full stop; the use of a superfluous item of punctuation, such as a comma or full stop, and the failure to use any punctuation between two discrete sentences. The most significant of these distinctive punctuation features was the use of a supernumerary punctuation item, inserted almost at random at several points in the known texts of the treasurer and the 'hate mail' texts. Here are some examples:

> 'by two rude and self important folks., or I fear that it may . . .'
> 'lies deceit, malice, and frivolous behaviour.'
> 'all of us are guilty of becoming very heated at the moment, which is very understandable as we all, enjoy the wonderful world of dogs . . .'

Capitalization

A number of words were consistently capitalized in both the known texts of the treasurer and the unknown 'hate mail'. These included words which were given an initial upper-case letter, and those which were capitalized throughout. The list of words capitalized in this way included: *Exhibitor, Breeder, Show President, Membership Secretary, Show License, Minutes, Check, Deputy Show President, Committee, Rang, ANYONE, NO TIME, ALL.*

Layout and text management

There were three striking features of layout and text management across the known and anonymous texts.

Method of dating

The treasurer has a very striking way of writing the date, which I have not seen used as a matter of routine by any other author in business letters, and that is that he invariably places the word 'Date' in front of the actual date. Usually, one tends to see this only in legal documents such as wills or contracts where the word 'Date' is inserted as a placeholder for people to write the actual date, often underneath their signature. On such occasions the word 'Signature' is also used as a placeholder to indicate where people are to sign. Sometimes there is a colon after the word 'Date'. The method, as described here, is found across all the treasurer's texts and the suspect texts.

Indentation of first paragraph

Another striking feature of the text layout, in addition to the somewhat idiosyncratic dating method referred to above, is the unusual method of indenting the first line of each paragraph. Two methods of paragraph indentation apply:

Method 1: The first line of the first paragraph of the text is heavily indented, but subsequent paragraphs are less indented.

Method 2: The first line of the first paragraph of the text is heavily indented, just as in Method 1 (above) but subsequent paragraphs are not indented at all.

All of the suspect texts and those of the Dog Club Treasurer are indented in this way, but none of the other texts are.

There are at least two other types of indentation in general use:

Method 3: No indentation of any paragraph in the text.

Method 4: Equal indentation of all paragraphs.

Neither the unknown texts nor the known texts by the treasurer use either of these latter methods. As previously stated, the treasurer and the writer of the anonymous texts each use the identical means of indentation, as described in Method 1 and Method 2 above.

Farewell salutation

The final category to be compared across the known texts of the treasurer and the unknown, anonymous texts, is that of the farewell salutation.

There is nothing particularly extraordinary about these farewell salutations, except that the known texts of the treasurer and the anonymous 'hate' texts use initial capitals in each case:

Table 4.1 *Comparison of closing salutations from the known to the unknown texts*	
Known	*Unknown*
Text 5: Yours Sincerely	Text 1: A Caring And Anxious Member
Text 6: Yours Sincerely	Text 2: A Caring Member
Text 7: Yours Faithfully	Text 3: With Best Wishes
Text 9: Yours Truly	Text 4: Yours Disgustedly
Text 10: With Best Wishes	
Text 12: With Best Wishes	

As can be seen from Table 4.1, in almost all cases the treasurer uses the slightly unconventional method of writing each word of the farewell salutation with an initial capital letter. The conventional method of writing the farewell salutation in English is, for example, 'Yours sincerely', 'Yours truly', etc., that is to say, the word 'Yours' is usually written with a capital letter, but the adverb, *sincerely, faithfully, truly*, etc., is written with an initial lower-case (small) letter. The method of writing the farewell salutation, as regards upper and lower-case letters, therefore, appears identical between the known texts of the treasurer, and the anonymous texts.

Summary of distinctive markers

In the *Dog Club Treasurer* case, there were several distinctive markers which the known texts of one of the candidates shared with the suspect texts. These included several important features. Among them were a number of orthographic and grammatical markers, a somewhat distinctive punctuation marker, the unusual initial capitalization of several words, and some aspects of text layout. There were eight distinctive markers in common between the Dog Club Treasurer and the unknown 'hate mail' texts.

Table 4.2 *Some orthographic features of the questioned texts*	
Marker	*Example*
Orthography	*apologies* for **apologize**
Grammar category confusion	*been* for **being**
Grammar category confusion	*to* for **too**
Superfluous punctuation	stop + comma for comma
Spurious capitalization	While it is not unusual to capitalize important nouns in a closed setting (such as a club) the capitalization of words like Check, Rang, etc. is far from conventional
Dating	e.g. 'DATE: September 9 1996'
Indentation	Different indentation for first and later paragraphs
Farewell salutation	e.g. 'Yours Sincerely' instead of the more usual 'Yours sincerely'

Bear in mind, not just that there are common points between the questioned and known texts, but that there are so many of them: the effect is cumulative, though – sadly – we cannot quantify it in a satisfactory, statistical way.

Nevertheless, it was felt that these eight distinctive features were significant enough to enable a report to be sent to the club president.[17] The committee then confronted the club treasurer who eventually admitted to authorship of the letters. This was a particularly successful case with a not unhappy ending (linguistically speaking). However, following our discussion on evidence acceptability in the previous chapter, several issues of methodology arise from cases like this.

Spelling and other markers

It is probably not unique for someone to misspell or write *apologize* as *apologies*.[18] However, to discover how common this is and then work out the probability of two authors among a small group having this feature in common would take considerable research into some suitable way of quantifying this kind of probability. The same applies to other misspellings and indeed to other marker categories. But in any case in a closed inquiry such as that of the Dog Club Treasurer, it is unnecessary to take a macro-corpus approach. The brief was to confirm or reject a *single* suspect from several candidates, not to unearth one individual from the entire population. Therefore how the population at large spells a particular word or uses a particular marker is really irrelevant. What we are interested in doing is distinguishing the behaviour of one individual with regard to the behaviour of other members of the group. This is because the author is not selected at random from the entire population of authors, but from a closed, finite set of authors, hence the term *closed* inquiry.

What is *scientific* evidence?

Above, the *Dog Club Treasurer* case was presented, but how would the evidence presented here be received by a court of law? Probably the attribution offered would have most difficulty in the USA, if it had to pass a strict interpretation of what is known as the Daubert test (as outlined in the previous chapter). As discussed, Daubert requires rigorous quantitative methodology, including an insistence on the expert being able to demonstrate error rates. The attribution made in the *Dog Club Treasurer* case was not made on the basis of quantitative data, but this does not mean that the method used was not scientific. In their seminal work on the design of social science inquiry King *et al.* (1994: 7) make clear that they 'do not regard quantitative research to be any more scientific than qualitative research'. In fact they view the word *scientific* here as a 'descriptor' not as a *term*, and candidly point out that it has many 'unwarranted and inappropriate connotations'. For King *et al.* the goal of scientific research is inference, of which there are two types, descriptive inference and explanatory inference, but we:

> cannot construct meaningful causal explanations without good description; description, in turn, loses most of its interest unless linked to some causal relationships . . . the relationship between description and explanation is interactive . . . Description and explanation both depend upon rules of scientific inference . . . we disagree with those who denigrate 'mere' description . . . [it] has a central role in all explanation . . . inference, whether descriptive or causal, quantitative or qualitative, is the ultimate goal of all good social science.
>
> (King *et al.*, 1994: 34)

King *et al.* further stress that the procedures we use must be transparent, or as they say 'public': 'Scientific research uses explicit, codified, and public methods to generate and analyze data whose reliability can therefore be assessed'. It is critical that methods are explicit and public because in this way any limitations can be dealt with: 'those limitations can be understood and, if possible, addressed'. In other words, according to King *et al.* the presence of limitations in a study is inevitable: there is little virtue in hiding them. As regards inference and reliability King *et al.* do not insist on 'known error rates' (as per Daubert), rather they think in terms of a 'reasonable estimate of uncertainty':

> Reaching perfectly certain conclusions from uncertain data is obviously impossible. Indeed, uncertainty is a central aspect of all research and all knowledge about the world. Without a *reasonable estimate of uncertainty*, a description of the real world or an inference about a causal effect in the real world is uninterpretable.
>
> (King *et al.*, 1994: 7; my italics)

This is a perfectly rational point: when we are being given information about something, we want to know how reliable that information is. 'How many times did . . .?' 'How often did . . .?' These are the kinds of question members of a jury, ordinary, lay people without specialist knowledge, would ask. Moreover, they would understand the answers, too, rather than the technical language of statistical probability. Hence, in making the attribution that I did, I believe I attempted no more than any 'sensible' person would have done in the same situation. I looked for the candidate whose texts were closest to the questioned texts and listed the points of comparison. In this regard I would argue that a strict adherence to Daubert and similar rule systems is counter-productive to fairness and justice in the legal system: the jury and other triers of fact are not statisticians, and so are forced to trust the scientist and the scientist's observations and opinions. Science is not and can never be impartial. In my view it would be far better for juries to be given expert evidence in ordinary language and to judge the value of that evidence for themselves. As things stand, the judge rules on the admissibility of experts in the absence of the jury. Even if the jury does not understand the technical aspects of the evidence they are given to understand that the expert has been sanctioned or approved by the court in some way. Under Lord Woolf's system in the United Kingdom, for example, only one expert will be admitted in any given court case. Judges themselves are not scientists: they depend on what the scientists tell them. They are just as liable as anyone else to be impressed by academic qualifications and/or reputations.

In the *Dog Club Treasurer* case, not one of the other candidates presented anything like the degree of similarity with the questioned texts as the club treasurer. However, this is just my opinion, based on observation, and – as noted before – in the law courts of some countries this kind of professional opinion would be acceptable, but in others it would not. In the end the linguist has to work with the data available and within the constraints imposed by the local legal system: on some occasions there is sufficient linguistic data to enable a full statistical analysis – most often there is only enough to enable a descriptive account to be made. This should not be taken as a negative point, because linguistic evidence can still benefit a case. For example, linguistic evidence can often be used at the investigative stage by law enforcement officers – such as in a missing person inquiry, or a hate mail investigation, and although this is still unusual, it is nevertheless on the increase.

The reader may be forgiven for wondering why I did not undertake a statistical investigation of the texts in the *Dog Club Treasurer* case. Previously, I have stated that there are many dangers in making attributions on the basis of statistical measurement when the samples are small, i.e. when

---

Exercise 4.1

Below are two texts/excerpts. Analyse them for their most notable characteristics and say whether, in your opinion, the two texts are by the same author. State your reasons. Note this is a qualitative assessment, but nevertheless you should still consider these texts as part of a serious inquiry (which they were).

1. Thank you for your call this past Sunday night. I am so glad you would check up on such a rumor before you would believe it. There is no one on the Brown side of the family who would believe such a rumor nor obviously spread a rumor that you were getting a divorce since you have always been loud and clear about that. I appreciate your confronting me about it so that we could clear it – and many other things – up.

2. Fred sees only one way of dealing with things – his way – and criticizes anyone who tries to do differently. Bert and I are firm believers that there is more than one way to resolve problems and that we can indeed go beyond violence and heartlessness to do so. Bert and I choose to be an example by the lives we live, the way we raise our children, by our farming techniques, by making inroads in the public education system, etc. Constant criticism is not part of our philosophy and we choose not to be around such negativity. Bert was coming to tell you these things the other night when you were not home. Maybe that is just as well. Bert and I are as different as day and night from you and Fred. I do wish you the very best and you have no idea how much I wish things were different but, Louisa, they are not and never will be. Fred has made that very clear. I have always been very concerned for you and for Sam and now for a new baby. You are always in my thoughts.

---

the questioned and known texts are short, or when not enough is known about the texts themselves. In the forensic context this is all too often the case, which is why courts need to take a flexible attitude to methodology and evidence presentation if forensic linguistics is to play a role in the criminal justice system. I am sure that as more cases involving forensic linguistics are brought before the courts, these difficulties will be understood. In the final analysis, the courts will be able to assess for themselves the value of particular kinds of linguistic evidence.

In Chapter 6 I will look at different types of authorship investigation. One of the types of investigation to be considered is known as the 'prominent feature' type of investigation. As the term suggests, this type of investigation is carried out when it appears that an author exhibits a particular prominent linguistic feature or set of features. In fact, the texts written by the treasurer in the *Dog Club* case would certainly appear to qualify for this kind of analysis.

Meanwhile, in the next chapter I will give an illustration of some of the dangers of using statistical results from short texts, rather than using descriptive and/or observational methodologies, which I believe in many cases can provide a superior inquiry technique.[19]

SUGGESTIONS FOR FURTHER READING

Gibbons, J. 1994 (ed.) *Language and the Law*, London: Longman, Chapter 15.

Hänlein, H. (1998) *Studies in Authorship Recognition: A Corpus-based Approach*, Frankfurt: Peter Lang, European University Studies, Chapter 6.

Svartvik, J. (1968) *The Evans Statements: A Case for Forensic Linguistics*, Göteborg: University of Göteborg.

CHAPTER 5

Sampling and authorship

In forensic cases, written texts and spoken language samples are often very short and so cannot be measured accurately. This means that most forensic linguistic reports will present results in a non-statistical format. However, in many countries courts do not consider non-statistical methods reliable, and so the probability of forensic linguistic evidence being rejected by courts is high.

In statistical terms what this amounts to is a sampling problem. You might be able to predict the result of an election based on the opinions of 100 voters sampled at random, though 1,000 would be much more preferable. However, you would certainly be very unlikely to make a successful prediction based on, say, the opinions of just three or four voters. In forensic linguistics, linguists and statisticians continue to look for ways of overcoming this problem of sample size.

INTER-AUTHOR VARIATION AND INTRA-AUTHOR VARIATION

Statistical measurement of authorship markers, though interesting, has so far had little success when applied to forensic work. Even if authorship markers in short texts were useful, the presence of variation within an author's oeuvre (and not just between authors) means that what is satisfactory as an authorship marker on one occasion may not necessarily be satisfactory on another, as Grant and Baker (2001) have observed (see Chapter 2). Moreover, what may be satisfactory between authors A and B may not work between authors A and C, B and C, and so on. One author can vary greatly from another author: this is known as inter-author variation. However, sometimes the amount of variation within just one author's work – intra-author variation – can be even higher than that between two authors.

To investigate this, I conducted three attribution tests (**A, B** and **C** in the table below) on two text excerpts (**1** and **2**) of 590 words each by Adam Smith, the eighteenth-century economist. These tests measure a range of values, including lexical density, long word density, etc:

Table 5.1 *Authorship testing of texts written by Adam Smith*

Text set	1	2
Results:		
A	387	338
B	363	346
C	367	384

I carried out a *t test* on the results. You may recall this test from Chapter 1 (pp. 18–19). The *t test* in fact compares two sets of texts, or two authorship markers, or indeed two of anything. You look for the closest pair out of all possible pairs. That's it. No further explanation necessary for immediate purposes.

In the case of the two texts by Adam Smith, all I did was to try to see how close Text 1 was to Text 2. Actually, it showed that Text 1 and Text 2 were not really like each other with regard to the values being tested: the tests yielded a probability of 0.37. Strictly speaking, this does not mean that Adam Smith was only 37 per cent like Adam Smith. However, it does seem to indicate that Adam Smith, like just about all other human beings, was capable of considerable variation in his writing style.

To make the investigation more interesting, I then introduced two texts by a second author, Thomas Malthus (1766–1834), another economist, like Smith. Guess what I found? Not that Smith and Malthus were very different from each other, or even that there was variation within Malthus' own work. On the contrary, what I found was that the amount of variation between Malthus and Smith was very low – in other words they were *very similar* to each other, with the result of the *t test* giving a probability of 0.92 (i.e. $p = 0.92$). Bearing in mind that previously Smith 1 was very unlike Smith 2, it now appeared – to put it crudely – that Malthus was more like Smith than Smith was! Finally, just to confuse matters, a *t test* was carried out across Malthus' own texts: Malthus was even less 'like' himself than Smith was: in fact his *t test* yielded the low probability of 0.26. Confused? Don't be. We expected Smith to be like Smith. He wasn't. We expected Malthus to be like Malthus. He wasn't. We expected Smith and Malthus to be different from each other. They weren't. In fact, Smith and Malthus were more like each other than each of them was like himself. Put simply.

What these tests show is that variation within a single author sometimes exceeds variation between authors: in other words, we are sometimes more like each other than we are like ourselves. This is in addition to the fact that we are sometimes not at all like ourselves!

Before I go any further, I feel the reader may be in need of another dose of statistical information, specifically to do with probability and how we go about 'proving' a hypothesis.

There is just one brief moral to this: I am not trying to discredit statistics or statisticians – only to point out that whoever uses statistics must have a regard for the truth. Also, let me make this point clear: in the age of computers, don't bother doing statistical calculations – that's what spreadsheets (e.g. Excel™ and Lotus™) are for. Let your computer do the work – it's easy!

DIVERSION ON SOME ASPECTS OF STATISTICS

Probability: we discussed this in Chapter 1, no less, but here is some more information. If we say something is very probable we mean that it is very *likely*. If we say something is very improbable we mean it is very *un*likely. To put a number to this, statisticians seem to think of 19 out of 20 as very probable or highly probable. They base this on the argument that if something happens 19 out of 20 times it is not likely to be accidental. The 'opposite' of 19/20 is 1/20, i.e. the two add up to 20/20 (or 1/1, which equals 1). Just as statisticians regard 19/20 as 'very probable' they consider 1/20 as 'very improbable', or having 'very low' probability. Recall that 1/1 (or 1) is total certainty, something that is largely unknown in nature – whatever anyone tells you!

However, for some purposes 19/20 – although high – is not high enough. Why not? Well, in forensic linguistics as in other forensic sciences, someone's life may depend on the expert's findings. If you were going to provide evidence which ultimately might impact on the court's view of a defendant's guilt or innocence you would want to have confidence in your testing methodology: in such a case 19/20 (or 95/100) might just not be enough and so it is necessary to sometimes work to a higher level of probability than 95 per cent, such as 99 per cent, or even 99.9 per cent, in other words 99/100 (0.99) or 999/1,000 (0.999). The opposite end of the spectrum is 1 chance out of 100, i.e. 1/100 or 0.01, or – even lower – 1 out of 1,000, i.e. 1/1,000 or 0.001.

So much for levels of probability, but what about 'hypothesis' testing? This is discussed elsewhere in detail, so for the time being I will just say this. When we want to demonstrate (note, I do not use the word *prove* but *demonstrate*) a phenomenon, we begin by testing its opposite. If we fail to demonstrate the opposite of the phenomenon, then we feel that our phenomenon has been successfully demonstrated. When we test the opposite of something we are said to be testing the 'null hypothesis'. The null hypothesis is the opposite of the 'research hypothesis'. The research hypothesis is, in fact, our 'theory'. It is what we are really interested in. Right, enough statistics, back to the texts in hand.

FURTHER TEXT TESTING

Above I discussed inter-author and intra-author variation based on a series of authorship tests. Subsequently, I ran the same set of tests as that described for another group of texts, this time between the authors Jane Austen and Anthony Trollope and some questioned text, actually authored by Trollope. These showed inter-author variation to be significantly higher than intra-author variation, and again *t tests* – to test probability – were applied, with the following results:

Table 5.2 t test *of Austen, Trollope and unknown*	
Austen–Trollope	<0.001
Austen–Unknown	0.005
Trollope–Unknown	**0.83**

This seems a not entirely unsatisfactory result, at least with respect to the fact that the test distinguishes Trollope and Austen from each other, and rejects Austen as the author of the unknown text. That is on the negative side. On the positive side, if we take $p > 0.95$ as a minimum, we see that the test fails to attribute the questioned text to its true author (0.83), but at least it does not reject the true author (Trollope in this case). Do we class this as a successful test? Yes, the test is successful, precisely because it shows us that the measurement is unreliable. It only works to the twin extent of: (a) successfully being able to reject the false candidate (Austen); and (b) successfully failing to reject the true candidate (Trollope). But despite these two positive points, a test that cannot successfully confirm the true candidate cannot be spoken of as a good test. Again the test was applied, this time to a set of articles by several UK journalists, namely Michael Dynes, Libby Purves and Carol Midgley. Again, work from one of the authors – Michael Dynes – was chosen to be the questioned text, the three texts were measured, and a *t test* was applied:

Table 5.3 t test *of Dynes, Midgley, Purves and unknown*	
Dynes–Midgley	<0.001
Dynes–Purves	<0.001
Midgley–Purves	0.04
Dynes–Unknown	**0.15**
Midgley–Unknown	<0.001
Purves–Unknown	<0.001

Once more we find that the test can reject the false candidates and distinguish between the candidates. However, once again the test does not make the appropriate attribution: it only goes as far as not rejecting Dynes as a false candidate, and so is very limited. Among other things, this demonstrates the experimental nature of research: it can take a long time to devise a successful discriminatory test.

Hence, thus far we seem to have a test which (a) has shown that intra-author variation can be higher than inter-author variation, and (b) has successfully distinguished between sets of authors on two occasions, but (c) has failed to attribute correctly on even one occasion.

As mentioned previously, the length of each of the texts in all of the above tests was 590 words (including the first texts introduced, economics texts of Malthus and Smith). I wondered what would happen if we tested longer excerpts. Would the results improve?

I chose lengths of 1,000 words and tested one set of texts, Trollope and Austen. The same set of text excerpts as before was chosen as the questioned texts. The measurements were *t tested*, with the following results:

Table 5.4 t test *of Austen, Trollope and unknown (1,000-word excerpts)*

Austen–Trollope	0.008
Austen–Unknown	0.0003
Trollope–Unknown	0.97

This was, by comparison, a very promising result: the test seemed able, at last, to discriminate between candidates, to reject the false candidate, and (almost) to make a positive attribution, at least above $p = 0.95$. Let us assume for the moment that $p > 0.95$ is sufficient to make an attribution. Can we celebrate yet? I doubt it: the text excerpts in this instance were 1,000 words in length. This is about three times the length of the average forensic text. Even if the authorship markers chosen for this test yielded $p > 0.99$, it would still not be a good forensic test. Why? At the risk of repeating myself, for the reason just stated – namely, that the test does not work for short texts. For the forensic linguist, it means nothing that the test is successful on longer texts.

I should point out, though, that the test does at least have some measure of consistency. At the opposite extreme, namely for short texts of 400 words, the following *t test* results were obtained:

Table 5.5 t test *of Austen, Trollope and unknown (400-word excerpts)*

Austen–Trollope	0.004
Austen–Unknown	<0.001
Trollope–Unknown	0.23

In other words, for *very* short texts (400 words) the result was even more unreliable than for short texts (590 words). For longer texts (1,000 words) the result was more reliable than for short texts. This is what I mean by the test having consistency, as shown in Table 5.6.

From Table 5.6 we see that as text length increases, the test is more likely

Table 5.6 *Showing the increase in* p *proportionate to text length*	
Length	*Probability*
400	0.23
590	0.83
1,000	0.97

to make a correct attribution. p (i.e. probability) increases with text length. Surely this is encouraging? Unfortunately, it only demonstrates the need for longer texts, and, as I have been at pains to point out, such texts are rarely, if ever, available in forensic work. For the above tests, I tested four texts and rejected any which yielded data very different from the rest (known as outlying data): but at least we had four texts to test. In many forensic cases, however, we might have only one or two texts, sometimes of minimal length, say 150 to 200 words.

This is why it is so difficult to provide courts with the kinds of 'scientific' evidence they require if they insist on purely statistical methods of reporting. In many cases we can provide attributions with, say, 95 per cent probability (or 5 per cent error rate) if texts are 1,000 words or more in length. However – again at the risk of repetition – texts in forensic cases are usually considerably shorter than 1,000 words.

AN EXPERIMENT IN MEASUREMENT STABILITY

In the previous section the aim was to show that authors can vary greatly with regard to measurements taken from within their own work, and that successful attribution will sometimes depend on the number of texts available and their length. In this section I would like to present the argument in a little more detail, and show the reader the phenomenon of *measurement stability*. For this series of tests I looked exclusively at lexical density, and then only with regard to the texts of one author. However, I believe this information can be extrapolated to almost all authorship markers – not just lexical density, and furthermore, that it could apply to most authors at one time or another.

I should first explain what I mean by measurement stability and how it can be demonstrated.

Statisticians refer to a statistical function called *deviation*, or *standard deviation*. It is the extent to which instances of a measure vary from the average (or mean). Let us consider a hypothetical case, where the lexical

Table 5.7 *Lexical density of four hypothetical texts*

1	40
2	39
3	40
4	41
Average	40

Lexical Density: The number of lexical words in a text divided by the total number of words in that text: a lexical word is one with content, e.g. *cat, dog, eat, fish*, as opposed to a 'grammar' word, such as *the, it, and*, etc.

density of four texts is obtained as 40 per cent, 39 per cent, 41 per cent and 40 per cent respectively, as shown by Table 5.7.

The average lexical density is 40 per cent, as shown. How much does each text vary from the average? Very little, as we can see, in fact 0 per cent, 1 per cent, 1 per cent and 0 per cent. The degree to which each text varies from the average is known as the *standard deviation*. The standard deviation in the present instance works out (following a complex formula, which you need not bother learning, given how easy it is to use computer spreadsheets) as 0.7 per cent. Do any of the texts vary significantly more than this from the average? No. Therefore, we can say that, given the data we have here *standard deviation* is low, in other words measurement stability is *high*.

Conversely, if we take another set of texts and the measurements vary significantly from each other – resulting in a relatively high deviation – then we will be able to say that measurement stability is *low*.

So much for the introductory example. Now let us look at an actual instance of *measurement of stability*.

For this test, four excerpts from Jane Austen were taken, and their lexical density measured at 200 words (hereafter 'w'), 400w, 600w and 1,000w, making sixteen measurements in all. The results are given in Table 5.8.

Table 5.8 *Showing the instability of measurement in shorter texts (deviation decreases with length)*

Words	200w	400w	600w	1,000w
Pride and Prejudice	0.43	0.48	0.45	0.434
Sense and Sensibility	0.46	0.43	0.42	0.426
Emma	0.46	0.46	0.44	0.432
Mansfield Park	0.51	0.48	0.46	0.446
Mean	0.46	0.46	0.44	0.43
Deviation	0.03	0.02	0.017	0.007

From these data it is seen that (in the present instance at least) mean lexical density reduces with length (0.46 at 200w, 0.43 at 1,000w), but more importantly that there is substantially less deviation at 1,000w than at 200w. In fact deviation decreases from 0.03 at 200w, to 0.02 at 400w, to 0.017 at 600w and, finally, to 0.007 at 1,000w. In other words it declines from 3 per cent to 7 one hundredths of a per cent. From the statistical point of view this is significant, and its message is very stark: the stability of this measure (and others like it) in short texts, say of 200 words, must be treated with caution. Put another way: look at the different lexical density values at 200 words, they vary from 0.43 to 0.51, whereas at 1,000 words they vary only from 0.426 to 0.446: this is a difference of only 2 per cent as opposed to 8 per cent. Moral of the story? Be careful how you interpret statistics from short texts. This does not mean you should not attempt statistical measurement of short texts, just that you need to treat your results with great care.

SUGGESTIONS FOR FURTHER READING

Olsson, J. (1997) 'The dictation and alteration of text', *Forensic Linguistics*, 4(2): 226–51.

CHAPTER 6

Single-text inquiries

First, a practical consideration for the reader. In this chapter we will have to discuss some aspects of text statistics in a little more depth than previously. If you have little or no knowledge of such matters *as mean, standard deviation, t testing* and *hypothesis testing*, you should read up as much as you can on these subjects as there is a limit to the amount of space that can be devoted to them in a text on forensic linguistics; also, I will of necessity confine my discussion to broad generalities. Besides the many good books on the subject of statistics the Internet itself is simply overflowing with resources on these subjects. You are advised to use them to increase your understanding of this chapter.

Now to the main thrust of this chapter: single-text investigations. What is a single-text investigation? As the name suggests, in the classic single-text investigation there is just one text: there are no candidate author texts. However, some investigations may present a number of candidate author texts which – for one reason or another – cannot be used. They may, for example, be too short, or there may be too many differences in register or mode between them and the questioned text. The end result is the same as if there were no candidate texts: the forensic linguist will focus exclusively on the single questioned text. There is another reason why an inquiry containing multiple texts may in the end come down to a single-text investigation, and that is because the questioned text indicates some kind of *duality*, e.g. dual authorship, dual mode or dual register. In such a case the forensic linguist may choose to focus exclusively on the questioned text, not because the other texts are not relevant but because the evidence of duality within the questioned text is powerful enough to enable attribution by indirect means (see below).

In the following sections we will discuss the different kinds of single-text investigation which can take place. First, let us discuss attribution in broad terms.

ATTRIBUTION BY INDIRECT MEANS

In a single-text inquiry, the strategy is not usually one of identification – perhaps because there are no suitable comparative texts – but one of *attribution by indirect means*. Note, attribution by indirect means is really nothing more than the search for textual duality.

TEXTUAL DUALITY

Textual duality is the umbrella term I use to describe a number of different phenomena which can occur in text, and which are often found in single-text investigations. Most commonly these relate to mode, authorship and register, but there are several other categories – as shown in Table 6.1.

When duality (of whatever kind) occurs in the text's creation or composition, the text may show some sign of this on the surface. Usually, one part of the text will be noticeably different from another part – but different in some systematic, structural way. Table 6.1 sets out the main kinds of textual duality.

Table 6.1 *Types of textual duality*	
Dual mode	Was the text dictated, spoken or written, or was it compiled from notes?
Dual authorship	Did several people have a hand in its authorship – in other words is there evidence of more than one style?
Dual register	Is there evidence of more than one register, e.g. colloquial *vs.* bureaucratic language?
Dual chronicity	Was it composed over a period of several hours or days, or even longer?
Dual physical production	Could some or all of it have been produced by hand and then put on a word processor or typewriter, or vice versa?
Dual discourse goals	What about the text's content: does the structure of the discourse reveal – usually only in parts of the text, and then somewhat disguised – a prejudice in favour of, or – alternatively – against, one or more of the participants (usually the nominal author)?

These general kinds of duality often manifest themselves in more specific instances of duality, such as *lexical duality, ideational duality, duality of referent*, etc. These terms will become clearer in the course of this chapter, as I will illustrate them with specific examples.

A good example of *textual duality* is the Derek Bentley statement (which is discussed elsewhere in this chapter and throughout the book). The reader may be aware that Derek Bentley and Chris Craig were involved in an incident in which a policeman was shot dead on the roof of a south London factory. Bentley was supposed to have dictated his statement to the police after his arrest, but on close examination the text did not show any signs of having been dictated, and in fact exhibited several other very curious authorship symptoms, which led me to believe the text was of *dual authorship*. There are many kinds of dual authorship. With the Bentley text, the claim was that it had been dictated, but actually it turned out to have been written. The opposite kind of inquiry is also possible: we could be presented with a text which was supposed to have been written, but which bears all the hallmarks of having been dictated, at least in parts. This is what I believe happened in a recent well-known murder case, which I will also be discussing in the course of this chapter.

Attribution by indirect means breaks down into two main types of investigation, which I term the **contrastive feature** type and the **register variation isolation** type. I will explain these in the following sections.

ATTRIBUTION INVESTIGATIONS

Type 1: Contrastive feature type

In the contrastive feature type of inquiry the investigator assesses whether there are stylistic or content differences across different sections of the text, such as:

- plain text alternating with or surrounded by a lexically rich section (*lexical duality*);

- change/s in method of reference (*duality of referent*), nomenclature, or even orthography;

- distribution of one or more high-frequency (or textually significant) lexical words exclusively within one section of the text (e.g. the use of the word *gun* in a well-known disputed text).

Note that appearance of the above phenomena does not necessarily imply grounds for suspicion. Forensic linguists always have to use their judgement, and to back up their reasons with further observations.

In the *Bentley* case, the suspicion was that the text had been produced by two or more authors – namely Bentley on the one hand and the police officers questioning him on the other. One possible clue in support of this was the contrast between the long sentences at the beginning and end of the text and the short sentences in the middle of the text. This is a slight generalization of the actual data, but a necessary one.

Example 1   Instances of long sentences in the outer sections of the Bentley text

Second sentence: We were stopped by our parents going out together, but we still continued going out with each other – I mean we have not gone out together until tonight.

Second-last sentence: I should have mentioned that after the plain clothes policeman got up the drainpipe and arrested me, another policeman in uniform followed and I heard someone call him 'Mac'.

Example 2   Instances of short sentences in the inner section of the Bentley text

14   There was a little iron gate at the side.
15   Chris then jumped over and I followed.
16   Chris then climbed up to the drainpipe and I followed.
17   Up to then Chris had not said anything.
18   We both got out on to the flat roof at the top.

The observations regarding sentence length opened up the possibility that there might be some important differences of meaning or communicative intent between the opening and closing sections of the text on the one hand, and the mid-section on the other, and in this regard, several observations were made.

Until W174 (the 174th word) Bentley's companion is referred to as *Craig* (three times) and then *Chris Craig* (once). From W174 onwards he is *Chris*. Why should the central character in the narrative be referred to in three distinct ways (note: this is an instance of duality – or, in this case, multiplicity – of referent)? It seemed strange, to say the least.

As a result, I decided to treat (tentatively) the first 174 words, with the sentences immediately around the other long sentence, sentence 43, as one section, with the body – or inner part – of the text, W174 to ± W500, as another section. I then measured these two sections for sentence length average and found, not surprisingly, that the outer section yielded a relatively high average, in this case 15 words per sentence, while W175–500 – the middle or inner part of the text – averaged much lower at 11.74 words per sentence. This meant that on average, sentences in the inner section were only four-fifths the length of sentences in the outer sections of the text. I wondered if this was significant and decided to do a statistical comparison between the outer and inner sections of the text.

Words like *statistical* or *statistics* should not cause alarm. All I will be doing is describing several very basic statistical tools we can use to compare two (or more) of anything, it does not matter what, from the weight and size of a piece of fruit, to the loudness of a sound. However, it happens that in the present case we are talking about how to compare sentence length averages in two texts or two sections of text.

SOME STATISTICAL JARGON

If you can do simple arithmetic, then you can do elementary statistics. However, don't expect to understand the whole procedure after one reading. Depending on your specific interest in forensic linguistics, this may not even be necessary.

The overall aim is to compare two texts or text excerpts, and to measure the differences between them in some way. Why are we interested in doing this? For a very important reason: if two texts or two sections of a text are significantly different from each other, then we may have to assume that there might be some kind of textual duality in progress – such as duality of authorship or mode (see Table 6.1). The following sections deal with the concepts that we need to understand.

The mean and *number (n)*: **mean** is just a technical way of saying *average*, so we should not be intimidated by it. Personally, I find the word *average* easier, but we should use *mean* because average can denote the statistical mode or median. To calculate the *mean* add up the values you want to test and divide by the number of values you are adding up. For instance, you have four sentences with 20, 30, 50 and 80 words each. First, add them up to obtain the total: 20 + 30 + 50 + 80. The total is 180 words. Now, to calculate the *mean* we divide this total by the number of sentences, 4. So, the *mean* is 180/4 = 45 words. There are two kinds of mean we need to use. The first is known as the mean of the sample (or sample mean), it is written $\bar{X}$, pronounced X-Bar. If we have two groups and take a sample mean of the values in each group then we get $\bar{X}_1$ and $\bar{X}_2$. The second type of mean we are interested in is the mean of the population, the population mean. It is written μ. The sample mean is easily calculated: the above example of four sentences with a mean of 45 words is an instance of a population mean ($\bar{X}$): we know all the values in this population because it is a very small population. However, in the case of a large population, μ is almost always impossible to know: this, in fact, is why we use $\bar{X}$ – as an estimate of the population mean. So in the case of a long text, for example, we could just sample excerpts for values like sentence length, and view our findings as *sample means*. However, it goes without saying that, if I am operating an ethical statistical policy in my reporting to you, then I need to tell you whether the mean I have given is a population mean or a sample mean.

N is our abbreviation for *number*, in this case the number of sentences in the test (*n* is also known as *population size*). So, in this case $\mu = 45$, with $n = 4$, i.e. a population size of 4. You need to know *n* because I could dishonestly give you a misleading average, and if I did not reveal the population size *n*, you might never know that the mean was misleading.

For example, if I have three cars and my neighbour has 1, it would scarcely be accurate to say that 'average car ownership' in my street is

(3 + 1 = 4/2 i.e.) 2. You would only really get to know this was a bogus mean if you also knew that $n = 2$. If someone tells you the mean is £3 or $2 or 55 years, or 2.4 children, or 17.6 dijeriedoos, always try to find out n, because otherwise you will not be able to assess the validity of the data you have been given. For instance, you may see an advertisement which refers to a survey in which '7 out of 10 householders . . .' stated the same thing regarding a particular product: I just wonder how many owners were actually interviewed – in other words, what was the size of n, the sample which was tested?

All of this is not designed to weigh you down with statistical knowledge – frankly, it is not necessary to become an expert – but just to enable you to be aware that there are a million ways of presenting the *actualité*, some of which are less honest than others.

THE STANDARD DEVIATION

So much for the sample mean, $\overline{X}$, and number, n, our first two concepts. Now for something more complex: standard deviation, written σ (pronounced 'sigma') in a population and 's' in a sample. Supposing I have $10, Pete has $5, Mary has $8, and Fred has $1,000,000. What is our mean wealth? It is of course the four amounts added up, and then divided by 4. This gives us each a mean of $250,005.80. Personally, I would like to have $250,000. I would be very happy. However, neither I nor my friends Pete and Mary have anything like this sum. This is why $250,000 is also a bogus mean, just like the mean number of cars per household referred to above. But it is bogus in a different way. The reason that the previous mean of two cars was bogus, was because the *sample size* was ridiculously small. If I wanted to know the average number of cars per household in my street I would need to take a much bigger sample (n) than two households. I would probably need to sample about 20 households in a street, say of 200 houses (providing of course the street did not incorporate two or more socially distinct areas). But in the case of four people having a mean amount of $250,000, what makes this a bogus mean is something slightly different. It is the fact that one of us is very far from the rest of us in terms of actual wealth. You will recall that we discussed *standard deviation* in the previous chapter, but we need to expand on it a little here to show how it can be manipulated by the unscrupulous. We need the *standard deviation* because we need to know the degree to which the sample is spread or dispersed from the mean.

So, let us look at the wealth of our four hypothetical individuals in more detail. This is shown in Table 6.2.

Intuitively we feel that it is misleading to take a mean in this case, because of the huge discrepancy between the wealth of the four individuals represented. Nevertheless, for comparison purposes we must take a mean, which is just marginally more than $250,000, as previously stated. Through the application of a complicated formula – the exact details of

76

Table 6.2 *Hypothetical amounts owned by our hypothetical people*	
Owner	*Amount ($)*
John	10
Pete	5
Mary	8
Fred	1,000,000

which you will find in Chapter 12 – we calculate that the individuals in Table 6.2 above *deviate* from the mean by approximately $433,000. This in fact is our standard deviation. It tells us what we suspected already, but in more formal terms, namely that the average in this case is misleading. In particular the actual amount owned by Fred – $1,000,000 – is nothing like the average attributed to him, namely $250,000.

In Fred's case the discrepancy between actual amount owned and the average amount owned is much greater than the rest of us. Put simply, Fred deviates from the average much more than the rest of us, nearly twice as much in fact (i.e. *two standard deviations*). This degree of deviation is *statistically significant*. This is an important technical term to learn: *statistically significant*. It says the difference is important enough for us to consider Fred as someone who comes from a *different population* than the rest of us.

To recap: if one member of the population is two or more *standard deviations* from the mean, then that member of the population might belong to a different population. There are more precise, more technical ways of saying this, but it boils down to the same thing.

What does all this mean in plain language and what has it got to do with forensic linguistics? The standard deviation measure is a powerful way of showing that one or more members in a sample are *significantly different* from the other members in that sample – what statisticians call dispersion from the mean: the spread away from the average.

In the above example, it is certainly the case that Fred is from a different population than the rest of us: he is wealthy, and we are all quite poor. We can tell this from the standard deviation. As I mentioned above, when we have one or more members of a sample differing from the rest by two or more standard deviations, then clearly it would seem to be the case that these members of the sample are not really from the same population as the rest (with apologies for the repetition). That is exactly the case I am proposing with the two sets of sentences from the Bentley text, that the middle or inner section of the text is significantly different from the outer section of the text.

I believe I *have* shown that they are different, and as far as I can tell the difference looks significant. But how can I demonstrate this 'scientifically'?

Well, to do this, I need to revisit another concept mentioned in the previous chapter, namely *hypothesis testing*.

HYPOTHESIS TESTING: A BRIEF, SIMPLIFIED EXAMPLE

Although statistics is frowned upon by many, we should not let it put us off, because it is a necessary part of understanding the forensic world. We don't have to become experts, but we do need to grasp the broad generalities. On the plus side we probably know far more about statistics than we realize. We are likely to know how long people in our country live, how many litres of milk the average person consumes in a year, the average distance people travel to work each day and many other such data. Being a simple-minded person, I refer to this kind of statistics, very unprofessionally, as 'average' statistics. We use it to calculate what the so-called average person is doing with their money, their job or their time. Even in general conversation, 'average' statistics is never far away: how much do they earn at such-and-such a factory? How old are the teachers in that school? How fast do the cars travel on this road?

There is a development from what I call average statistics, and that is to do with the *difference* between two sets of people or things. So, when we watch a game of football, baseball or cricket, the commentators will be reeling off statistics to us throughout the game: how many innings, how many passes, how many catches, how many home runs, how many fours, sixes, etc. All of this will be given to us for one purpose: to compare one player or team with another player or team. Who scored more home runs, Babe Ruth or Shoeless Joe Jackson? Who took more wickets, Richie Benaud or Ian Botham? Did Pelé or Maradona score more goals? This kind of statistics I refer to as 'difference' statistics. On the face of it finding the difference between two things is quite easy, you just subtract the one from the other. So, in the case of the Bentley texts, surely all we need to do is to take 15, the average length of sentence in group A and subtract 11.74, the average length of sentence in group B? However, all this gives us is the *arithmetic difference*, it doesn't tell us what we really need to know: how *important* is the difference between the two groups – in other words what is the *significance* of the difference?

The perceptive reader will have observed that in order to calculate the *difference* between two groups I first need to know the *average* in each group. Remember, above, how I said individual scores are used to calculate first the average and then the standard deviation? Now, however, we need to take things a step further.

As we have seen above, one of the main aims in *statistics* is to discover how significant the difference between A and B is – whatever A and B are. If I were a botanist, A and B might be two different growing conditions given to a species of flower. If I were a geologist, A and B might be the different sizes of quartz rock found at separate locations. If I were a chemical pathologist, A and B might be the presence or absence of a certain poison in two different blood samples. As a forensic linguist, however, A and B are often a lot simpler than any of these. In the present case, A is one set of sentences in a text and B is another set of sentences in the same text, although of course there's nothing to stop A and B being sets of sentences from two *different* texts, instead of from the *same* text. Regardless of whether the sentences are from the same text or different texts, what I need to establish is whether these groups of sentences are different from each other in some important way, and I don't just mean a little bit different, but, as we have noted above, *statistically significantly different*. The meaning of this term will become apparent in due course.

So, where do we begin?

The answer may surprise you: with a theory. Actually, we call it a hypothesis, we begin with a hypothesis but, perversely, we state its opposite, universally called the *null hypothesis*. Remember, we talked about finding the significant difference between two things, A and B, for example? Well, when we state the *null hypothesis*, we effectively say that there is *no* significant difference (i.e. there is a *null* difference) between A and B. It's more scientific. It says, you're conducting an experiment, and for the sake of transparency, you are beginning by testing the *null hypothesis*. Of course it isn't true at all, what you're really interested in is the *research hypothesis*, in other words your real live theory. This may, for example, be that the two sets of sentences in Bentley's alleged statement were by two different authors. For many cases in forensic linguistics, one of the best ways to test the null hypothesis is to *t-test* it. This was introduced in previous chapters, but we need to expand on it a little here.

T-testing: In a *t test* we compare the averages of two populations such as ages, ice-creams or sentences in a text. There are a number of different types of *t test*. This one looks at two samples (the two sample test) which are not related (independent samples) and which are not even necessarily the same size as each other.

One final point which is of importance: this is to do with something called *tails*. You can have a one-tail test or a two-tail test. Supposing we are analysing apples from two different crops, A and B. Put simply, if you have reason to believe the apples in group A will be larger than the apples in group B or vice versa, then you do a *one-tail* test (because *one* answer is likely). On the other hand, if you have no reason to believe that the apples in either sample will be larger than those in the other, then you do a *two-tail* test. This is because *two* answers ('larger' and 'smaller') are possible.

There are many ways of doing the mathematics for *t-testing*, depending on the type of *t test* we're doing, but the underlying principle behind *all* of them is the same. In its simplified form the *t test* is nothing more than a difference between the two averages, divided by the difference between their standard deviations, such as:

$$t = \frac{\overline{X}_1 - \overline{X}_2}{s_1 - s_2}$$

> Where X is the sample mean and s is
>
> the sample deviation.

On the other hand, in tests where we might assume no difference between the population and sample means, we would begin with

$$(\overline{X}_1 - \overline{X}_2) - (\mu_1 - \mu_2)$$

> Where μ is the population mean.

After this we divide by the standard deviations.

The point is, whichever path we choose – and it will depend on circumstances too complex to go into here – a *t test* is basically just the difference between two means divided by the difference between two standard deviations or their estimates. Of course, purists will argue that the above is a very inexact description, and leaves too much latitude, since even this formula has many variations. However, I would argue that the above gives you a working idea of what *t-testing* is about, which is as much as I set out to do in the first place. Remember, we began with the simple task of calculating the mean of a sample, $\overline{X}$. We followed this by talking about *sample size* (n). We then talked about how some values within a population might be very different from the average just calculated. The statistic of all of these differences is called the *standard deviation*. Finally, we showed how each of these items in the statistical gun battery could be used to calculate a thing called *t*, as in *t testing* – something of a redundancy really, because the t in *t test* actually stands for *test* itself, or experiment. The upshot of all of the above is that in the Bentley text we found that the *t test* yielded a very low probability that the two sets of sentences were from the same text, a probability of 0.03 in fact (see '*Hypothesis test*', below. In other words they showed a high probability that the two sets of sentences were not from the same text. In the hypothesis test below I express this more formally. Note that H_0 is the null hypothesis I referred to earlier, while H_1 is the actual test hypothesis, known as the alternate or research hypothesis.

Hypothesis test

If in a given text two sets of sentences were found to average 15 words ($n = 17$) and 11.74 words ($n = 27$), with a standard deviation of 6 and 3.6 respectively.

H_0: $p > 0.05$ H_1: $p < 0.05$

Where H_0 is that the sentences come from the same population, and H_1 is that they come from different populations.

From the data: $p = 0.03$

$\therefore$ H_0 is rejected at the $p < 0.05$ level.

In the above hypothesis test '$p = 0.03$' means that the probability of the two sets of sentences originating from the same text is 0.03 (i.e. 3 per cent). This is considerably below the 0.05 (5 per cent) level, and so therefore I believe it is safe to reject the null hypothesis (at this level). By saying that the null hypothesis is rejected at the 0.05 level, I mean that there is a less than 5 per cent chance that we are rejecting H_0 incorrectly. Note that in rejecting the null hypothesis I am not directly inferring that there are two styles in, and therefore two authors of, the Bentley text, but that the presence of two styles cannot be discounted because there are, according to the data, two different distributions of sentence length averages. On the basis of the above calculations and the hypothesis test just demonstrated, I therefore concluded that the Bentley text was of dual authorship (see Olsson, 2000, for more detail). In the following section I will look at less formal – but still scientific – ways of testing for differences within texts.

In this section I presented a brief introduction to text statistics, with a view to giving the reader a quick flavour of how to compare two text excerpts in a single text inquiry. A simplified example of hypothesis testing was given.

THE RAMSEY NOTE: SINGLE OR DUAL AUTHORSHIP?

In the previous example we showed how the Bentley text displayed two distinct sentence length means in two sections of the text. In that example I concluded that the Bentley text was of dual authorship. The Ramsey text represents another (albeit different type of) example of a contrastive feature investigation. However, does this necessarily mean that the text was of dual authorship? The reader will be aware of the tragic murder of JonBénet Ramsey, a 6-year-old girl, in Boulder, Colorado, on Christmas Day, 1996. In this case a ransom note was found shortly before the discovery of the body. Probably, in the entire history of American crime there have been few forensic texts which have been the subject of greater speculation than the Ramsey ransom note. The parents of the child were among the earliest suspects, and some of the questions concerning the ransom note therefore involved them: did they write the note, and, if they did, was there an earlier draft? Did they write the note together? Did the father dictate it to the mother, or the mother to the father? On the other hand, if the parents were not involved, did two kidnappers write the note? The note is shown in full as Forensic text 6.1.

One of the first things that struck me about the Ramsey note[20] was the use of 'we' and 'I'. It is not uncommon for writers to use both pronouns, whether they are involved in single or multiple authorship. However, as the reader will notice from the above text, the use of 'I' is confined to just

Forensic text 6.1   The text of the Ramsey ransom note

Mr. Ramsey,
Listen carefully! We are a group of individuals that represent a small foreign faction. We do respect your bussiness but not the country that it serves. At this time we have your daughter in our posession. She is safe and unharmed and if you want her to see 1997, you must follow our instructions to the letter.

You will withdraw $118,000.00 from your account. $100,000 will be in $100 bills and the remaining $18,000 in $20 bills. Make sure that you bring an adequate size attache to the bank. When you get home you will put the money in a brown paper bag. I will call you between 8 and 10 am tomorrow to instruct you on delivery. The delivery will be exhausting so I advise you to be rested. If we monitor you getting the money early, we might call you early to arrange an earlier delivery of the money and hence a earlier pick-up of your daughter.

Any deviation of my instructions will result in the immediate execution of your daughter. You will also be denied her remains for proper burial. The two gentlemen watching over your daughter do not particularly like you so I advise you not to provoke them.

Speaking to anyone about your situation, such as Police, F.B.I., etc., will result in your daughter being beheaded. If we catch you talking to a stray dog, she dies. If you alert bank authorities, she dies.

If the money is in any way marked or tampered with, she dies. You will be scanned for electronic devices and if any are found, she dies. You can try to deceive us, but be warned that we are familiar with Law enforcement countermeasures and tactics. You stand a 99% chance of killing your daughter if you try to out smart us. Follow our instructions and you stand 100% chance of getting her back. You and your family are under constant scrutiny as well as the authorities. Don't try to grow a brain John. You are not the only fat cat around so don't think that killing will be difficult.

Don't underestimate us John. Use that good southern common sense of yours. It is up to you now John!
    (Victory!)
    (S.B.T.C.)

one part of the text, from halfway in the second paragraph to the end of the third paragraph: 'I will call you . . . I advise you not to provoke them'.

> **Forensic Text 6.2**   Localized distributions: 'I', 'my'
>
> . . . *I* will call you between 8 and 10 am tomorrow to instruct you on delivery. The delivery will be exhausting so *I* advise you to be rested. If we monitor you getting the money early, we might call you early to arrange an earlier delivery of the money and hence a earlier pick-up of your daughter.
>   Any deviation of *my* instructions will result in the immediate execution of your daughter. You will also be denied her remains for proper burial. The two gentlemen watching over your daughter do not particularly like you so *I* advise you not to provoke them . . .

This seemed interesting. Why should 'I' be confined to just this one part of the text. Coincidentally (apparently) the word 'delivery' also occurs just in the same part of the text as 'I': '. . . instruct you on *delivery . . . delivery* will be exhausting . . . arrange an earlier *delivery*'. I wondered, therefore, whether the author, feeling that insufficient information had been given with regard to *delivery*, inserted this section at a later stage in an earlier draft: by accident, perhaps, this person had used 'I' rather than 'we' in just this part of the text. If this were the case, it might lend support to the notion that there were two authors.

I then examined the rest of the text to look for other points of comparison, which was when I realized that there were several instances of the same kind of restricted circulation (i.e. localized occurrence of a particular word or phrase). For example the phrase 'she dies' is limited in scope to just one group of successive clauses: 'If we catch you talking to a stray dog, *she dies*. If you alert bank authorities, *she dies*. If the money . . . tampered with, *she dies*.' We do not find the phrase 'she dies' anywhere else in the text, except just in this one small area.

> **Forensic text 6.3**   Localized distributions: 'she dies'
>
> . . . *she dies*. If you alert bank authorities, *she dies*. If the money is in any way marked or tampered with, *she dies*. You will be scanned for electronic devices and if any are found, *she dies* . . .

There are two other instances of this kind of distribution in the text: for instance, note that the dollar amounts are all localized to one area.

> **Forensic text 6.4**   Localized distributions: '$'
>
> ... $118,000.00 from your account. $100,000 will be in $100 bills and the remaining $18,000 in $20 ...

The other localized distribution is: 'John' (Mr Ramsey's first name). This is restricted in distribution to just the last few sentences of the text:

> **Forensic text 6.5**   Localized distributions: 'John'
>
> ... Don't try to grow a brain *John*. You are not the only fat cat around so don't think that killing will be difficult. Don't underestimate us *John*. Use that good southern common sense of yours. It is up to you now *John*! ...

Hence we see that there are several instances of localized repetition in the Ramsey text. This would indicate that the localization of a single word, such as 'I' to one part of the text is not unusual in this text. In other words, whatever else we might be tempted to conclude about this text, we have no grounds for assuming it is a dual authorship text. At least we have no grounds on the basis of the localized change of pronoun use from 'we' (which is found throughout the text) to 'I', found in just one section of the text.

The above is just an outline of the reasoning process in considering whether the text was of dual or single authorship. Below, I recap these points in a more systematic fashion: the reader will recall that I began with a hypothesis, as described in the previous section.

Hypothesis
The Ramsey text is of dual authorship.

- Observation: an instance possibly supporting the hypothesis is the localized distribution of 'I' – confined to one small section of the text, coincident with the word 'delivery'.

- Tentative conclusion: when we find one section of a text notably different from the rest we may be inclined to view the text as having dual authorship.

- Further observation: there are several other instances of localized distribution, such as '$', 'she dies', and 'John' in the text.

- Conclusion: because localized distribution is common in this text, there is no single section of the text which is structurally different from the rest. Therefore there is no reason to suppose that a second author was involved in the production of the text.

At this stage I will refer to Popper's formula for reasoning modification. This is the observation that we modify our reasoning depending on experience, starting with a hypothesis formed on the basis of an initial observation:

$$P_n - TS - EE - P_{n+1}$$

which can be translated as follows – on being confronted with a problem (P_n) we attempt a trial solution (TS). Later we modify this, mainly by error elimination (EE) which then produces a revised appraisal of P_n, now P_{n+1}.

In my reasoning of the Ramsey text, I followed a typical Popper-style sequence:

- I found myself confronted with a problem, P_n: is the text of dual authorship?

- I found a possible clue and on this basis offered a trial solution, TS: the text could be of dual authorship.

- I conducted some further observations in order to eliminate any possibility of error, EE. There were other instances of the phenomenon that had led me to my first tentative solution.

- I therefore revised my tentative observation, and re-stated the situation or hypothesis as P_{n+1} – namely that the text was not of dual authorship.

I offer the above not as an ideal example of authorship testing, but merely as an alternative way of applying the scientific method where there is insufficient data to undertake a statistical analysis. Readers should be aware that there are many valid ways of making deductions. Rigid statistical analyses, attractive as the outcomes they present might appear to be, are not necessarily the only way to reach definitive conclusions. There are many ways of arriving at a state of *relative* certainty – which is all we can reasonably hope for in a world in which little is certain.

Type 2: The register variation isolation inquiry

The Gilfoyle 'suicide' letter: two styles?

Previously we suggested several ways in which the presence of multiple styles could be detected in a text. Among these were the following:

- a lexically rich, or otherwise apparently florid section of text, preceded and/or followed by text in a plainer style (or the reverse);

- an excerpt whose vital measurements (word length average, lexical density, sentence length average, etc.) differ markedly from surrounding text;

- an excerpt which is at variance, factually or in terms of ideas, with surrounding text.

The register variation isolation type begins with an investigation of register within a text. It is closely related to that of the contrastive feature type of inquiry which examines different sets of stylistic features in different sections of the text. The register variation isolation type examines the possibility of two registers or modes: either the text contains a *formal* and an *informal* register, or it contains signs of *spoken* and *written* language. In the case of the Bentley text at first there appeared to be two registers or modes. However, the second 'register' – the mid-section of the text previously referred to – turned out to be nothing of the kind: rather it seemed to be an attempt at emulating spoken language. This is why we could not designate the Bentley investigation as being of the register variation isolation type. However, another text, the Gilfoyle 'suicide' text does offer the possibility of such an investigation, because there was an early claim that the suicide texts had been dictated to the deceased. In other words in the case of the Gilfoyle 'suicide' text, there was a claim that the text consisted of more than one mode, i.e. that it was both dictated and written. This is exactly the kind of text that the register variation isolation type of investigation is designed to address, as will become clear in the following paragraphs.

When first looking at the Gilfoyle texts, the most striking feature of the alleged suicide letter (referred to here as 'S1') is the frequent occurrence of such phrases as, 'pain and heartache', 'family and friends', 'change or alter', 'goals and dreams', 'pain and suffering', etc. On analysing these phrases in more detail, they seem to be pairs of close collocates: for example *suffering* is a **collocate** of *pain*, *friends* is a collocate of *family*, etc. What is a *collocate*? To understand this, consider the concept of a language *corpus*, a body of language. More particularly, a corpus is a vast collection of samples of natural language (spoken and written). We use such a body of language, or corpus, to analyse language, to understand how it is used and – in the present instance – to look at words which routinely occur near each other: such words are called collocations or collocates.

The lexical words of the pair of collocates (e.g. *pain*, *suffering*) usually enter into a metaphoric relationship with each other, for example:

1. Synonymy (similar meaning).

2. Meronymy (part–whole).

3. Antonymy (opposite meaning).

The pairs of words in these metaphoric relationships are referred to as *couplets*. There are a number of these couplets in the questioned Gilfoyle suicide text, S1, as shown in the bold-type sections of Forensic text 6.6.

> **Forensic text 6.6**   Excerpt from the Gilfoyle 'suicide' text
>
> Dear Eddie,
>   . . . Don't blame yourself Eddie it's not your fault, I've caused **all your pain and heartache**. I've destroyed **you and your life**. I just hope you can rebuild everything and **realize your goals and dreams**.
>
> I'm sorry for hurting my **family**, your **family** and my **friends** but most of all hurting you . . .
>
> . . . I can't **change or alter** what I've done but if I could I would. They say time heals a broken heart. I hope your heart heals pretty quick. I don't want you to waste anymore of your life. Its time to turn the clock **forward instead of backwards** and go forward . . .
>
> . . . I apologise for all the **pain and suffering** . . .

On close examination it turns out that the paragraphs containing this couplet style use predominantly phrasal *and* (and phrasal *or*), whereas in the other paragraphs mostly it is only clausal *and* which occurs, see examples below:

> **Example 3**   Instances of phrasal 'and' and clausal 'and'
>
> *Phrasal 'and'*: 'pain *and* heartache' – phrasal *and* usually connects two words or phrases
> *Clausal 'and'*: '. . . tell them I love them *and* that I'm sorry for everything.' – clausal *and* usually connects two clauses.

As Biber observes (Biber, 1988: 245) clausal *and* is usually more indicative of speech than written language. By contrast, phrasal *and* is often symptomatic of written language. It also happens that those paragraphs containing couplets show a higher word length average than the paragraphs which do not contain the couplets, as can be seen from Tables 6.3 and 6.4.

Table 6.3 *Word length averages for paragraphs containing couplets*

Paragraph	Word length average
2	4.67
3	3.93
7	3.94
8	4.21
Average	4.19

Table 6.4 *Word length averages for paragraphs not containing couplets*

Paragraph	Word length average
1	3.46
4	3.64
5	3.74
6	3.58
Average	3.6

You will recall the notion of the *null hypothesis*, given earlier. Assuming the null hypothesis, these data yielded an average probability of $p = 0.04$ for the word length averages of the couplet paragraphs to be of the same population as the non-couplet paragraphs. In other words – since $p < 0.05$ (i.e. p is less than 5 per cent) the indication was that they were from different populations, texts or events. Following this observation it was then noted that the sentences in the paragraphs[21] containing couplets seemed to be shorter than the sentences in paragraphs not containing couplets. Measuring the sentences of the paragraphs yielded the following values:

Table 6.5 *Gilfoyle S1 sentence length average for paragraphs containing couplets*

Paragraph	Sentence length average
2	6.8
3	12.5
7	10.2
8	9.25
Average	9.69

Table 6.6 *Gilfoyle S1 sentence length average for paragraphs not containing couplets*

Paragraph	Sentence length average
1	15.25
4	15.25
5	9
6	9.57
Average	12.27

Again assuming the null hypothesis, the calculation was made that only paragraph 2 of the couplet paragraphs showed $p < 0.05$ with respect to being of the same population as the non-couplet paragraphs. Of the non-couplet paragraphs only 1 and 4 showed $p < 0.05$ with respect to being of the same population as the couplet paragraphs. All of the other paragraphs showed $p > 0.05$ – in other words the null hypothesis could not be rejected with reference to sentence length averages. In plain terms this means that we can note the fact that the sentences in the coupleted paragraphs are on average shorter than the non-coupleted paragraphs, but our scientific proof is not as strong as we would like. Luckily we have better proof with regard to word length differences between the couplet and non-couplet paragraphs.

Style in the Gilfoyle 'suicide' note: S1

Above we noted that S1, the alleged suicide note in the Gilfoyle case, appeared to contain two distinct kinds of paragraph, as summarized in Table 6.7.

Two points arise from the differences between the textual measurements of the couplet paragraphs and the non-couplet paragraphs: (a) do they indicate the presence of more than one style and (b) if so, what kind of style difference do they indicate?

The reader will recall that *long words* are more typical of written language than they are of spoken language (Biber, 1988: 104–5), as are short, simple sentences (Olsson, 2000: 24). A similar point was made by De Vito some years ago when comparing written with 'oral' language:

> written samples differed from the oral 'in that they included more words that were difficult, had greater verbal diversity, had greater density of ideas, and contained more sentences that were grammatically simple'.
> (De Vito, 1965: 128)

If we add to these claims the observation that phrasal 'and' is itself more characteristic of written language, it does seem more and more possible that we are dealing with a difference of language mode between the two types of paragraph in the alleged suicide note, S1.

If the above observations are correct, all the signs seem to point to parts

Table 6.7 *Style differences between paragraph types in S1*

Style 1 Paragraph	Style 2 Paragraph	Null hypothesis
Paragraphs contain couplet metaphors	Non-couplet paragraphs	n.a.
Phrasal 'and'	Clausal 'and'	n.a.
Short sentences	Long sentences	failed
Long words	Short words	NH rejected

of S1 having been dictated or spoken, while the couplet paragraphs – inserted later (for reasons which I will allege will become clear in the next section) – may have been written. However, the question is how sure are we? If we move the discussion from the topic of textual measurements (word length, sentence length, etc.) to one of content – will we find real, linguistic differences between these paragraphs and the non-couplet paragraphs? This will be the focus of the next section.

The theme of the couplet paragraphs

In this section we will move from differences of measurement across the two supposedly different types of paragraph in the 'suicide' text, to questions of content. As will be plain to the reader, our argument that a given text contains two distinct styles would be more convincing if we could demonstrate not just differences of measurement, but actual differences of content as well.

Looking closely at paragraphs 2, 3, 7 and 8 in S1 we see that the notions of blame and fault occur several times. For example, immediately after claiming that 'I' decided to 'put an end to everything' the author of S1 says:

> Don't blame yourself Eddie it's not your fault.

Note that this is much more than just a casual acceptance of blame. The repetition of *blame* through *fault* makes it very emphatic. In the very next sentence, for example, further blame is placed on Paula:

> I've caused all your pain and heartache. I've destroyed you and your life.

It seems the author is anxious that whoever reads this letter should lay all the blame on Paula and not on anybody else. The next paragraph, which is also a couplet paragraph, restates the recent apologies: 'I'm sorry for hurting my family, your family and my friends but most of all hurting you', and continues with more self reproaches. It is Paula's *stupidity* which is to blame, and Paula's *moaning and nagging*. Hence, in these two couplet paragraphs there is absolutely no doubt that the author wishes the reader to understand that Paula is to blame for everything.

After further expressions of regret on 'Paula's' part in paragraph 7 ('I can't change or alter what I've done but if could I would') this theme of self-blame continues in paragraph 8, which is the last paragraph of the text: 'I apologise for all the pain and suffering I have caused by taking my own life. I don't mean to cause any problems for anyone, no-one is to blame except myself'. This is a further restatement of the previous self-blame sections of the text. Note that the other sections of the text are not absolutely devoid of blame for Paula, rather they are concerned with other matters in addition to some degree of self-criticism. They are, however, not by any means as fault-finding or critical of Paula as the paragraphs mentioned here.

The other questioned text in Paula's handwriting (S2) also contains two couplet paragraphs. These are, first:

> **Forensic text 6.7** Opening paragraph of Gilfoyle S2 text
>
> I am sorry for what I am about to write, but I can't go on living a lie anymore. I've **cheated & lied** to you. I just can't carry on anymore. I am having to write it down on paper as I can't tell you face to face.

> **Forensic text 6.8** Closing paragraph of Gilfoyle S2 text
>
> You must go on and forget me and my family its all down to you now. You have been great with me over the whole situation. I couldn't have been so calm about it as you have been. But as you said you only stayed because of the baby it was not for me. I wonder what my **family and friends** will say, it's going to be interesting. *I hope they don't blame you*, I will tell them everything once I'm gone.

Curiously, both these couplet paragraphs (though, admittedly, they contain fewer couplets than S1) also contain admissions of guilt and self-blame: 'I've cheated & lied to you', and 'I hope they don't blame you', among other, less direct forms.

Hence, both S1 and S2 seem to have couplet paragraphs devoted to the issue of blaming Paula. Both sets of couplet paragraphs are at the beginning and end of the text and not in the middle. The couplet paragraphs in S1 have several distinctive features – listed above – which lead us to believe they may have originated as written text while the remainder of S1 may have originated as spoken/dictated. In any case in S1 the couplet paragraphs seem to be in a different style to that of the non-couplet paragraphs. These differences are less obvious in S2.

It seems possible that these couplet paragraphs were inserted after the main text was already outlined: certainly they add nothing material to the information of the text. But although their informational content is low, they evidently have a specific function: to lay as much blame as possible on Paula. But that is not their only purpose. Their second purpose is a silent, almost unspoken one: to exonerate or even to praise Eddie. However, this purpose, though almost subliminal is not entirely absent: 'you have been great with me over the whole situation' (in S2) for example, is just one of the items of apparent praise for Eddie, while S1 does not venture any further than: 'no-one is to blame except myself'. Since Eddie had already been told 'Don't blame yourself' and 'it's not your fault' we can only assume that the 'no-one' in 'no-one is to blame except myself' once again exonerates Eddie and does not refer to anyone else.

It is not unusual for suicide notes to contain elements of self-accusation, nor is it unusual for suicide notes to attempt to exonerate a spouse or other loved one. However, what is unusual about S1 is that two significant portions of it, paragraphs 2, 3 and paragraphs 7, 8 seem to be in a markedly different style or register from the rest of the text, and it so happens that just these two sections exonerate – several times – Eddie Gilfoyle, while at the same time blaming – several times – Paula.

Finally, when we turn to S2 we see the same thing there. Again, there are two couplet sections. Again these occur at the beginning and end of the text. Again these exonerate Eddie and, again, they blame Paula. On close examination both texts break down into two types of subtext: information and blame. The information section is predominantly contained in the non-couplet sections of the text, while the blame sections of the text are predominantly co-located with the couplets.

Two-style hypothesis in the Gilfoyle 'suicide' letter

This brief style analysis of the Gilfoyle 'suicide' text has had as its aim the demonstration of multiple styles in text, just as the earlier analysis of the Bentley text did. It is therefore appropriate to review the nature of the claim.

Hypothesis

There are two styles in the Gilfoyle 'suicide' letter and the alleged 'confession' letter.

Observations

1 Each of the above texts has several paragraphs containing couplets.
2 These couplets are not found in the rest of the text.
3 The coupleted paragraphs in S1 have certain other distinctive features, such as longer words and shorter sentences and phrasal 'and'. Of these features only that of longer word length averages is statistically significant. This was the same feature found to be statistically significant between the two different styles in the Bentley text.

Conclusion

The text appears to contain two distinct styles. The purpose of the coupleted paragraphs seems to have been to lay as much blame as possible on Paula, while exonerating Eddie. With regard to this aspect of self-incrimination the Gilfoyle 'suicide' text seems to be similarly structured to the Bentley text, and possibly certain other kinds of questioned text of dual authorship. Like the Bentley text, S1 is a first-person text. Just as with the Bentley text, this makes the process of self-blame and/or self-incrimination much easier than otherwise.

Inferences

What inferences can be drawn from the above analysis? A second author will be introduced into the text creation process to originate a second line of thinking, or to emphasize an existing line of thinking which has not hitherto (in the view of one or other party to the text) been given enough emphasis. This controlling author – the police officers in the case of the Bentley text and, apparently, Eddie Gilfoyle in the case of the Gilfoyle text – is then able to indulge in self-advancement, self-exoneration and/or blame of the other party. However, depending on how the text is produced, the presence of the second author may be detectable using certain key measurements such as word length average and sentence length average. If significant differences are found in any of these areas, which can be linked to other style or content differences, then this would appear to be further confirmation that the text contains two styles. Both the Gilfoyle and the Bentley text would, on this basis, be prime candidates for consideration as texts of dual authorship.

Conclusion

In the previous two sections the two main attribution investigative strategies were considered, the contrastive feature type and the register isolation variation type. These two types were seen to have several important similarities. In each case the text contained a marked duality of style. These dualities were finally attributed to dual or multiple authorship on the one hand, or dual register or dual mode on the other.

Type 3: Prominent-feature type

Prominent-feature type is the term I use in referring to an investigation in which a candidate presents a style of writing with very distinctive, or prominent, features. Very often there is only one text in this kind of investigation – hence its inclusion in a chapter on single-text investigations. However, there are cases where there are many texts within such an inquiry.

Prominent-feature cases differ from *contrastive-feature* cases where, typically, we find one set of features in one or more sections of the text contrasting with another set of features in one or more other sections of the text.

As a type of investigation the prominent-feature type is relatively rare, and in fact breaks down into two sub-types. In the first sub-type there is an adequate number of texts of good length from each of several candidates. This is the *comparative–prominent feature* sub-type, so called because we are able to compare features across a set of candidates. The case of the Dog Club Treasurer, discussed in Chapter 4, is a good example of this kind of investigation. We had several features, they were all fairly prominent (in the sense of unusual) and we could compare the work of several authors across a number of texts. So much for the comparative–prominent feature type of investigation.

In the second type of investigation, no candidates other than the suspect author are under examination, and so this is just known as the prominent-feature type, of which the Lindbergh case of the early 1930s is perhaps the pre-eminent example.

The Lindbergh case

The infant son of Charles Lindbergh and Anne Morrow Lindbergh, Charles Lindbergh Jnr, was kidnapped on 1 March, 1932, and subsequently murdered. The note left at the scene of the crime by the perpetrator is given in Forensic text 6.9.

Forensic text 6.9   The first Lindbergh ransom note

Dear Sir!

   Have 50000$ redy with 2500$ in 20$ bills 1500$ in 10$ bills and 1000$ in 5$ bills. After 2–4 days we will inform you were to deliver the Mony.

We warn you for making anyding public or for notify the polise the child is in gut car.

Indication for all letters are singnature and 3 holes.

This was just one of many ransom notes written by the kidnapper. Among many other features, note that the various sums ($2500, $1500, $1000) do not add up to the total demanded, i.e. $50,000: in fact they add up to exactly one-tenth of the ransom amount, i.e. $5000. In other letters we have various phonological clues to the probable L1 (first language) of the writer being German, for example 'covert' for *covered*, 'boad' for *boat*, 'supway' for *subway* and 'simble' for *simple*. There is also 'Haus' (initial capital) for *house*.

   Even making allowances for the writer of the ransom notes not being very experienced at writing English, there are numerous instances of non-standard English in the letters which indicates not just that the writer had difficulties in communication because of a different L1, but other – perhaps neurolinguistic – problems as well.

   For example, consider the following excerpt:

Forensic text 6.10   Lindbergh ransom note

It is realy necessary to make a world affair out of this, or to get your baby back as soon as possible to settle those affair in a quick way will be better for both

---

Confusion between questions and statements

In the above excerpt it seems the writer was actually asking a question and not making a statement. In referring to the publicity generated by the crime, he says: 'It is realy necessary to make a world affair . . .' but since he offers the alternative, 'or to get your baby back as soon as possible' it seems to me he really intends to ask a question: 'Is it really necessary to make a world affair . . .?'

In the same letter he appears to claim that the baby is being well cared for: '. . . don't be afraid about the baby-keeping care of us day and night'. But here he has the baby 'keeping care of *us*' (my italics) – in other words the baby is doing the caring, and not the adults.

In the same letter he says: 'We know very well what it means to us' in referring to the way in which the Lindberghs have (according to him) publicized the crime. It is evident (to me at least) that he probably means '*You* know very well what it means to us', rather than 'We know . . .' since this precedes a demand for an increase in the ransom money.

We also have adverbs for adjectives: 'impossibly' for *impossible* and, also, 'impollibly' for *impossible*, and on occasion nouns for adjectives, e.g. 'innocence' for *innocent*. Therefore, when we add these various instances of the kidnapper's language together, we note:

- a tendency to mix actor–patient roles;
- a tendency to confuse statements with questions;
- mixing of grammatical categories, e.g. nouns for adjectives, adverbs for adjectives;
- confusion of first-person with second-person pronouns;
- confusion of consonantal sounds, e.g. 's' for 'l' and/or the creation of new words based on existing ones, e.g. *impollibly* for *impossible*.

There is one other curious feature of this writer's language, and that is the insertion of superfluous syllables in words, for example 'Lindberbergh' for 'Lindbergh' in one of the letters. This is in addition to the confusion of categories noted above, the several apparently 'nonsense' sentences already noted, and the apparent creation of new words seems to indicate some kind of neurolinguistic disability, possibly Wernicke's[22] aphasia.

However, so far we have referred only to the written letters by the 'unknown' ransom letter writer. How can we relate these to the suspect in the case, Bruno Hauptmann? Do we have any record of his *known* language use? Fortunately, we have an audio-recording of a speech made by Hauptmann to the world's press and media at the time of his conviction for the murder of the child.

Forensic text 6.11 Hauptmann's speech: an early audio-recording

i want to tell the people of america dat i am absolutel innocent of the crime of the murder my conviction was agreed to file and never for the **Lindenbergh** baby and i never would burst in the admonium and i vant do appeal to all people everyvhere to aist me in dis time, the defence ment must be raised to carry my appeal to a higher court, before god i am absolute innocent i have told all i know about the crime.[23]

I believe that this speech excerpt contains many of the same features as the language of the ransom notes, including the spurious insertion of meaningless syllables into words, e.g. *Lindenbergh* (see *Lindberbergh* in the ransom letter – below):

Forensic text 6.12   Comparative text from the kidnapper

dear Sir. please handel incloced letter to Col. Lindbergh. It is in Mr. **Lindbergergh** interest not to notify the Police. dear Sir, Mr.Condon may act as go-between. You may give him the 70000$. make one packet the size will bee about . . . (sketch of a box) we have notify your already in what kind of bills. We warn you not to set any trapp in any way. If you or someone els will notify the Police ther will be a further delay After we have the mony in hand we will tell you where to find your boy You may have a airplain redy it is about 150 mil awy. But befor telling you the adr. a delay of 8 houers will be between.

There are also clauses that have no meaning in the speech, such as 'was agreed to file and never for the Lindenbergh baby', invented words, e.g. *admonium*, confusion of categories (*absolutel* and *absolute* for *absolutely*), and even the mixing up and/or extension of functions, e.g. *handle* (spelled *handel*) for 'hand', i.e. *hand* to someone, or *hand* over to someone. In addition there are several consonantal substitutions, such as /d/ for /t/ which accord with the suspect's written language. Finally there is what I take to be an inadvertent admission: 'I have told all I know about the crime'. If Hauptmann was not involved, why would he have known about 'the crime'? If he had no involvement, then it would not have been 'the crime' but 'the incidents', 'events', etc. If he was innocent, why should he have known anything?

Exercise 6.1

Below are some excerpts from a variety of texts. In your view is the writer in each case a native or non-native speaker of English?

1. I decided to dig down into my memory and extricate a few anecdotes.
2. If you have any questions or comments, feel free to write it down in the following box.
3. All types of accommodation are located on good pitches and are provided with garden furniture and a full inventory.
4. Israel has used the weapon before in the conflict with the Palestinians.
5. Does Europe not run the risk of falling apart if it enlarges to the borders of the continent?

There have been many conspiracy theories about the Lindbergh kidnapping, including that the parents of Charles Jnr, had kidnapped and murdered their own child, that the Lindbergh baby was seen many years later, alive and well, that Hauptmann was framed, and so forth. To date I have not seen any comments on the language evidence in this crime – above I have presented only a brief summary of this. As to the question of individual style, I believe Hauptmann's style of language use is so marked because of his apparent disability that not only does it transcend genre (compare the ransom notes with the appeal for help to the press), but also it transcends mode, i.e. speech *vs.* writing, and – indeed – even register: informal notes as compared to the formality of an appeal. This is why I have classified this inquiry as one of *prominent-feature identification*, i.e. the features of this speaker's style are so prominent that they are not very difficult to identify, regardless of whether we find them in speech or writing, or in a formal or informal context. We are fortunate to have an audio-recording of Hauptmann's actual words at the end of the trial which provide many parallels with the written language of the ransom notes, making the language evidence[24] against him very strong.

McMenamin (1993: 3–28) gives another example of a comparative–prominent feature authorship inquiry, with regard to the 'Mrs Brown' diary (referred to earlier). In that case there was good reason to believe that the diary could only have been written by Mr Brown or Mrs Brown. This made the authorship candidature a closed one – the candidates were drawn from a closed 'circle' where – any suspicion of dual authorship aside – the task is usually one of weighing the relative styles of the two candidates and providing evidence in favour of one or the other. In the Brown case McMenamin was able to do this because, as previously indicated, there were a number of prominent linguistic features in the corpus of one of the candidates which accorded closely with a number of features found in the questioned text. In the Lindbergh case we were fortunate because someone had thought to preserve an audio tape for more than seventy years, presumably because they had realized its historical importance to the case. In *State* v. *Brown*, on the other hand, it is the fact that there were only two candidate authors, one of whom had a quite distinctive style, which enabled the identification to be made. The prominent-feature type of investigation is, almost by definition, a descriptive study. As such there are two ways in which it can be used: either as an investigative tool or, if admitted into evidence, merely as an aid to the trier of fact, rather than as hard scientific evidence. In that case the forensic linguist simply offers the evidence as a series of observations, and it is up to the court how such evidence is used.

CHAPTER CONCLUSION

In this chapter, *single-text* authorship inquiries were classified by (a) indirect attribution and (b) identification. Attribution investigations were further divided into two categories, (i) contrastive feature types and (ii) register variation isolation types; while identification investigations were shown to consist mainly of prominent-feature types. It was felt that these types of investigation strategy would answer most *forensic* inquiry scenarios, because in general it is rare for a statistical identification study to be necessary, and even where it is necessary it is not always possible, given the real-world limitations of much forensic text.

In the next chapter I will consider an important aspect of authorship studies, that of authorship profiling. This is not a psychological type of study, as the title might suggest, but rather studies different aspects of authorship and how these might be combined to form an author profile – i.e. the profile of an individual as an author, rather than the profile of an author as an individual, in other words, the sum of authorship characteristics which describe that author *qua* author. Such profiling may be of immense use to law enforcement and other investigative agencies when faced with anonymous text which may contain threats of terrorism or other mass dangers.

SUGGESTIONS FOR FURTHER READING

Coulthard, M. (ed.) (1992) *Advances in Spoken Discourse Analysis*, London: Routledge, Chapter 12.

Authorship profiling

A further tool in the forensic linguist's authorship armoury is now considered: authorship profiling. The reader will be aware that this is not the same as psychological or personality profiling. In other words the focus is not on exploring the writer's 'personality' or 'character'. These constructs have no meaning for the forensic linguist, whose sole interest here is in obtaining linguistic information about the writer, some of which may be helpful in the course of an investigation. In the following section this will be illustrated with an example.

THE ANTHRAX 'SCARE'

The reader will be aware of the anthrax scare which followed the September 11, 2001 attack on the Trade Center and the Pentagon. At that time, envelopes – disguised to look like harmless communications from schoolchildren – were received by several prominent public individuals: these envelopes contained the poison anthrax.

At the time it was thought by a number of commentators that the anthrax attacks formed part of the alleged Al-Qaida assault on America, and among the first questions asked – regarding the envelopes and their written content – was whether the writer was (a) a native speaker of English or some language which used the Roman alphabet – possibly English – (abbreviated L1 = 'E'), or (b) a speaker of one of the languages which uses Arabic writing for its script – a list which includes Arabic, Farsi, Urdu and Punjabi as spoken in Pakistan – (abbreviated L1 = 'A'). A key part of the question is, of course, the role of linguistic evidence in such an inquiry.

It was decided to attempt to answer this question with reference to the envelope and text sent to the leader of the US senate, Senator Daschle, a copy of which is shown below.

Note that some consideration of the handwriting here is necessary, but this should not be taken as a handwriting analysis, or as an exercise in what is popularly known as 'graphology'. Those subjects are not usually of direct interest to forensic linguists. Rather, what is of interest is the connection between handwriting and language – and the use of both as *linguistic* evidence. However, as the following paragraphs show, it is not always easy to avoid some trespass, however reluctant, into the field of document examination.

STYLE OF PRINTING

The following paragraphs represent a somewhat hesitant foray into a field about which I know nothing, namely document examination – yet it is important to make this journey in order to offer a few preliminary observations about the language. I hope the reader will forgive this departure.

The first task was to examine the style of printing: we might be tempted to think that L1 = 'A' because of the apparently very simple style of printing, i.e. large, rounded letters sloping downward. It might be imagined that this is an Arabic-script L1 who does not have much experience of English and therefore needs to print, rather than write cursively. However, the printing is far from uniform in style: it shows a mixture of large and small upper-case letters and, indeed, some of the letters are almost lower case in appearance, e.g. the 'o' letters in *school*. This mixture of large and small capital letters might indicate that the true writing style of this writer could be a 'proper' cursive style in which upper and lower- (or 'title') case letters are used. This could signal that the writer is possibly a native speaker of English (i.e. L1 = 'E'), or has been well educated in English and is simply printing in order to disguise his/her handwriting or to create the impression of a child's handwriting (hence the text relating to '4th Grade' in the upper left hand corner of the envelope).

However, there is another factor which might contribute to our thinking of this writer as a non-native user of English and that is the apparent overall inclination of the writing to the right. It might be thought that, since Arabic is written from right to left, the writer is having problems adapting to a left–right orientation, thus causing the baseline to wander down to the right. However, the inclination of the baseline angle does not seem to be because of a difficulty with left–right writing rather than right–left writing, it is to do with the writer's natural style. If an example of this writer's genuine writing (in the Roman alphabet) is ever found, it seems almost inevitable that there will actually be a sloping of the script downward and to the right in some way. Note that the bottom of the right descender of the letter A – always upper case in this writer's printing of the envelope – is always lower than the left.

> **Exercise 7.1**
>
> The discussion of these texts brings up the issue of credibility in text in general. When we read something, what do we believe? What does the text attempt to make us believe? Does it succeed or fail? Why/why not? Attempt to answer these questions with the excerpt from the anonymous smear mail note below:
>
> DEAR BILL,
>
> I SUPPOSE YOU THOUGHT I WOULD FORGET BUT YOU ARE WRONG HOW COULD I FORGET A RAT LIKE YOU. I HAVE SENT A LETTER WITH ALL YOUR PAST DETAILS TO THE PRESIDENT. ALL YOUR DEBTS AND PAST MISSDEMEANOURS. IF YOU DON'T RESIGN FROM THE COUNCIL IMMEDIATELY THE PRESS WILL PRINT A LIST OF ALL YOUR DEBTS BOTH LOCALLY AND NATIONALLY . . . YOU MIGHT BE ABLE TO FOOL SOME PEOPLE BUT NOT ME. YOU FORGET I HAVE KNOWN YOU FOR ALL OF YOUR LIFE.

LACK OF PUNCTUATION

The fact that a return address (albeit fictitious with an incorrect or false zip code) is provided neatly top left shows that the writer seems comfortable with writing letters of different sizes. Moreover, the shapes of the letters are reasonably consistent across the different sizes. This writer does not have any difficulty with the Roman alphabet.

The false return address, incidentally, might be evidence of the writer's overall deceit, i.e. to use the evidence of the text of the envelope to deceive: this indicates that the style of handwriting is also being used to deceive, i.e. textually – that is to say it appears to be confirmatory of the style of writing/printing being disguised rather than natural. One other indication of the writer possibly being Arabic is an apparent underuse of punctuation. Other analysts, e.g. Jonathan Charteris-Black have observed that Arabic speakers (among others) of English tend to underuse punctuation in English. However, the Daschle envelope does not contain many opportunities for punctuation, other than, for instance, 'N.J.' and 'D.C.' both of which appear to be punctuated as abbreviations in any case. This means that in reality there is no basis for believing that this writer is either of Arabic origin or has an Arabic script L1, such as Farsi, Urdu, Pakistani Punjabi, etc. However, there is one clue which has so far not been discussed in any detail.

MIX OF LARGE AND SMALL UPPER-CASE LETTERS

Above, the appearance of the mix of large and small upper-case letters in the address was discussed. This may have come about because of the kind of address found, for example, on a number of Internet pages, i.e.: 'Senator Thomas A. Daschle. 509 Senate Hart Office Building . . .' Here the text is a mix of upper and lower case (a style known as title case). This could be the kind of candidate material for the source text of the address on the Daschle envelope. The writer may have felt there was not enough room for the Senator's first name or initials, hence these were omitted. However, even despite such an address being a possible candidate for the source of the envelope, it still does not answer the question – why did the writer transpose large and small upper-case letters for title case?

FAMILIARITY WITH ROMAN ALPHABET?

The apparent transposition of upper and lower-case printed letters, into large and small caps (i.e. upper-case letters), a completely different kind of printing, seems very curious: it requires much more thought than straightforward upper/lower-case copying, which is in any case closer to 'normal' handwriting. This is hardly 'least effort'. However, the fact that the writer combines large and small caps so well is almost definite proof of the writer as an L1 English speaker. Here there is evidence of someone who is able to transpose upper and lower-case into large and small caps, seemingly without thinking about it. This is clearly a person who knows how to manipulate the language, even down to its most basic elements, in this case something evidently quite banal and simple, i.e. the use of printed letters in a particular way.

The contents of the envelope are interesting, in particular the way the date is written: month + day + year. This is the standard American way of writing the date. The British, for example, use the day + month + year format, while the Chinese use the year + month + day format. Others often use the year + day + month format. However, most Arab countries use the same form as that used in the USA. The full text of the letter inside the envelope (according to www.dawn.com) reads: '09–11–01. You can not stop us. We have this anthrax. You die now. Are you afraid? Death to America. Death to Israel. Allah is Great'.

This is very similar to that received by Tom Brokaw, which reads: '09–11–01. This is next. Take penacilin[25] now. Death to America. Death to Israel. Allah is Great'. Note the terseness of the style. It is far from easy for a learner of English to use the language in this concise, precise way. Moreover, it is probably indicative of someone with a good education and – paradoxically – someone who is used to doing a lot of writing. The misspelling ('penacilin') and the pseudo-pidgin style 'You die now' are probably just red herrings and should be ignored.

CONCLUSION

In this chapter a brief demonstration of author profiling was given. Given the necessary emphasis on some aspects of presentation, the analysis may have sometimes appeared not unlike questioned document examination work – which, despite a brief diversion into that territory, it is not.

It should also be stressed that this analysis did not relate to psychology or personality profiling, topics as to whose merits the author offers no opinion. Rather, author profiling relates to the author's use of language and what it tells the analyst about the writer linguistically. As such it is still an inexact science, and one which – like other branches of forensic linguistics – will require the benefit of case examples in order to be of value. However, it may have value in certain kinds of investigations where risk needs to be assessed, for example, stalking, terrorism, hate mail, etc. or in those situations where it is important to assess the genuineness of the text as well as degree of risk.

SUGGESTIONS FOR FURTHER READING

McMenamin, Gerald R. (1993) *Forensic Stylistics*, Amsterdam: Elsevier.

CHAPTER 8

Detecting plagiarism

INTRODUCTION

In this chapter I will briefly consider some aspects of plagiarism, in particular how to measure text to ascertain whether plagiarism has taken place. First, though, it is my intention to consider some examples of what may be considered a form of academic plagiarism. Although these examples have a humorous twist to them, there is nevertheless a serious intent in bringing them to the reader's attention, as will be seen.

I am going to give some examples of what may constitute plagiarism. I am offering these prior to attempting an actual definition of plagiarism for reasons that will become obvious to the reader.

Plagiarism is the theft of the words and ideas of others . . . note, by writing that sentence without acknowledgement I may just have committed plagiarism. Why? Because I may have seen those words or something similar to them on the Internet and therefore they could have been created by someone else. For example, according to the Harvard Extension School:

Plagiarism is the theft of someone else's ideas and work.[26]

Black Hills State University entirely agrees with the Harvard Extension School.[27] Word for word, in fact: 'Plagiarism is the theft of someone else's ideas and work'. San José State University, concurs, also word for word: 'Plagiarism is the theft of someone else's ideas and work'.[28]

In fact these *exact* words were found on many university websites, with paraphrases on literally hundreds of others, if not thousands. I wondered who had borrowed from whom.

The key question here is whether it is possible for two authors acting independently of each other to produce the same formulation of words, such as that shown above ('Plagiarism is the theft of someone else's ideas and work'). Of course, universities are probably cleverer than ordinary people such as you and I are, so it is possible they have some other way of doing this, some kind of academic telepathy, perhaps! In order to test the probability of two authors independently producing the same string of words I first formulated a working hypothesis, namely that there would be some kind of maximum number of identical words which could be produced by two authors acting separately from and independently of each other (academic telepathy aside!).

At the same time, what I dreaded most was that two authors of similar educational attainments writing on the same subject could easily produce short sentences or strings which were identical, especially if they contained very common or high-frequency words, or ideas or thoughts. If that were the case it would certainly subvert the chances of proving many cases of word-for-word plagiarism where 'only' short texts or excerpts were at issue.

On the other hand, in line with my policy of simplicity in forensic linguistics, it had to be the case that we could demonstrate plagiarism even with regard to very short passages of text. For this purpose a maximum verbal string of some kind – beyond whose length it would at the very least be *unlikely* that two authors could produce identical phrases – would be a very useful notion to work with. Provisionally I called this putative phenomenon the *maximum string of coincidence*. I postulated that, fixed phrases aside, there was some kind of golden rule which stated that x number of words (or letters or characters) was this maximum string of coincidence regardless of whether the individual words in the string were of low or high frequency, whether they were short or long, lexical or otherwise.

Following this it seemed to me that the best way to determine whether such a phenomenon existed was by means of searching the Internet. The reader will be aware of how powerful modern search engines are. One in particular claims to have over two billion pages on its database. Nobody knows the average number of words per Internet page, but at a conservative estimate two billion pages probably represents approximately 30 million books. Let us assume, for the sake of argument, that only one third of these are in English. Again, this is a conservative estimate, because English is – for all sorts of reasons both good and bad – the language of choice on the Internet.

Using one of the Internet's most powerful search engines, I soon discovered that strings of 30 or even 20 words were absolutely beyond this maximum string of coincidence. Even strings of 10 words did not seem to occur more than once.

Having begun the search with what now seemed to be long strings (i.e. 10, 20 and 30 words) I now decided to approach the problem from the other direction: I would start by searching for very short strings, one, two, three, four words, etc. I already knew that the maximum string of coincidence – if it existed – was less than ten words, but just how many words, letters or characters would it be?

Supposing we took a ridiculously common word, like *the*, for instance. The word *the* occurs in virtually every document or text in the language: not surprisingly, because it is the most common word in English. It is extremely unlikely that anyone would level a charge of plagiarism against either you or me if both of us happened to use this word in our (allegedly) independently produced term papers. Indeed it is almost inevitable that we would both use the word *the*, not once but many times, since it is the most common word in the English language. The same applies to almost any other word by itself, for example *experiment*: just like *the*, no reasonable person would charge either one of us with plagiarism if we both happened to have the word *experiment* in our independently produced term papers. There are 4,760,000 uses of the word *experiment* on our search engine (at the time of writing), making it a word of fairly low frequency. *Dog* for instance, occurs 14,200,000 times, while *life* occurs 78,600,000 times. *Dog* is probably a medium-frequency word, while *life* is a high-frequency word. On the other hand *the* occurs 2.6 billion times on the particular search engine in question, and so this is an extremely high-frequency word. *Tempestuous* on the other hand, is very low in frequency, with barely 50,000 occurrences. For convenience sake, I present these frequencies in Table 8.1.

Table 8.1 *Examples of words of varying frequency found on an Internet search engine*

the	2,600,000,000
life	78,600,000
dog	14,200,000
experiment	4,760,000
tempestuous	50,000

As you might predict, when we start stringing words together, the frequencies begin to come down somewhat dramatically. Thus, when we connect *the* with *experiment* to get *the experiment* we find only 692,000 instances of this phrase. On the other hand *by experiment* is even rarer, with no more than 26,900 uses. This still would not suggest plagiarism, the fact that you and I both included the phrase *by experiment* in our term papers. However, if the phrase is now extended to read *determined by experiment*, the number of instances of its occurrence again drops sharply, this time to 1,790. Extending the phrase still further to *be determined by experiment* I found only 920 occurrences. When I went one step further and searched for *may be determined by experiment* only 13 instances appeared. Note that each time I add a word to the phrase or string, the count of incidences reduces – this is entirely predictable and something I have found in virtually every experiment like this I have performed. Finally, in searching for the six word string . . . *question may be determined by experiment*, I found no instances in the search engine in question on the Internet.[29] These results are tabulated as follows:

Table 8.2 *Showing the reduced frequency of the increased string or phrase*

String	Words	Characters	Instances	Density
experiment*	1	10	4,760,000	0.000006[†]
by experiment	2	12	26,900	1.29e–5
determined by experiment	3	22	1,790	8.633ee–7
be determined by experiment	4	24	920	4.43e–7
may be determined by experiment	5	27	13	6.26e–9
question may be determined by experiment	6	35	0	0

* all string measurements are given without counting spaces
† density = target word count/estimated total word count

Table 8.3 *Showing reduction in instances is in proportion to string length*

String	Words	Characters	Instances	Density
The example	2	10	1,510,000	0.000002
The example given	3	15	38,800	
The example given here	4	19	1,540	
The example given here is	5	21	550	
The example given here is taken	6	26	3	≈ 0
The example given here is taken from	7	30	3	
The example given here is taken from a	8	31	0	

The experiment in Table 8.2 seems to suggest that a string of about 6 words, or 35 characters or letters, might be something like the maximum string of coincidence. However, this is just on the basis of one trial, and so I present another trial above. This time I tested for the phrase *the example given here is taken from a book*. The results are given in Table 8.3.

As before the highest density item is the shortest phrase or part phrase, in this case *the example*. In the previous example the maximum string seemed to be between 27 and 35 characters. Here it seems to be at exactly 31 characters. I took another phrase at random: *some of these results are given in the table below*.

As with the previous examples this experiment showed an apparent maximum of around 31 characters. However, note that the similar phrase 'some of *the* results are given in the table below' is more common (i.e. substituting the word *these* for *the*), and yields an apparent maximum of 39 characters (or letters), 8 more characters than the above example.

Similar results (i.e. showing a maximum of 31 characters or letters) were obtained with other phrases, some chosen from popular Internet sites, for example 'thousands of fans lined the streets to greet/cheer/' . . . etc., 'the result was a triumph of modern technology . . .', etc.

What all of these results seem to suggest is that a phrase or string (which is not a fixed phrase or part of a fixed phrase) of more than 31 characters is extremely unlikely to occur twice in a corpus of some 800,000,000,000 words. Erring on the side of caution, we could perhaps extend our definition of the maximum string to, say, 40 characters, in order to accommodate more common phrases and strings.

Turning back to our earlier example of the wording found on university plagiarism sites 'Plagiarism is the theft of someone else's ideas and

Table 8.4 *A further example of the relationship between frequency and string length*

String	Words	Characters	Instances	Density
Some	1	4	136,000,000	0.00017
Some of	2	6	6,300,000	0.000008
Some of these	3	11	2,360,000	0.000003
Some of these results	4	18	6,030	0.00000001
Some of these results are	5	21	1,260	0.000000002
Some of these results are given	6	26	23	0.00000000003
Some of these results are given in	7	28	18	0.00000000002
Some of these results are given in the	8	31	1	0.000000000001
Some of these results are given in the table	9	36		–
Some of these results are given in the table below	10	41		–

work', we note that this string is 47 characters in length, well outside the maximum string we have arrived at by empirical means. It therefore seems unlikely that the universities which feature this phrase on their plagiarism websites will have arrived at this phrase independently of each other. How unlikely? According to an average of the results given above, the probability seems to be less than 0.000000000001. This is so far below the normal levels of probability we measure (e.g. 0.05, 0.01, etc.) that we can, effectively refer to it as zero probability, that is to say, p is nearly 0. Of course the possibility is that these various university sites gave each other permission to use the phrase in question, and didn't really plagiarize it at all. Another possibility is that some of the university sites that use these kinds of phrases borrowed them accidentally, unintentionally. However, as most students are aware, even 'unintentional plagiarism is still plagiarism'. At least, so says the University of Missouri, the University of

Massachusetts, Long Beach City College and Stony Brook State University of New York, all word for word reproducing a string of exactly 40 characters.

Some universities are very precise about the seriousness of the crime of plagiarism. For instance according to a leading faculty member of the Max Planck Institute in Germany:

> the university insists that instructors report every case of plagiarism to the Academic Judiciary Committee, which keeps records of all cases. The recommended penalty for plagiarism is failure for the course. Unintentional plagiarism is still plagiarism.

The trouble is that someone else, namely a member of the faculty at Stony Brook – five thousand kilometres away in the USA – also has these very words –

> the university insists that instructors report every case of plagiarism to the Academic Judiciary Committee (which keeps records of all cases). The recommended penalty for plagiarism is failure for the course. Unintentional plagiarism is still plagiarism.

That is, if we count the insertion of parentheses as insignificant!

CONCLUSION ON DETECTING WORD-FOR-WORD PLAGIARISM

We can postulate an instance of word-for-word plagiarism if identical strings of more than 40 characters occur in two or more texts alleged to have been produced independently of each other (fixed phrases aside). Of course we would be unlikely to criticize a writer for just one such phrase or string. The likelihood is that we would expect at least half a dozen such strings to occur across two or more texts before being able to level an accusation of plagiarism against a writer. In reality, though, word-for-word plagiarists usually plunder much longer excerpts from their victims. However, we have discussed extremely short examples here in order to illustrate the simplicity and power of the method given.

On the Internet and elsewhere you will find many highly sophisticated pieces of software which claim to be able to detect plagiarism. In reality it is one of the simplest forensic linguistic skills to exercise, and no great software, other than search engines, is required.

However, there is one important question we have neglected to answer: how would you find a suspect phrase or sentence, or longer passage, in a text you feel lacks in originality in some way? It is one thing to show that a sentence or phrase may be found in other texts, but how does the forensic linguist locate such offending phrases and sentences in the first place? At first glance, it seems like looking for a needle in a haystack.

There are two ways of locating suspect passages: if a passage seems familiar or strange, copy it or an excerpt of it and paste this into the search box of an Internet search engine, first placing it between quotation marks. If this does not yield any results, try working with a really short extract, anything between four and nine words in length. If you are still unable to pinpoint the offending passage but feel that the text somehow just does not 'add up', then measure several sections of the text, including the suspect section, for lexical density, average word length, sentence length, unique word density, and so on. Look for sections of the suspect text which show these values to be at variance with other sections. Preferably, you would have a number of prior examples of the individual's work – samples taken prior to the suspect incident. If the student normally exhibits low lexical density, average word length, medium sentence length, etc., but in the offending passage shows a different pattern, e.g. high lexical density, high word length average, etc., then you are justified in being suspicious. If the plagiarism cannot be sourced on the Internet, try consulting a list of the individual's library borrowings (if regulations allow). There are of course, several other techniques, such as checking for mixed orthography, i.e. American spelling in the same text as British spelling; abbreviations or contractions mixed with words or phrases in their full form; formal and colloquial language in the same text, etc. Yet further techniques, not related to word-for-word plagiarism, are discussed in the next section.

MOSAIC PLAGIARISM

In the previous section only word-for-word plagiarism was discussed. Another very important kind of plagiarism is *mosaic plagiarism*.

Mosaic plagiarism involves interspersing the plagiarist's own language with that of the victim's. The mosaic plagiarist does not take the trouble to originate work, but adapts the work of others by changing key words and phrases.

However, this paraphrasing is done without acknowledgement to the source and, as an added illustration of the lack of originality, the mosaic plagiarist often repeats each idea, concept or event of the original text, more or less in the precise order in which it is found.

A striking instance of this kind of plagiarism is cited by Richard Marius on his Harvard website (according to J. Bondy at de Pauw).[30] The original text was from Marc Raeff in his 1966 work entitled *The Decembrists*, plagiarized by G. R. V. Barratt in his introduction to an anthology entitled *The Decembrist Memoirs* (1974).

Part of the source passage reads as follows:

> December 14, 1825, was the day set for taking the oath of allegiance to the new Emperor, Nicholas I. Only a few days earlier, on November 27, when news of the death of Alexander I had reached the capital, an oath of allegiance had been taken to Nicholas's older brother, Grand Duke Constantine,

Viceroy of Poland. But in accordance with the act of renunciation he had made in 1819, Constantine had refused the crown.

The plagiarized section reads:

> December 14, 1825, was the day on which the Guards' regiments in Petersburg were to swear solemn allegiance to Nicholas I, the new Emperor. Less than three weeks before, when news of the death of Alexander I had reached the capital from Taganrog on the sea of Azov, an oath, no less solemn and binding, had been taken to Nicholas's elder brother, the Grand Duke Constantine, viceroy of Poland. Constantine, however, had declined to be emperor, in accordance with two separate acts of renunciation made in 1819 and, secretly, in 1822.

We can see that in the original the style is fairly plain: 'taking the oath of allegiance'; 'an oath of allegiance had been taken'. In the copy passage, however, these ideas are expressed in a florid manner: 'to swear solemn allegiance'; 'an oath, no less solemn and binding'. However, despite these attempts at disguise the two passages have more than 50 per cent lexical words in common with each other, and virtually every single event and/or incident is duplicated in the copy passage *in sequence*. However, we would need to be more precise than this – we would need to test specifically for mosaic plagiarism. How would we do this? We could begin by building a corpus of pairs of texts. Each text in the pair of texts would be of the same genre, of similar length, and written at roughly the same time as the other text in the pair. Excerpts would be fairly short, probably no more than 300–400 words in length.

The aim would be to establish a norm of lexical similarity or identity between each text in each pair of texts: what percentage of words do the two excerpts have in common? Previous experience suggests that two texts of approximately 250 words in length with 30 per cent (or more) of lexical words identical to each other are unlikely to have been produced independently of each other.

In the above example we found 50 per cent lexical identity between the suspect and the source text. This is unusually high. This level of lexical identity strongly suggests that the later text was indeed taken from the earlier. Just as telling as the degree of lexical identity is the sequence of ideas found in both texts. In the above example, the copy text follows the identical train of thought and incident that the original does. Sometimes, also, we find that critical measurements across the two texts yield strikingly similar results. For example, in the above case the two texts were measured for comma density, period (full stop) density, word length average and lexical density, giving the results shown in Table 8.5.

As can be seen, the two sets of results are very similar. Add this to the high lexical identity (i.e. number of words in common) between the two pieces and the fact that the copy piece follows the same train of thought and incident as the original, and we have a strong indication of mosaic plagiarism.

Table 8.5 Showing the closeness of measurements between the original and the copy texts

Density	Original	Copy
Stops	0.12	0.15
Commas	0.04	0.03
Word length	4.47	4.68
Lexical density	0.54	0.53

If you are presented with two similar texts, one of which is a clear mosaic of the other and wish to know which is the source text, then there are generally two clues: the source text is almost invariably shorter and less florid (or pompous) than the plagiarizing text.[31] Mosaic plagiarists always seem to have the need to ornament the original, in their bid to mask it. Sentences are longer, as in the above example, as is also word length.

One curious measure in the above example is that of lexical density. Note that the copyist was unable to exceed the source text in lexical density, dropping slightly below the original value in fact.

Lexical density is a very important measure. As a writer you will find it difficult to achieve a high lexical density unless your text is conceptually and intellectually rich. Text which lacks a density of ideas is seldom also lexically dense. In the above example the copy passage has higher word length and higher sentence length averages than the original. It is almost axiomatic that the text with the higher word and sentence length averages should also have a higher lexical density. However, in the above example we have a mixed result: high word length average, high sentence length average, but (slightly) lower lexical density. Note also that, despite

Exercise 8.1

Consider the two excerpts below (courtesy of Drew University website):

1. "Such 'story myths' are not told for their entertainment value. They provide answers to questions people ask about life, about society and about the world in which they live".
2. Specifically, story myths are not for entertainment purposes rather they serve as answers to questions people ask about life, about society and about the world in which they live.

In your view – and bearing in mind comments in other parts of this chapter – which of these is likely to be the original and which the paraphrased version? Also, assuming plagiarism had taken place, how would you assess the degree of copying involved?

Example 4
Martin Luther King's version of a sentence also found in the earlier PhD dissertation of Dr Jack Boozer

Correlation means correspondence of data in the sense of a correspondence between religious symbols and that which is symbolized by them. It is upon the assumption of this correspondence that all utterances about God's nature are made. This correspondence is actual in the logos nature of God and the logos nature of man.

Example 5
Dr Jack Boozer's attested earlier version:

Correlation means correspondence of data in the sense of a correspondence between religious symbols and that which is symbolized by them. It is upon the assumption of this correspondence that all utterances about God's nature are made. This correspondence is actual in the logos–nature of God and the logos–nature of man.

the higher word length average in the copy text, some of the phrases containing these longer words are pompous and tendentious: 'no less solemn and binding', for example. The copy text is not lexically rich – it simply appears to be so at first glance. The observant reader may have spotted two strings in the copy text which were word-for-word plagiaries of the original? One string was 50 characters in length, while the other was only 36.

One plagiarist who did not take the trouble to mosaic his thesis was Martin Luther King, Jr. This work happens to have a number of passages in common with the earlier work of Dr Jack Boozer. Theodore Pappas (1998) has found many such instances in Martin Luther King's work, of which the 53-word *verbatim* example above is not atypical.

What are the chances of Martin Luther King, Jr. having produced this string of language independently? A non-statistician would probably say 'nil': however, as professional forensic linguists we would have to say 'less than 0.05' or 'less than 0.01'.

SUGGESTIONS FOR FURTHER READING

Johnson, A. (1997) 'Textual kidnapping – a case of plagiarism among three student texts?', *Forensic Linguistics Journal*, 4(2): 210–25.

CHAPTER 9

Veracity in language

TRUE OR FALSE?

How do we react when we hear that someone has been accused of child abuse? Can we detect whether the witness is telling the truth or lying? This was the dilemma that faced Swedish psychologist Arne Trankell in a well-known 1950s child abuse case. Trankell developed his method, using the statements of the 5-year-old alleged victim and his mother to analyse what had happened (Rogers, 1990, online). In his reconstruction of the incident behind the accusation, Trankell was able to expose many inconsistencies in the evidence, and as a result the defendant was acquitted. Trankell later published an account of what had led to the accusations and the trial (Trankell, 1958), and in this way the science of 'witness psychology' was born (Rogers, *ibid.*). Its aim was to evaluate witness statements – in whole or in part – as true or false.

THE ORIGINS OF STATEMENT ANALYSIS

Even before Trankell proposed analysis of witness statements as a way of evaluating witness veracity, Undeutsch had already begun to develop Statement Validity Analysis (SVA), the core proposal of which was that memory-based experiences and fantasy-based experiences differ from each other (Undeutsch, 1967). Statement Reality Analysis (SRA) and Criteria-Based Statement Analysis (CBSA) are broadly similar to SVA. Although SVA began with child abuse cases, it has since been adapted for use in all kinds of criminal and civil investigations.

MEMORY

The tenets of SVA and the related disciplines mentioned above are psychology based. The key element is memory. A genuine, memory-based experience will differ significantly from a manufactured, falsified or fantasized experience. The two important dimensions are content and quality (Undeutsch, *ibid*). The false experience will lack both. Psychologists score witness statements on a range of criteria – from characters and themes to sequence of events. Veracity is determined not only by the presence of such criteria, but is also based on whether criteria are weakly present, strongly present, etc. Criteria include logical structure, unusual or extraneous details, etc. (Triandafilou *et al.*, online).

121

STATEMENT ANALYSIS IN LINGUISTICS

Statement analysis in linguistics is somewhat different from the SVA of psychology. For one thing, linguistics cannot easily base its findings on concepts such as *memory, fantasy, truth* or *veracity*. If we are to analyse statements as linguists we need to look at purely linguistic issues: narrative structure, sequence of events, association of narrator with events, and so on.

Some time ago, police forces in the United States found that statements written out by witnesses were easier to evaluate than verbal evidence obtained from interviews. As this practice spread across the country, a number of basic 'rules of the game' were discovered, enabling police officers to distinguish between the factual and the invented. Not surprisingly, many of the observations made by law enforcement professionals about statement analysis turn out to have close parallels in narrative theory and other branches of linguistics.

NARRATIVE ANALYSIS AND REPORT ANALYSIS

The two basic types of statement analysis relate to *narratives* and *reports*. Witnesses and defendants narrate their knowledge of an incident, while in other cases people report a missing person, a robbery, etc. Some incidents lend themselves to a combination of both genres, e.g. you come home and find your house has been burgled. You relate the incident as a *narrative*, but then you need to make a *report* of any stolen or damaged items, perhaps for insurance purposes. The witness narrative tends to be in the first person, while claim reports usually background the first person and concentrate on the missing person or the stolen property.

THE STRUCTURE OF FIRST-PERSON NARRATIVES

In attempting to find the structure of first-person narratives there are two approaches we can take. We can collect a corpus of narratives, and then survey them in order to draw up a style profile, or we can consider each narrative on its own merits and look for stylistic inconsistencies within each narrative.

The first, top-down approach assumes that there is such a thing as an ideal or model first-person narrative, to which all narratives should conform, and that failure to do so on the part of a narrative makes it 'ill-formed' in some way. The second, bottom-up approach makes no assumption about the structure of narratives in general, but looks for a norm for each of a range of values within the individual text. Significant deviation from this individual text norm might lead us to believe that the narrative is ill-formed. In this chapter we will confine ourselves to the 'top-down' approach. It is easier and more practical, and there is good reason to believe that first-person 'fact' narratives are fairly consistent as to their properties, thus enabling us to observe and record inconsistencies without too many problems.

FIRST-PERSON NARRATIVES

So, what is a well-formed witness/defendant narrative like? Evidence suggests that usually it is spontaneous and concise, and appears to conform to a number of criteria, the most important of which are summarized in Table 9.1[32] (to be explained in detail in the section 'Categories in Narrative', pp. 125–133).

Table 9.1 *Characteristics of a well-formed witness narrative*

	Criterion/category	Description
1	Time	Events take place in given time period without gaps
2	Place	Key places in narrative are introduced as they appear
3	Sequence	Events are described in sequence
4	Descriptions, superfluity	Extraneous and superfluous details are absent
5	Tense	Simple past tense

PRINCIPLES OF EVALUATING NARRATIVE

Above we listed a number of categories which we would use to judge the 'veracity' of a witness or defendant narrative.[33] However, veracity is a psychological construct, and as such is not directly observable. Instead I prefer the notion of *speaker commitment* to appraise veracity in language. How is speaker commitment assessed? Broadly speaking, if we are committed to what we are saying we tend to be brief and to the point, we tell it 'like it is', as the saying goes – we do not hedge. On the other hand if we do not believe what we are saying or if we do not believe *in* what we are saying, we will probably beat about the bush, we will be hesitant and non-committal, and even the sequence of events we are describing will most likely be somewhat disordered. We will certainly not be demonstrating speaker commitment. Table 9.2 summarizes the key differences between what we may term *associative language* strategies on the one hand and *distancing language* strategies on the other.

The idea behind Table 9.2 is to show that usually when the speaker or writer uses simple, congruent forms of language, in logically ordered sequence, then this individual is most probably 'associating' with the narrative. Under these circumstances the speaker relationship with veracity is said to be high because speaker commitment is high. On the other hand, when speakers wish to distance themselves from their language, this is best achieved by using formal language, by placing narratives out of sequence, and/or by avoiding logical, ordered structures. In this case the relationship between speaker and veracity is probably low.

Table 9.2 *Speaker/writer distance*

Observation	Deduced language strategy	Probable speaker commitment	Probable relationship with veracity
Speaker/writer uses simple, congruent forms, logical, sequential structures	Associative	High	High
Speaker uses elaborate 'polite' or formal forms, convoluted, roundabout non-sequential, 'illogical' structures	Distancing	Low	Low

METHODS OF STATEMENT TAKING

Great Britain

How are police statements taken in Britain? Has it always been the case that the defendant's words were faithfully recorded? Traditionally, statements were dictated by witnesses and defendants to police scribes. If carried out legally (according to Judge's Rules, 1952), a dictated statement could be an excellent way of narrating an incident. At its best, it was spontaneous, brief and concise. It gave no more details than were required to investigate the crime further, and because the defendant was at liberty to stop dictating at any time, the chances of self-incrimination were low. However, transcription difficulties aside, the system was open to abuse if those taking the dictation were unscrupulous, and several famous cases of disputed statements surfaced from the 1960s onwards. Eventually, audio and later video-recording of interviews became mandatory, so that nowadays, when the interviewing process is completed, a written summary of the tapes is produced by the police. Prosecution and defence legal teams are given copies of these tapes and may dispute the written version if they wish prior to trial. All sides agree the final version and serious disputes as to content are rare.

United States

In the USA, police forces use a number of different methods, from contemporaneous interview notes to audio and video-recording, to the current practice adopted by many states, of getting the witness to write down their own statement. The statement is then analysed category by category (see next section for explanation of categories). A photocopy of the statement is taken, and inconsistencies are marked in colour-codes, or some other method. In important cases two or more officers are each given their own copy of the statement and they mark it up independently of each other. In the days before statement analysis, however, other methods were used to take statements from defendants in the USA, and some of these were clearly open to abuse, just like their British counterparts.

In the next section each statement category will be explained and illustrated with examples, and the reader will be shown how to mark-up a statement.

CATEGORIES IN NARRATIVE

At this stage I will give examples of the previously listed categories (see Table 9.1) from genuine witness statements – both American and British, and I will show how statement analysis can be used to identify inconsistencies.

CATEGORIES OF WITNESS NARRATIVES: *TIME*

Time is important both in terms of scale and in terms of continuity. In a well-formed narrative we expect the narrator to be fairly precise about when events occurred, but not over precise. For example, in this statement allegedly dictated by Timothy John Evans, he refers to events which occurred over a two-day period several weeks earlier:

Text 9.1   (excerpt):

I went to the pictures – A.B.C. Lancaster Road, known as Royalty, at 4.30 p.m. I came out when the film was finished, I think about 7.15 p.m. I went home sat down and switched the wireless on. I made a cup of tea. My wife was nagging till I went to bed at 10 p.m. I got up at 6 a.m. next day, made a cup of tea, My wife got up to make a feed for the baby at 6.15 a.m.

There are two comments we can make about this excerpt and the frequency with which times of day are given in it. First, most people can scarcely remember what time they did something on the previous day, *let alone* the time of day they did something several weeks earlier, and this applies particularly to events outside our normal daily routine. If I go to the cinema, it is unlikely I will first look at my watch to see what time I enter the cinema, and similarly, I am equally unlikely to look at my watch again the moment I come out. Even if I do note the time, why should I remember it several weeks later?

In fact the whole passage is suspicious. How would Evans remember – so long after the event – that he came home, sat down, switched the wireless on and then made a cup of tea, in that order? Even if he could remember these petty details, why would he narrate them? What relevance do they have to the crime?

Now let us look at the gaps in the times given and the information he left out. If he went to the cinema that afternoon, and if it was important for him to remember the time he went in and the time he came out – how is it he does not mention the name of the film, or whether he bought popcorn, or who he sat next to or spoke to, or how much he paid for the ticket?

Furthermore, are we to believe that Evans sat in his chair drinking the one cup of tea from the time he got home until he went to bed 'at 10 p.m.'? Now look at the following excerpt from the same statement. Analyse it in terms of its treatment of time, and see what else you can observe about it, with reference to whether it is well or ill-formed:

Text 9.2   Excerpt from Timothy John Evans's statement

I got home about 10.30 p.m. I walked in she started to row again so I went straight to bed. I got up Tuesday morning and went straight to work. I come home at night about 6.30 p.m. my wife started to argue again, so I hit her across the face with my flat hand. She then hit me back with her hand. In a fit of temper I grabbed a piece of rope from a chair which I had brought home off my van and strangled her with it. I then took her into the bedroom and laid her on the bed with the rope still tied round her neck. Before 10 p.m. that night I carried my wife's body downstairs to the kitchen of Mr Kitchener's flat as I knew he was away in hospital.

MARKING-UP: BEFORE YOU BEGIN

If your text is on a word processor or web page, print it out first and work with pen and ink, preferably in different colours for each of the analysis categories. Otherwise, if working from a hard copy, make several photocopies of the text, retaining the master copy safely to one side. Practise typing and writing the text out several times, just to familiarize yourself with it. Make careful note of any unusual spellings, punctuation methods, layout styles, etc.

MARKING-UP *TIME*

In marking-up a narrative statement for **time**, first note actual times given, e.g. '4.30 p.m.'. Look for gaps in 'real-world' time. Look for sections of the text where there are clusters of stated times as opposed to sections of the text where all mention of specific times is absent. Where a specific time is mentioned, ask yourself what its relevance is. At this stage do not mark the text up for **sequence**, though you can make notes about it for later mark-up.

CATEGORIES OF WITNESS NARRATIVES: *PLACE*

Here is an excerpt from a statement by Texas prisoner Max Soffar, who has been on death row since 1981 in connection with the Houston Bowling Alley Murders, in which three people died and one was seriously injured.

> **Text 9.3** (excerpt):
>
> One thing that I didn't tell the truth on was that Lat Bloomfield and I did this thing when we first got to the bowling alley, not like I said about being there in the parking lot for awhile. Lat drove in and we were in his brown thunderbird. Lat pulled right to the front door so that the passenger side was next to the bowling alley. I think that there was a couple of cars in the parking lot when Lat pulled to the door.

It may not be immediately apparent, but the above excerpt contains several opportunities for self-incrimination on the part of the narrator. As will be seen, each of these opportunities relates to *place*.

First, we note that the narrator begins with an admission of untruth, 'not like I said about being there in the parking lot . . .'. I have not listed *admission of untruth* as a separate category within statement analysis, because it is relatively rare and at this stage it is probably better for students to concentrate on the most common categories.

However, it is almost always suspicious, because it invariably throws the narrative out of sequence – either in terms of time or, as here, in terms of place. The next mention of place relates to 'the front door'. However, first we have mention that it was Lat who was driving, and that they were in Lat's 'brown thunderbird'. Why do we need to know the Thunderbird was brown? This is an unnecessary detail, and moreover, it creates a gap between Lat driving in and Lat pulling to the front door. But what is the relevance that the passenger side is next to the bowling alley? Why are we told this at this stage, unless it is to show that the narrator himself would logically have been the first person to enter the bowling alley, since he was the passenger? Also, what is the relevance of there being 'a couple of cars in the parking lot', unless it is to provide the opportunity for the production of a witness later on? So, when we analyse this section of the text closely, we can see at least three opportunities for self-incrimination:

1. Allegedly Soffar claims to have lied about being in the parking lot 'for awhile' [*sic.*] before entering the bowling alley.

2. Allegedly Soffar positions the passenger side of the car (his side) as nearest the front door of the bowling alley (where the crime took place).

3. Soffar allegedly gives details of the car's colour and type: since this is irrelevant to the actual crime (especially the colour of the car, in view of the fact that the crime took place at midnight) we can only conclude that it was part of the 'self'-incrimination process, as was possibly the claim of 'other cars' in the car park.

Analyse the following text excerpt from the same Max Soffar statement. Ask yourself why some details are being included and what is being omitted. Confine your answer to matters relating to the theme of *place*.

> **Text 9.4   Excerpt from Max Soffar's statement**
>
> Lat drove and we had the windows down to his car. He made a right on the highway and drove down for a little bit and then turned around and came back past the bowling alley. I asked him why he shot the dudes and he said he shot the dude for raising up and playing hero. He said he made me shoot the other two so that I would be as guilty as him if we got caught. I put the gun under the front seat after I reloaded it and it only had one live bullet in it before reloading. I don't know where the gun is now.

MARKING-UP *PLACE*

Whenever a location is mentioned, or an event that occurs at a location, note it carefully and ask yourself why that event or that place is being mentioned at just this point in the text. Is it really relevant to the narrative? Is the detail excessive?

MARKING-UP AND TEXT OBSERVATION TIPS

As you will have printed out several copies of the target text, do not hesitate to make as many handwritten notes as you want on each copy. Be open to all possible ideas, but be prepared to argue for and defend each one of these ideas rigorously. Discuss text details with other students. Learn to present an oral argument and to defend it. Your arguments must be substantial and structured, not slick. Imagine you are already a forensic linguist having to defend your position to a cross-examining barrister or attorney. Look for similar examples from other texts.

CATEGORIES OF WITNESS NARRATIVE: *SEQUENCE*

In the following excerpt, Frank Kuecken is supposedly relaying the events of a night on which a pizza bar assistant was killed. Later, after Kuecken 'confessed' several other youths unconnected with Kuecken admitted their part in the crime. Kuecken was eventually released and all charges were dropped.

Text 9.5   Excerpt from statement attributed to Frank Kuecken

Q: Who were you with on October 21, 2000 around 10 p.m.?
A: F.J.
Q: Were you in a vehicle and if so, who's [*sic.*] vehicle?
A: Mine, '68' Ford F-100 black.
Q: Did you and F.J. go to Mancino's Pizza in New Baltimore on October 21, 2000 and if so what time?
A: Yes. 9:50 p.m.
Q: What did F.J. do at Mancino's Pizza?
A: Went in and ripped the kid off.
Q: How do you know F.J. ripped the kid off?
A: He told me when he came out.

In the above excerpt, the questioning supposedly begins with a question relating to a specified time, namely '10 p.m'. but then later refers to an earlier time, namely '9.50 p.m.'. While it is not difficult to understand the importance of a question like 'where were you at 10 p.m.?', the fact that the text then refers to an earlier time is puzzling, and while it is relatively easy to think in terms of a time on the hour, or even on the half hour, times such as 50 minutes past the hour are not that easy to remember after several weeks. So, in this excerpt it is the fact that the times are given out of sequence that highlights the spurious nature of at least some of the information the excerpt supposedly imparts. Notice also the 'thinness' of the information in this sequence: there is no substance or depth to the answers, which have a rehearsed feel to them.

Analyse the following excerpt from the Derek Bentley statement for sequence. In terms of other categories, what mental process does the phrase 'I should have mentioned' illustrate? Why do you think this section has been inserted. Bearing in mind that this is where the text ends, what is the significance of 'killed'?

Text 9.6   Excerpt from Bentley text

I should have mentioned that after the plain clothes policeman got up the drainpipe and arrested me, another policeman in uniform followed and I heard someone call him 'Mac'. He was with us when the other policeman was killed.

MARKING-UP *SEQUENCE*

We can tell out-of-sequence sections fairly easily: when there is loss of focus, such as in the appearance of private verbs, and – as we will see shortly – when there is an alteration of tense, or an inconsistency of tense. When sequence is lost, ask yourself what the inserted text is designed to achieve.

CATEGORIES OF WITNESS NARRATIVE: *DESCRIPTIONS, SUPERFLUITY*

In fact-narratives, detailed descriptions are rare, just as they usually are in casual conversation. In fact detailed descriptions are something we most often find in such environments as fiction, academic journals and docu-mentaries. This is why, when we do come across them in fact-narratives, they seem out of place, and so we mark them up as worthy of note. One description that has always intrigued me is the following from the Bentley statement:

> I could see he was hurt as a lot of blood came from his forehead just above his nose.

The reader will be aware that the incidents related in the Bentley statement took place on a dark winter's night on a rooftop in south London. The speaker was at least 30 feet from the police officer who had been shot. He could not possibly have seen blood, far less exactly where it came from. Moreover, we all know a person's forehead is 'just above [his] nose', so why tell us? It is superfluous because it is common knowledge.

Rather, it seems to be the case that this part of the statement is being designed to paint a picture of horror. Put simply, details such as these were inserted into so-called defendant statements to shock juries and eventually, newspaper audiences. They seem to have borne little relationship to what was actually said by the defendant.

It is not possible from 30 feet away to say that blood is coming from 'just' above the nose, simply because 'just' in this sense implies precision, the kind of precision that would not have been available to an observer from that distance under those conditions.

In this sentence, the excess of detail – inserted to add realism as well as horror – makes the narrator lose focus. Attention is distracted from the narrative to produce a separate cognitive effort.

Look at the following excerpt from Evans' NH1 statement, and see if you can find any examples of detailed descriptions or superfluous information.

> **Text 9.7** Excerpt from Timothy John Evans' NH1 statement
>
> I strangled her with a piece of rope and took her down to the flat below the same night whilst the old man was in hospital. I waited till the Christies downstairs had gone to bed, then took her to the wash house after midnight. This was on the Tuesday 8th November. On Thursday evening after I came home from work I strangled my baby in our bedroom with my tie and later that night I took her down into the wash house after Christies had gone to bed.

MARKING-UP: *DESCRIPTIONS, SUPERFLUITY*

Look for information which the listener or reader does not need to know, or for information which is intended for the *overhearer* (Goffman, 1981: 133–4) especially a jury, the media, etc. Previously we referred to examples of time and place which were superfluous or 'excessive'. The above examples are similar in nature.

CATEGORIES OF WITNESS NARRATIVE: *TENSE/ASPECT*

First-person fact-narratives are almost entirely in the simple past tense. Where sentences are not in this tense then the lack of sequence could indicate an insertion of some kind. Consider this from the Bentley statement:

> When we came to the place where you found me, Chris looked in the window. There was a little iron gate at the side. Chris then jumped over and I followed. Chris then climbed up to the drainpipe and I followed. Up to then Chris had not said anything. We both got out on to the flat roof at the top.

Note that all the sentences use the simple past, except the second last one: 'Up to then Chris had not said anything'. This is a spontaneous denial – what could its purpose be, except to set up the narrator for his later denial about knowing the gun was going to be used, which in turn was followed by a denial of knowledge of a gun?

Consider the following excerpt from Max Soffar's statement. Look at tense changes and ask yourself why those changes occur. What do they add to the narrative? The last sentence of this excerpt is in fact the end of the statement. What impression is the overhearer left with?

> **Text 9.8** Excerpt from Max Soffar's statement
>
> We went to my house and did some preludin and Lat said he was afraid someone had seen his car so he went and took it home. He walked back over to my house that night and we did the rest of the pills. We stayed up all day and went out to the park the next day. I was scared and that is the reason that I did not tell the whole truth before and I feel like shit and feel bad about what happened and ought to take my punishment for it. I think Lat and me both ought to pay for what we did.

MARK-UP OF *TENSE/ASPECT*

The most common non-simple past tense in narratives is past perfect. However, it is not always a cause for suspicion: only usually where clauses relate to something outside of the present focus of the narrative. It is really the combination of change of tense and loss of focus that is most likely to signal narrative inconsistency.

OTHER CATEGORIES

As previously indicated, there are many possible categories for the analysis of statements – the above five constitute what seem to be the most significant for evaluating veracity. In the following paragraphs I illustrate several others which, though significant, have not been encountered as frequently as those mentioned in the previous sections.

Character naming

Elsewhere I mention 'Craig' becoming 'Chris Craig' which then becomes 'Chris' – in the Bentley text. Manifestly this is highly suspicious. In a fact-narrative of less than 600 words, it seems very strange to have three different ways of referring to a close friend.

Register

Also in the Bentley text we see several curious instances of mixing register. The *police* are mostly *police* except for one part when Bentley supposedly refers to a *copper*.[34] Generally there are no contractions in the text – but where they do appear, there is a cluster of them. In other words we appear to have more than one register in the text – a formal one and an informal one. Mixing register in any genre, except perhaps fiction, is rare, and it is certainly unusual in fact-narratives.

133

Pronoun omission

Remember these sentences from Frank Kuecken's statement?

Q: What did F.J. do at Mancino's Pizza?
A: Went in and ripped the kid off.

Why does the speaker drop the first person pronoun in 'Went in and ripped the kid off'? This appears to be a distancing feature. It seems that either the speaker himself has omitted the pronoun because he does not really endorse his own words, or the person transcribing the text has made this alteration. If you look closely at the Kuecken interview you will see that the answers are very terse and seem prepared, almost mechanical. The statement seems to read almost like a Bogart script.

CONCLUSION

In this chapter the reader has been shown a great many different techniques in the handling of statements, whether oral or written, uninterrupted or in interview form. A number of categories under which statements could be analysed have been given. As pointed out, there are many further possible categories, and some of these were illustrated. It is hoped that this chapter will equip the student of forensic linguistics with the raw material of statement analysis and handling.

PRACTICE TEXT

Below is a text on which to practise your statement analysis techniques. The first half of the text has been marked-up for you. You might wish to photocopy the text and mark-up the second half. While marking-up the text, you might like to think about answers to the four questions below. Note that question 4 is not a psychology/mental health question – you are being asked to evaluate the veracity of the speaker's words, nothing more than that.

1. Does the statement narrate the crime?

2. Does the defendant admit the crime unequivocally?

3. Does the defendant face up to the crime?

4. Do you believe the defendant when she says she was 'an absolute mental case' at the time and what is the significance of the adjective 'absolute'? What is the evidence?

Text 9.9 The Susan Smith written statement

When I left my home on Tuesday, October 25, I was **very emotionally** distraught. I didn't want to live anymore! I felt like things could never get any worse. When I left home, I *was going to* ride around a little while and then go to my mom's. As I rode **and rode and rode**, I felt **even more anxiety** coming upon me about not wanting to live. I felt I couldn't be a good mom anymore, but I didn't want my children to grow up without a mom. I felt I had to end our lives to protect us from any grief **or harm**. I had never felt so lonely **and so sad** in my entire life. I was in love with someone. **very much**, but he didn't love me and never would. I had a **very** difficult time accepting that. But I had hurt him **very much**, and I could see why he could never love me. When I was @ John D. Long Lake, I had never felt **so** scared and unsure **as I did then**. I wanted to end my life so bad and was in my car ready to go down that ramp into the water, and I did go part way, but I stopped. I went again and stopped. I then got out of the car and stood by the car a **nervous** wreck. Why was I feeling this way? Why was everything **so** bad in my life? I had no answers to these questions. I dropped to the lowest when I allowed my children to go down that ramp into the water without me. I took off running and screaming "Oh God! Oh God, no!" What have I done? Why did you let this

Annotations
Loss of narrative to mental focus
Change of tense: mental projection – intention
'rode and rode and rode' – overstatement; quality of narrative suffers, ditto 'even more anxiety'
Excessive: grief **or harm**, **so** sad, **very** much, etc.
Loss of focus to mental state
Overstatement given previous descriptions

135

happen? I wanted to turn around so bad and go back, but I knew it was too late. I was an **absolute mental** case! I couldn't believe what I had done. I love my children with all my (a picture of a heart). That will never change. I have prayed to them for forgiveness and hope that they will find it in their (a picture of a heart) to forgive me. I never meant to hurt them!! I am sorry for what has happened and I know that I need some help. I don't think I will ever be able to forgive myself for what I have done. My children, Michael and Alex, are with our Heavenly Father now, and I know that they will never be hurt again. As a mom, that means more than words could ever say.

I knew from day one, the truth would prevail, but I was so scared I didn't know what to do. It was very tough emotionally to sit and watch my family hurt like they did. It was time to bring a piece of mind to everyone, including myself. My children deserve to have the best, and now they will. I broke down on Thursday, Nov. 3, and told Sheriff Howard Wells the truth. It wasn't easy, but after the truth was out, I felt like the world was lifted off my shoulders. I know now that it is going to be a tough and long road ahead of me. At this very moment, I don't feel I will be able to handle what's coming, but I have prayed to God that he gave me the strength to survive each day and to face those times and situations in my life that will be extremely painful. I have put my total faith in God, and he will take care of me.

> **'I knew'**: Almost all that follows up until the end of the text is really a projection of 'I knew', once again reducing the narrative to a mental projection of knowledge (in hindsight). This considerably weakens (and therefore devalues) the narrative.

[Signed] Susan V. Smith
[Dated] 11/3/94 5:05 p.m.

ENDNOTE ON VERACITY ANALYSIS OF REPORTS

The main function of veracity analysis is as an aid to investigation. A court would probably only accept this kind of analysis in rare instances – and then usually only if there were plenty of additional supportive evidence. This applies both to statements and reports.

In many respects **reports** are very similar to **narratives** except that narratives are almost always undertaken using the simple past tense. Reports usually deal with missing persons, burglaries, stolen goods, etc. In the previous section you looked at Susan Smith's statement. Prior to making her confession Susan Smith claimed that her children had been kidnapped by a carjacker. This is what she said on video tape:

Text 9.10   Susan Smith's claim regarding her children's abduction

all he ever told me was shutup or i'll kill you (break) and i just screamed i said what are you doing he said shutup and drive and had a gun and he was (. . .) poking it in my side you know and told me to drive (.) and I (.) so I drove

---

Later Susan Smith and her estranged husband appeared on television at a news conference. This is what they had to say:

Text 9.11   Smith news conference appealing for return of their children

SUSAN: I have been to the Lord in prayers every day with my family and by myself with my husband it just seems so unfair that somebody could take such two beautiful children

HUSBAND: please do not give up on these two little boys and the search for their return safe home to us

---

Exercise 9.1

Mark up and evaluate the most important features of the above text fragments, as per the previously discussed categories.

Exercise 9.2

Read the statement below, in which the author reports an alleged case of sexual assault. State whether, in your view, the statement is genuine or false. Give reasons for either view.

Text 9.12   Statement alleging sexual assault[35]

Upon arrival at Joe's Club, (date April Xth, 200- ⟨. . . . . .day⟩) I had entered the lounge area to have a drink and dinner. I was approached verbally by a man (mid 30's) as walking to a seat just 2 away from him. The words I remember most from any conversation that may have taken place that evening were "where you been? What took you so long?" I do no recall if/what I responded with in turn.

I then ordered a bourbon and coke while waiting for my order of "crab rolls." I wish I had more recolection of people or words exchanged, as this is where my mind is having trouble remembering. My food had arrived, enjoyed it with a glass of water topped with a lemon, finished my dinner and ordered 1 last drink, with all intentions of leaving at that point. if my memory is treating me well I had been offered another drink – hesitated but accepted offer. At this time I remember clearly going to the rest room. Upon my return, I casually had my 3rd Bourbon and Coke, while conversation was minimal and do remember paying most of my attention to the television directly in front of me.

Some time in the evening I do receall speaking to, one which was a bartender, James Smith & younger brother, Ben ?? These 2 are child-hood – neiborhood acquaintances – I wish I could recall any of which conversations in the evening but unfortunatelly cannot as of today.

From this point, honestly things are neither here nor there in my head. Can not seem to decifer any actual instances.

I can say that approx. times were last recolection of 8pm or 9pm roughly. I woke with my alarm clock staring the time of 10:03 am. I frantically went to check on my son, he was not there. After becoming somewhat aware of my surroundings I then realized the only clothing I had on was my sleeveless dress, sweater, which was worn the day of April Xth under my blue dress jacket, which all clothing now in pocession/ evidence. No under clothing as well. My sheets were soiled in what appeared, to me, as to be a mixture of slight blood and my own urine. In discust and pure confusion I stripped the fitted sheet from my bed and replaced it with a fresh one . . . first phone call was to my mother, with my little knowledge at that time our conversation was brief, just enough to know my son, Hugh, was safe and at daycare . . .(this info as of 4–12, mom stated it was 10 or 15 min after 10 am when she received my phone call.)

She was angry and we ended the phone call. Various phone calls including Mary Williams and Sam Walker, 2 close personal friends. . . after a few conversations and tears shed with them, I then decided to call the local police to report this incedent.

(rewind: first call after mom was to close friend Darleen Brown → she gave me a number to the crisis line. moments later I discussed the situation "BRIEFLY" with a lady there . . . She (not purposely) gave me the intention if I were to report, nothing could be done on the little info I had.) So back to the police call I got disconnected, strangly, as another call was coming in. I had called my neighbor in # 94 a sally Edwards to see if she had heard or seen any thing → she came home and stated times home and awake 8:30 pm to 11pm → nothing. Sally stayed w/ me and that's when (all within moments) the 2 police officers arrived. Spoke to Ofcr. Macnamara.

All of stated information IS true & correct to the best of my knowledge. 4/12/02

(Wendy M. Mullins)

SUGGESTIONS FOR FURTHER READING

Trankell, A. (1958) 'Was Lars sexually assaulted? A study in the reliability of witnesses and of experts', *The Journal of Abnormal and Social Psychology*, 50: 385–95.

CHAPTER 10

Forensic text types

This chapter is primarily concerned with investigative linguistics, that is to say the aim is to provide the investigator with methods of text analysis on a text-type basis rather than to provide the court with scientifically evaluated evidence.

In referring to text types found in forensic linguistics we are really referring to a number of different contexts of situation, each of which generates one or more text types. For instance, a kidnap situation is typically seen to generate at least one ransom demand. It may also generate threats not directly related to the hostage. In that case the context of the situation is not just the kidnapping itself, but might include several other factors, for example the kidnapper's previous criminal activities, relationship with law enforcement, etc. The text types which will be discussed in this chapter are as follows:

- emergency calls;
- ransom demands and other threat communications;
- suicide letters;
- final death row statements;
- confessions and denials by public figures.

Not every type of forensic text is discussed here, because many are dealt with extensively in other chapters or sections of the book. For example, Chapter 4 discussed the authorship of a series of anonymous hate mail texts, while Chapter 7 looked at authorship profiling in a well-known trick mail case. In addition, the chapter on statement analysis included extensive commentary on witness and defendant statements, confessions and claim reports.

In this chapter we will present some of the main features of each of the types listed above, some aspects of a 'typical'[36] context of situation applicable to that text type, and a comparison between genuine and simulated texts and/or situations pertaining to that text type, where applicable. The amount of space devoted to each section will depend in part at least on my own experiences with that text type.

The first situation we will look at is that of the emergency call. The ability to distinguish genuine from simulated emergency situations is a necessary skill for any emergency operator, because of the need to deploy resources effectively. Learning about emergency calls is a good introduction to this whole idea of genuineness *vs.* simulation in text types.

EMERGENCY CALLS

Before we begin our study of this section, you might like to attempt Exercise 10.1

> ### Exercise 10.1   Emergency call
>
> Imagine your car has caught fire. Luckily you managed to get everybody out of the vehicle and you are all now standing at a safe distance from it. You get out your mobile/cell phone and start to call the emergency services. Write down the first thing you would say to the emergency operator. Head the example 'Forensic Linguistic Exercise'.

Until now we have mostly been discussing written text, but looking at emergency calls will give us an opportunity to analyse spoken forensic language. As a matter of fact, statement analysis (see Chapter 9) can be applied to written or spoken language, and in a later chapter we will be discussing *voice identification*. Additionally, several of the text types to be discussed in this chapter sometimes take a spoken rather than a written form. The reader will therefore see that this book presents plenty of opportunities to analyse spoken, as well as written data.

The most important feature of any emergency call is probably *urgency*. The situation the caller is in seems urgent to that caller, even if the caller may have misjudged the situation. However, the linguist will generally find that it is not particularly helpful to attempt definitions of urgency, or 'sense of urgency' or related concepts. This is because notions such as *urgency* are essentially psychological constructs which can manifest themselves in a variety of ways.

Rather, it seems useful to focus on something more familiar and perhaps slightly less subjective to linguists, namely the notion of information.

But first let us consider the role of the emergency operator, an individual we can conceive of as, typically, very experienced, and with good visualization of a number of scenarios, and one who – in most circumstances – can speedily evaluate the quality of information being received. Note that the concept of 'quality of information' in the abstract cannot compare with the day-to-day experience of the operator who is directly involved in the actual operation of collecting intelligence moment by moment in an emergency situation: it means, quite simply, the ability to sift primarily linguistic information in potentially deadly circumstances and to come up with the required response in a timely manner. The emergency services operator needs to evaluate the degree of threat, within seconds if possible. These situations are made more fraught by what can only be described as a great social evil – the making of hoax or malicious calls. People who make what are known as malicious calls, can sound just as distressed as genuine callers, or they can portray an apparent calm in the face of adversity or fear: this is why it is not useful for the linguist to think in terms of notions such as *urgency* at the emotive level.

Below is an exchange[37] between a caller, a male security guard and an emergency services operator. Inaudible speech is indicated by a dash.

Text 10.1   Emergency[38] Call 1[39]

1 Hello can I help you?
2 Yes security guard here XYZ Electronics at the ABC canal.
3 Yes?
4 I've just been walking on the back well there's **smoke** coming out of one of our **roofs**. So, could you tell the fire service our *curt*ain shop there's a lot of **chemicals** and what **have** you in there.
5 Uh. Right. Is it XYZ Electronics.
6 Yeah.
7 ABC Industrial Estate.
8 That's right.
9 By the ABC Canal?
10 Yeah. What I'll **do** I'll make my way round the **back** and I'll leave the gates **open** for them.
11 Right and it's **smoke** is it?
12 Yeah. Smoke coming out of the **roof**.
13 From the **roof**?
14 I haven't been there to investigate but I'll –
15 Right – are you . . . any of the chemicals that are *kept* there?
16 I *could*n't really tell you.
17 Are they just –
18 chemicals from the –
19 So –
20 phuric acid is in there.
21 It's *what* sorry?
22 Sulphuric acid is in there.
23 Okay, don't *worry* now, we're on our way there.
24 Thank you.
25 Thank you. Bye.

Legend:
Bold: emphasis
underlined: overlap
Italic: rising voice pitch

One way to evaluate a conversation like this is to take a piece of paper and, laying it across the page of the book, cover the entire conversation except the first line. Study that line, and then expose the next line. Do this line by line. In this way you will be able, in part at least, to see the text as it unfolds. As you do so, ask yourself what kind of information is being passed between the caller and the operator, and what the quality of that information is. What does the operator know at any one moment in time? Is the operator's information being increased significantly with every turn? This latter point is very important: there must be a sense in which information continues to be added to throughout the exchange. You will see that at a particular point in time the operator has enough information and makes moves to terminate the call.

In notating these calls I have concentrated on just three elements of each conversation. First, I am interested to know the extent to which there is cooperation between caller and operator at any one time. I take it as axiomatic that cooperation means the full, frank and timely answering of any questions in addition to the spontaneous offering of any information regarded as essential. Hesitations, incomplete or overly short answers, and any signs of evasiveness on the part of the caller must indicate that there is something wrong: i.e. that the caller might be making a false or hoax call (medical or other reasons apart).

One of the most striking symptoms of a genuine call is the interlocking of turns: what we seem to be looking for is a slight overlap between turns, probably measured as no more than a few hundredths of a second, between speakers.

In my analysis of these calls I indicate this kind of overlap by underlining the last few letters or syllables of the outgoing turn and the first few letters or syllables of the incoming turn (depending on the amount of overlap):

> From the roof?
> I haven't been there to investigate but I'll –

In this sequence the operator is trying to ascertain the visible source of the smoke. She says: 'From the roof?' Note that 'roof' is underlined here. This means that the next turn overlaps with this word, or part of it, because we see that what the caller says is also underlined: 'I haven't been there . . .'.

So, what this notation means is that the caller does not wait for the operator to finish the information request. Rather, we can imagine that the caller is listening very intently, and is ready with an answer even before the operator has finished asking the question. This would appear to show a willingness on the part of the caller to cooperate, particularly as the content of the turn appears relevant to what the operator needs to know at that point. We can surmise that if the caller were not willing to cooperate, then in all probability attendance to the operator's needs would be much less. What does cooperation mean, in the narrow sense in which we are using the word here? Strictly speaking it is a term, not a word, in this context. It means the caller is continuously adding or seeking to add to the information being given to the operator. The caller knows that for the call to be successful, information must be incremental.

An emergency call seems, therefore, to have at its core a relationship of trust between caller and operator. The operator trusts the caller to give accurate and timely information, and the caller in turn trusts the operator to ask only the most pertinent questions. The entire call moves on a trajectory from nil knowledge on the part of the operator to the maximum amount of knowledge that the caller can impart in the minimum possible period of time. This makes an emergency call unlike any other type of service encounter. Although it is true that both operator and caller have needs and can supply needs, over and above this the caller and the operator have a common goal: to activate the appropriate assistance as speedily as possible. There is a clear understanding that the key to this process is information. Note that I do not qualify information here, by calling it 'good', or 'accurate', for example. If an exchange in which information is to be imparted lacks these characteristics then what is being exchanged is not information. Information is *per se* 'accurate', 'good', etc.

Regarding the mark-up process – my own somewhat minimal version of the complex art of CA (conversational analysis) the second element of the conversation I concentrate on is that of intonational emphasis (i.e. verbally stressing a word or syllable):

> I've just been walking on the back well there's **smoke** coming out of one of our **roofs**.

As can be seen from the above excerpt from the call, the speaker emphasizes two words *smoke* and *roofs*. I would contend that this is part of the speaker's commitment to information. He is emphasizing the two most informative (pertinent, relevant, etc.) words in the sentence. We can imagine that even if the operator had somehow missed every other word in the sentence, the two words *smoke* and *roofs* would have been heard. Speech emphasis is very important in emergency calls, and is quite unlike 'normal' conversational emphasis.

Finally, there is rising voice pitch, which I highlight because it tells us two things. If the caller repeatedly uses rising pitch at the end of each turn, then it may indicate lack of commitment. If the operator uses rising pitch it may mean either that the operator doubts the call, or is seeking clarification. When someone is doubtful of what we say, or appears to need clarification, then in 'normal' conversation we have the opportunity to commit firmly to what we want to say, or we have the option of modifying what we have said, or even backing away from it. Therefore, it would seem when the operator uses rising pitch (indicated with *italic* type), the caller has the opportunity to commit or to withdraw.

I have confined my analysis to these three elements of phonetic output: overlap, emphasis and rising pitch. There are many other possible aspects of emergency call phonetic output which could be highlighted. However, I have avoided mention of these with the specific aim of keeping the analysis as uncomplicated as possible, while still retaining essential information. I believe these three elements alone can give us most of the information we need when analysing emergency calls. This does not exempt the student forensic linguist from pursuing the topic at a deeper level and finding out more about how to analyse emergency calls.

In the following paragraphs there will be several opportunities to see each of these, and other non-phonetic features of emergency calls in action. Let us consider the first two lines of the above emergency call:

1 Hello can I help you?

2 Yes security guard here XYZ Electronics at the ABC canal.

Turn 1 is the operator speaking. Note that the greeting 'can I help you' is something of a politeness ritual. It could be argued that the caller is 'helping' the fire service by providing it with information, rather than that the operator is actually helping the caller. Similarly it could be argued that 'can I help you' is an invitation by the operator to the caller to begin.

In Turn 2 the caller identifies himself. He does so in a way which seems brief and concise. He first states his function, then the name of his company, and finally where the company is located. Even if, at that moment, the caller were cut off, the operator would know where to send assistance – assuming the call to be genuine. The fact that the assistance is apparently required at an electronics company might give the operator further valuable information as to how to respond.

The operator next says:

3 Yes?

This 'yes' seems to mean several things: 'Yes, I've got that' and 'Yes, carry on'. It could also mean, 'Yes, fine, now give me some details'.

Note that the brevity of the answer could mean the operator is looking favourably on the call, i.e. disposed to treat it as genuine. We could also say that now that the caller has apparently established his credentials, the operator wants him to continue. Hence the perfunctory 'Yes?'. Using a speech act model we could say that a number of moves have been made. The operator first invites the caller to give his information, the caller takes up the invitation, gives some basic information and then waits for the operator to issue another request. The operator does so, with this perfunctory 'Yes?'. In some ways this is a very unusual service encounter. The operator is actually behaving like a customer and the caller is behaving like someone providing a service. Curiously, both speakers seem to take this situation entirely for granted. They both appear to understand that this is what an emergency call consists of, or rather that this is what *this* emergency call consists of at just *this* moment.

The caller continues:

4 I've just been walking on the back well there's **smoke** coming out of one of our **roofs**. So, could you tell the fire service our ***curt***ain shop there's a lot of **chem**icals and what **have** you in th<u>ere</u>.

Turn 4 seems slightly garbled. Although the caller knows what he is saying, he seems to want to get the information out fairly quickly. Do you think he is genuine, or does this indicate that he is anxious to get off the line? Again, I would suggest questions asked in this way do not interest the linguist. What we are really interested in is the information being given. We need to look at the current information in the context of the information previously given. Previously, in Turn 2 the caller gave his job title or function, his company and location. Now he is giving his reasons for calling. He is describing the real world conditions which are of relevance to the service he is implicitly requesting. Note how, as he comes to the end of what he is saying, he is no longer providing a service, i.e. information. Rather, he is requesting help. What has been achieved so far? The caller has provided the background information to the call: his function – which impacts on his reason for calling – and the location of the incident. Only then does he give the actual reason for his call: '. . . there's smoke coming out of one of our roofs'. Compare this with Emergency Call 2.

Text 10.2   Emergency Call 2

1 Fire service.
2 Ah mm our shed is on *fire* at the *bottom* of the *garden*.
3 Right, what's the address <u>please</u>.
4 172 Smith Street Mt Pleasant.
5 172 Smith Street Mt *Pleasant*?
6 Yeah.
7 <u>Right</u> what's your *tele*phone <u>number</u>?
8 <u>555</u> –.
9 Yeah.
10 5555.
11 <u>Right</u> okay we'll be along right a*way*.

What are the main differences between the previous call and this one? In the previous call the security guard first gives his own credentials by stating who he is, perhaps because he may consider that he is dealing with fellow professionals, and they would give him immediate credibility if they know who they are dealing with. In the second call the speaker, a female householder, appears to hesitate momentarily, but then launches right into her reason for calling. She does not give her name, but she implies that her concern in the matter is one of ownership, '. . . *our* shed . . .' this is tantamount to saying: 'I am the owner of a property where the shed is on fire'. In other words she states her relationship to the event just as the security guard did in the previous call.

The second caller therefore appears to have a vested interest in calling, a valid reason, which can be compared with the security guard's reason: he is an employee of the factory, one who is charged with special responsibilities, i.e. <u>security</u>. That is his reason for calling. However, the operator asks the second caller for her telephone number. She did not ask the first caller for his telephone number. Is she being sexist, or is it possible that she has some doubts about the second caller? However, these doubts seem to be dispelled by the fact that the second caller gives her telephone number without any hesitation. Note that the operator actually acknowledges the first part of the caller's number before the caller is able to give the whole number:

7 Right what's your telephone number?

8 555 –.

9 Yeah.

10 5555.

It is possible that the operator is acknowledging not just the number, but also the caller's right to make the call: in other words the operator is accepting the call as genuine. Why do we say this? Because the caller co-operates immediately – she gives her telephone number unhesitatingly. The operator interjects with 'yeah' after the code portion has been given, indicating her awareness of this co-operation.

Just as with other types of conversation, the caller and the operator co-operate with each other. They work together for a common goal. It is understood by both parties that the real power must reside with the operator. This is after all an emergency service. In practice this means that the caller must co-operate with the operator: the operator is the authority.

However, the operator makes this as easy as possible for the caller. She does not put obstacles in the caller's way. The caller may choose to give information in any order, as long as it is given promptly. Sometimes, though, depending on the level of threat to the caller, the order will be important. All of this the operator makes allowances for.

Any request for information must be responded to immediately, so that if the operator asks for the telephone number and the telephone number is not forthcoming, or there is undue hesitation, the operator will become suspicious, unless there is good reason for the delay.

Consider the following call. At what point does it become apparent that there is something unusual about this call?

Text 10.3   Emergency Call 3

1 Hello fire service can I help you?
2 [ ]
3 Hello?
4 Hello there's a fire in Bennets Bowling *Green*.
5 In *where*?
6 Bennets Bowling *Green*.
7 Bennets *Bowl*ing Green?
8 Yes.
9 Uh. Right and where in Bennets is it?
10 In the *site*.
11 Is it in the *street*?
12 No the **Bowling Green**.
13 Yeah, uh, is the Be- is the Bowling *Green* in the street?
14 No.
15 No. It's not in the street at *all*?
16 No.
17 Is it in the *park*?

> 18 No, it's just in the Bo- in the actual Bowling Green.
> 19 Right and it's just in Bennets is *it*?
> 20 Yes.
> 21 And what what's on fire there?
> 22 Whaa?
> 23 What's on **fire** in the Bowling Green?
> 24 Yes. Um. The shelter *thing*.
> 25 The shelter?
> 26 Yes.
> 27 Uh. Right and you're definitely telling me the **truth** now?
> 28 Yeah, yeah, I'm **telling** you the truth.
> 29 Okay then we'll send them alo*ng* straight away.

In this call (the caller is a young child) we start to see signs of something wrong almost immediately. Turn 2 is what we call an empty turn. An empty turn means nothing is said in answer to a greeting or request. There could be valid reasons for this, for example deafness, or some other disability on the part of the caller, so at this stage we keep an open mind. Instinctively, when an operator gets an empty turn, the operator will start to listen for other signs – for example unexplained hesitations and pauses. In the next turn the caller says: 'Hello there's a fire in Bennets Bowling Green'. Not only is a third 'hello' now being exchanged, but the actual topic of the sentence, the reason for the call is further delayed, postponed by this apparently superfluous greeting. Moreover, it is not the case that something is **on** fire, rather that there is 'a fire', i.e. a fire exists. The phrase 'a fire' – as mentioned above – is much less urgent than 'on fire'. 'A fire' is impersonal, even non-threatening, but when the phrase is 'on fire' then there would appear to be a stronger suggestion of actual danger.

Hence in this example, the perceived level of threat on the part of the caller seems very low, while the level of caller co-operation is also low: it is not until Turn 5 to Turn 6 that we see any overlap between turns.

Later we see that the caller is giving very little information about the 'fire'. It takes to Turn 24 to ascertain that it is the 'shelter' which is on fire, and then it turns out not to be a shelter as such, just a 'shelter thing'. Note also the following sequence, as an example of the function of rising voice pitch:

4 Hello there's a fire in Bennets Bowling *Green*.

5 In *where*?

6 Bennets Bowling *Green*.

7 Bennets Bowling *Green*?

8 Yes.

9 Uh. Right and where in Bennets is it?

10 In the *site*.

In this sequence of turns we note, firstly, that there are few overlaps between turns. This seems to indicate an undue slowness, possibly due to lack of co-operation, on the caller's part. However, the operator is aware that the caller is a very young child, possibly less than 10 years of age. She must, therefore, tread carefully. However, as the turns progress, it seems that not only is there a lack of overlap, but that the caller keeps raising the pitch of her voice at the end of each turn. In other words it seems that the operator keeps trying to get commitment out of the caller, but fails to do so.

This call is characteristic of hoax calls: there are long pauses between turns, some turns are not at all informative, and the accumulation of information is painfully slow. Finally, the operator – who appears to have been making allowances for the youth of the caller up until now – asks: 'Right, you're definitely telling me the truth now?' to which the caller hastily asserts 'Yeah, yeah I'm telling you the truth'.

It is evident, however, that the operator gives no credence to the call: she has not bothered to take the caller's name or address. Note that she does not ask for the caller's telephone number because the call is being made from a telephone booth, so we cannot use the absence of this question as an indicator that the operator accepts the call as genuine (as in the case of the security guard).

EMERGENCY CALL MODEL: A SKETCH

Previously we suggested that the best way to evaluate emergency calls might be to construct some kind of information model, and then to test this model against what we actually encounter. Having now looked at a few emergency calls, we can perhaps sketch out a possible sequence of events in the model emergency call:

Emergency centre response
Reason for calling/role of caller
Location of emergency
Nature of emergency

Before the caller can begin to relate the event the emergency centre must respond. Hence 'Emergency centre response'. This can take many forms, but is often phrased as a greeting, e.g. 'Hello' followed by an apparent offer to help such as, 'Can I help you?'.

Next the caller proceeds to give details of the emergency. This information can be in any order, and may possibly best be summed up in the six wh-words *who, what, why, where, when, how.*

Who: The person who is calling, either by name, function of person calling, or relationship to the incident, e.g. security guard, owner, neighbour, passer-by.
What: The (detailed) nature of the emergency, e.g. shed fire, factory fire, etc.
Why: Why the person is calling (if not previously covered).
Where: The location of the emergency.
When: When the emergency began or when the caller became aware of it.
How: How the emergency started or was caused.

SEQUENCE OF DETAILS, IMPLIED INFORMATION, CONFLICT AVOIDANCE

The sequence of details given to the operator may not always be important to our model, for instance it probably does not matter if we know where the fire is before we know what kind of fire it is. However, the sequence is important from the point of view of what it tells us about the incident and the caller's relation to the incident. For example, in Emergency Call 1 the caller begins with his relationship to the incident. In other words he foregrounds his own relationship to the emergency. In Emergency Call 2 the caller does the same but does it in a different way, she implies her relationship to the incident with the use of the word 'our', as in 'our shed is on fire at the bottom of the garden'. In numerous other calls I have analysed we hear callers beginning with their own involvement in the situation. This can take the form of stating a job function, claiming ownership, being the neighbour of a victim, being a victim or potential victim, or even just being a passer-by.

Of course, the caller could begin with stating the location of the incident. There is no reason for this not to happen. However, the operator would very rapidly expect the caller to state or imply their own relationship to the incident.

In the following call excerpt we see that, as in the second call above, the caller does not state her precise role in the incident – in this instance because the call has come through on a secure line.

Text 10.4   Emergency Call 4

1   Um we've got a --- running into into a house.
2   Right anyone trapped?
3   Uh no not that we're aware of. um one woman has actually gone through the window and has landed in the lounge of the house so obviously there could be problems with um petrol coming from the vehicle and I'm sure there's – damage to the house.
4   Right but.
5   But you're not aware there's anybody trapped there.

Note that the gravity of the emergency does require that the caller gives considerable detail to the operator. Curiously, whereas the police officer is focused on the possibility of a fuel spillage into the house, the operator is more concerned with whether any of the crash victims are trapped in the vehicle. Each side has their priorities, but each side accommodates the other and lives with the other's priorities, without conflict. Contrast this with line 28 of Emergency Call 3, where the caller impatiently asserts that she is telling the truth 'Yeah, yeah'. Clearly, in that situation there is the potential for conflict, whereas in a genuine call the potential for conflict is generally much less, or is avoided. The police officer takes account of what the operator needs to know, but is anxious to put over her point at the same time. Despite their differences there is no hostility and no conflict, just an understanding of the needs of the other.[40]

As far as the model is concerned, therefore, co-operation is critical. Part of this co-operation is, as we have just stated, lack of confrontation. We could surmise that people who are genuinely co-operating with each other will tend to avoid confrontation wherever possible.

EMERGENCY CALLS: CONCLUSION

In this section we have looked at some aspects of emergency calls, specifically fire emergency calls, though police, ambulance and other emergency service calls could also be considered. We have seen that there is great variety in the presentation of information in emergency calls. We cannot propose a fixed order of information, and it is not always easy to tell the difference between genuine and malicious calls. For the operator at the end of a telephone line, having to make instant decisions on where to deploy resources, it is even more difficult. However (with the proviso that these are generalities and not hard and fast rules), we can propose that a genuine emergency call usually has several constituents, which we can consider under three headings:

1 Components of the call.

2 Attitude of the caller.

3 Aspects of phonetic output.

Call components

- information about the incident, especially <u>where</u> and <u>what</u>;
- the relationship of the caller to the incident.

Attitude of the caller

- commitment by the caller to relay the details of the emergency;
- co-operation of the caller with the operator – a willingness to answer questions fully, promptly, and accurately;
- absence of conflict or confrontation from the caller, even if confronted as to the genuineness of the call.

We can also, to some extent, predict some of the physical or phonetic features of the emergency call:

Aspects of phonetic output

- overlap between turns, especially from the caller, indicating co-operation;
- emphasis of important, salient items of information;
- avoidance of sentence-final rising voice pitch except where repetition or clarification is required or where there is immediate cause for alarm.

RANSOM DEMANDS AND OTHER THREAT TEXTS

Threat texts (which can be spoken or written, or even videoed) have something in common with malicious emergency calls: the sender of the text or the person making the call are usually anonymous. The recipient of the malicious text and the person receiving the malicious call are both at a disadvantage: violence of one form or another is being perpetrated against them by someone who is unseen.

It seems axiomatic that the essence of a ransom demand is the demand for a ransom, but the truth is – in my view at least – that it is the *threat* component which is really the most important part of any ransom note.

Threats are the counterparts of promises. If one person threatens to cause death or injury to another unless x is done, then the person making the threat is implying that they will not carry out the threat if the required condition is fulfilled. This is why ransom demands are so complex: they appear to contain a conditional promise: 'If you do X, or pay Y, we will return Z to you'. However, it is very important that the wording of the condition be considered carefully, because very often the kidnapper has no intention of returning the hostage, alive or dead. In the Lindbergh case the family is asked: 'It is realy [sic.] necessary to make a world affair out of this, or to get your baby back as soon as possible'. Making allowances for the writer's difficulties as a non-native speaker possibly with some kind of aphasia, we note that the return of the child is backgrounded to the second clause of the sentence, rather than, for example, 'To get your baby back . . .'. This backgrounding of the 'claim', i.e. that the baby will be returned, makes this a somewhat vague commitment, to say the least.

However, even if the threat were more direct, e.g. 'if you want your baby back . . .', we note that this is still not a commitment to return the kidnap victim. It is an equivocal conditional clause: the result is not stated in terms of certainty. It is very different from 'You will get your baby back if you do x, y or z' or, for example, 'Do x, y or z and you will get your baby back . . .'. These two latter examples can be referred to as *cause and effect* clauses, *Do A and B will follow*. I would suggest that usually a ransom demand which does not contain an unequivocal *cause and effect* clause could indicate a detrimental result for the hostage.

Therefore, we need to bear in mind how far removed 'to get your baby back . . .' is from 'You will get your baby back if you do this' or 'Do this and you will get your baby back'.

Clearly in the Lindbergh case, one cannot gather any commitment from the ransom demand as to the child's return. It has long been suspected that the child was dead before he was removed from the premises by Hauptmann – having been dropped from the ladder. If so, Hauptmann would have had to conceal the child's death, and so continued to press for a ransom payment (which he received). So, it seems that the real, underlying move in the Lindbergh kidnap notes is one of making a threat while appearing to make a promise. There is a real threat to the child in the language. This is bound up with the conditional 'promise' of the child's return and the false claim as to the child's state of health. As an exercise you might like to write several threats disguised as conditional promises and award them varying degrees of merit as regards their actual *vs.* apparent commitment. Label them 'Class Exercise: forensic linguistics' at the top, just to make sure that they cannot be inadvertently misinterpreted!

Recall from Chapter 3, that the first note sent by Hauptmann contained this clause: 'We warn you for making anydig public or for notify the polise the child is in gute care'. Here the kidnapper claims the child is in good hands. However, the note would have to have been written before the perpetrator entered the premises, and so we see immediately that the claim is false, since the kidnapper had not even encountered the child when he wrote the note. How did he know that the child was not ill on that day, for example? Note: there are several instances of ransom demands written prior to the crime taking place.

When kidnappers (or perpetrators of other, similar violent crimes) make claims they are not in a position to verify at the time of making them, we need to respond quickly and decisively: we are probably dealing with a perpetrator who is lying to us and will therefore not hesitate to break any so-called 'promise'.

HATE MAIL

Ransom demands are not the only kinds of threat text. In fact threat texts probably require a book by themselves since they are so diverse in character and, unfortunately, all too common. They include threats to expose public officials or company executives unless such individuals resign, for example:

Forensic text 10.1   An anonymous hate-threat letter

DEAR BILL,

I SUPPOSE YOU THOUGHT I WOULD FORGET BUT YOU ARE WRONG HOW COULD I FORGET A RAT LIKE YOU. I HAVE SENT A LETTER WITH ALL YOUR PAST DETAILS TO THE CHIEF EXECUTIVE. ALL YOUR DEBTS AND PAST MISSDEMEANORS [*sic*]. IF YOU DONT RESIGN FROM THE SENATE IMMEDIATELY THE PRESS WILL PRINT A LIST OF ALL YOUR DEBTS BOTH LOCALLY AND NATIONALLY. I ALSO KNOW OF THE BRIBES PAID TO THE UNDESIRABLES TO VOTE FOR YOU. YOUR BEHAVIOR IN MEXICO ALSO LEAVES ME WONDERING WHY YOU BOTHERED TO GO. IT CERTAINLY WAS,NT TO PAY HOMAGE TO THE DEAD AS YOU WERE NEVER SOBER. WHAT WOULD THE LOCALS THINK OF THAT. I ALSO KNOW OF THE MONEY YOU HAVE POCKETED FROM THE MONEY RAISED FOR THE CELEBRATIONS YOU MIGHT BE ABLE TO FOOL SOME PEOPLE BUT NOT ME. YOU FORGET I HAVE KNOWN YOU FOR ALL OF YOUR LIFE. GO BACK INTO YOUR RAT HOLE WHERE YOU BELONG AND STAY THERE.

?????

The above letter was received by a client of mine some years ago, and contained a number of apparent accusations. However, if we really want to accuse someone of something – instead of just smearing them – then usually we would be more direct about it: 'You stole such-and-such an amount of money from so-and-so' or, 'You owe money to so-and-so and such-and-such'. If someone claims to know of 'money you have pocketed' then they should know something about the amount, when it was taken, etc., otherwise we are entitled to think they are just gossiping or propagating scandal. In fact, if someone wants to accuse another person of theft, all they have to do is to report the crime to the law enforcement authorities. In other words, the writer's intention in sending this letter does not seem to be the substantiating of 'claims' as to genuine wrongdoing, but rather to distress the addressee with threats.

So, it seems that the threat in the above letter is not like the threat in the ransom note: the writer is not in possession of anything that the addressee will want returned. There is a conditional, which can be summed up as: 'Resign or I expose you'. The real threat here is to the recipient's peace of mind and health. The most the recipient can do is to resign, i.e. give in to the writer's demands, but even that is no guarantee that the recipient will be left alone by the writer. On the other hand in a hostage situation, if the ransom is paid and the kidnap victim is returned, that is generally the end of the matter as far as the person paying the ransom is concerned, at least in respect of any contact between kidnapper and ransom payer. Suppose 'Bill' in the above letter did resign? Would he be left alone? The chances are the writer would subsequently demand he left the area, or sold his business, etc.[41] We should be aware that there is no limit to what blackmailers can and will demand of their victims.

That is the key difference between the letter to 'Bill' demanding his resignation and, say, a hostage note. A hostage note is not a threat accompanied by blackmail, it is a threat accompanied by a demand. It appears to hold out a promise. When, however, we evaluate the 'promise' (i.e. to return the victim) we very often find that it is not a real promise, just the appearance of a promise. The real object of hate mail is just that, to express hatred by appearing to threaten someone. However, there is no actual threat because in reality the person making the threat is rarely in a position to carry it out. Just as the writer of the hostage note does not always deliver on the promise to return the victim, so too the hate mail writer does not always deliver on the threat to 'expose' the recipient.

Earlier we looked at the anthrax letters. At first glance these seemed to be almost pure examples of trick mail, i.e. the recipient was tricked into believing the letter was harmless, and therefore opened it. No demand was made to the addressee, no promises were made to the addressee. The threat component in those letters was not within the letters themselves, but was really directed at members of the public, any one of whom, it was implied, could receive such a letter – hence the mass mobilization of postal workers to prevent the successful transmission of such letters through the US postal system. People were genuinely afraid they might be sent such a letter, and in fact several were. The campaign was very successful in its aim of causing widespread fear, partly helped by the media. The anthrax letters contained elements not only of trick mail and threat mail, but also terror mail, that is to say they used a relatively few letters to conduct a nationwide campaign of terror. The person who sent them can truly be described as a terrorist, since he/she used all of the methods and ingredients employed by terrorists in carrying out acts of terrorism: surprise, fear and publicity, in all of which the terrorist (as we have noted) was very successful. When you have analysed many anonymous letters of all types, you begin to see a common pattern emerging. After a while the terrorist, the kidnapper and the sender of hate mail begin to seem remarkably similar to each other: their communicative aim is identical, namely to victimize others through terror and pain or the threat of terror and pain. The only difference is one of degree. The common component is *threat* (or appearance of threat), as summed up in Table 10.1.

Table 10.1	*Threat type in relation to context*	
Context	*Primary threat*	*Secondary threat*
Kidnap	Death or injury to victim	Negative effect on the recipient of the ransom demand
Anonymous hate mail	Exposure or embarrassment	Possibility of repeat letter
Trick mail	Death or injury to recipient	Perceived mass danger

CONCLUSION

I believe the foregoing indicates that different types of threat mail – of which we have considered only a few – have far more in common with each other than otherwise. Any form of threat mail constitutes a danger to those to whom it is sent, to those to whom it refers, and – in some cases – to other individuals as well.

SUICIDE LETTERS

In this section we will first evaluate several known genuine and simulated suicide[42] texts, and we will then consider the Gilfoyle 'suicide' text in the light of these observations. A suicide note, to have credibility, must – in my view – be seen to be making a definite proposition although the situational context of the proposition may not always be clear to the casual reader, as for instance in the text below:

Forensic text 10.2

I hope this is what you wanted.

(Schneidman and Farberow, 1957)

This is the entire text of what is believed to be a genuine suicide note. We know nothing about the circumstances of the victim's death, other than that the Los Angeles County Coroner found the death to be one of suicide, and that Schneidman and Farberow (1957) appear to have evaluated the text in the same way.[43]

For the addressee of the text, the context behind the sentence 'I hope this is what you wanted' may or may not have been apparent, but the casual reader – i.e. one who has no knowledge of the participants, the events or the circumstances – would probably have to take such a note almost on trust.

However, even though the context may not be apparent to us we can, I believe, recognize the elements of a proposition. Although this may entail using a degree of imagination, this is a licence that we can to some extent allow ourselves in investigative linguistics, though we cannot do so in evidential forensic linguistics.

First of all, though, we need to distinguish between the apparent locution and illocution of the text. We can imagine that the writer does not literally intend to provide the addressee with what the addressee wants, since the phrase 'I hope this is what you wanted', said in a certain way, and under certain circumstances, can mean 'I know this is <u>not</u> what you want, and that is why I am giving it to you'. In other words, it may be the intention of the writer in this text to thwart or spite the addressee rather than to provide the addressee with something the addressee has stated he/she wants. The proposition, therefore, behind this text could be an intention to make the addressee suffer or feel guilt as a result of the writer's death.

Further – as regards the proposition itself (if it is a proposition) – whereas normally we might say 'I hope this is what you **want**' in this text the writer says '. . . what you want**ed**', implying that there is nothing the addressee can do now because it is too late. This really does seem to show the writer's intention <u>not</u> to provide the addressee with what the addressee wants: the verb is in the past tense.

By contrast with the previous seven-word text, the following text is much longer and, apparently, more descriptive:

Forensic text 10.3

Dear Mom, In the last week a number of occurrances [*sic*] have forced me into a position where I feel my life is not worth continuing. Friday I lost the job I have held for the past seven years. When I told my wife she packed her bags and left me. For six years she has been living with me, not for me but for my money.

Mom please take care of Mary for me. I'm leaving and I don't want Betty to have her. I have nothing left to live for so I'm just checking out – I love you Mom, Bill

(Schneidman and Farberow, 1957)

Consider the first sentence of the text: 'In the last week a number of occurrances [*sic*.] have forced me into a position where I feel my life is not worth continuing'. This sentence does appear to contain a proposition, namely: '. . . my life is not worth continuing'. But is this really a proposition, or is it just informational? One thing that may tell us that this is informational rather than propositional is the fact that the clause apparently containing the proposition is not thematic to the sentence. The sentence consists of two clauses 'a number of occurrances [*sic.*] have forced me into a position' and its dependent clause 'where I feel my life is not worth continuing'. The first clause is preceded by an adverbial phrase of time 'in the last week' and the subject of the clause is an indefinite subject 'a number of occurrances'. In fact the second clause is not 'my life is not worth continuing', nor even 'I feel my life is not worth continuing', but is a dependent clause 'where I feel my life is not worth continuing'. Thus, if the proposition is part of a non-thematic, backgrounded subordinate clause, I am sure we are legitimately able to view the proposition with some scepticism, since it is axiomatic – in the model we have been proposing throughout this chapter – that prop-ositional content is in proportion to thematicity. Moreover, consider the phrase 'my life is not worth *continuing*'. This is very different from 'my life is not worth living'. In the latter case, the verb is much more powerful and personal: 'to live'. But in the former case 'continuing' is an impersonal, middle verb, i.e. 'to continue one's life'. Even the choice of tense weakens the propositional value of the sentence: '. . . my life is not worth continu-ing' as opposed to 'I don't want to continue my life' – itself not as strong as 'I don't want to carry on living' or the even more direct 'I don't want to live' or – to take matters a step further – 'I want to die'.

The previous two texts, the one genuine and the other simulated, were perhaps not that easy to 'read' as to their genuineness. However, consider the following note:

Forensic text 10.4

Dearest Mary. This is to say goodbye. I have not told you because I did not want you to worry, but I have been feeling bad for 2 years with my heart. I knew that if I went to a doctor I would lose my job. I think this is best for all concerned. I am in the car in the garage. Call the police but please don't come out there. I love you very much, darling.

Goodbye.

Bill

(Schneidman and Farberow, 1957)

Here we have I believe, a classic suicide note: it is brief, concise and highly propositional and yet there seems to be a degree of evasiveness. It begins: 'This is to say goodbye'. The context of 'this' is 'this note', 'this communi-cation', but also, I believe, 'this act', i.e. of suicide. This is a very direct opening, one which is not easy to misinterpret. The letter states what the problem is, the fact that the writer felt he could not discuss the problem with 'Mary', and – as sometimes happens in suicide contexts – the desire not to be seen dead by the loved one. As with many suicide notes we sense – too late of course – that there was a perceived communication impasse between writer and addressee. Indeed, it is almost as if the suicide note is the only way in which this impasse could be overcome, or even just addressed. As with many other suicide notes, it seems that the text and the suicide act are one, with the suicide note having something of the status (in the writer's mind at least) of the act itself. In examples like this where we find formulations like 'I did not want you to worry . . .' it sometimes turns out that the writer – here claiming to have had heart trouble – is actually hiding something from the addressee, for example a debt, an undisclosed crime, an affair, etc. Whether or not the writer is telling the truth about the reason for the suicide, the text is still highly propositional in regard to the act of suicide, and is very clear about the purpose of the note, about what he could or could not tell the addressee, and his resolve: 'I think this is best for all concerned'.

In summary, I believe the following points can be made about suicide notes.

- A suicide note should contain an unequivocal proposition, even if it is bizarre or unusual.

- The proposition is normally to do with the act of suicide itself and/or with the communication (i.e. the suicide note).

- The proposition needs to be simply phrased: it should be thematic (i.e. the first clause of the sentence/clause complex); it should be direct; it should be directed at the addressee, and relevant to the writer's relationship with the addressee.

- Where mention is made as to necessity for (or even 'desirability' of) the act of suicide, the suicide note should be unequivocal about the writer's view that this is not just the best course of action, but the only course of action.

- Genuine suicide notes tend to be short, mostly fewer than 300 words in length. There is usually little or no extraneous material.

- The situational context of the suicide note is not always obvious – as in Forensic Text 10.2, for example, and usually the reader has to deduce it. It is rarely stated directly. Even where it is stated 'directly', the reader cannot necessarily take the context for granted.

THE GILFOYLE 'SUICIDE' NOTE: GENUINE OR SIMULATED?

In the previous section we considered several genuine and simulated suicide texts with a view to suggesting that genuine suicide texts have certain linguistic characteristics. In the chapter on authorship, we looked at the Gilfoyle texts from the point of view of style. However, supposing we ignored – for the moment – the observations we made on the authorship of the Gilfoyle texts and considered the texts afresh, purely from the point of view of their genuineness. Is there anything in the so-called Gilfoyle 'suicide' text which would enable us to say whether the text is a genuine suicide note or a simulated one?

Consider the opening paragraph of the Gilfoyle text:

> I've decided to put an end to everything and in doing so ended a chapter in my life that I can't face up to any longer. I don't want to have this baby that I'm carrying. I wish now that I had got rid of it. When I was thinking about it I wouldn't be hurting the way I am now.

This is not a proposition. In fact it reads more like a preamble to a speech. Why do I say it is not a proposition? The opening sentence of any text, especially one as important as a suicide note, is always critical. 'I've decided to put an end to everything' might have been convincing if it were not for three things: first, the emphasis is on the decision, the mental action not the physical. The writer does not say 'I am ending it all' but 'I've *decided* to . . .'. Second, what is 'everything', and why 'put an end to *everything*'? Why not just 'end everything' rather than '*put an end* to everything' – in other words why nominalize a perfectly straightforward verb like 'end'. The third thing that is striking is that having claimed to have decided to 'put an end to everything' the writer states that this is to end 'a chapter in my life'. However, it seems to me, we would end a chapter in our life, in order to avoid something unpleasant, or the continuation of something unpleasant, rather than end *everything* in order to end a *chapter*. As such, this is a meronymy/hyponymy issue: life contains events, not events life, just as books contain chapters and not the other way around. In fact it is slightly more than a meronymy/hyponymy issue: Paula Gilfoyle's death is the end of *a chapter* in Eddie Gilfoyle's life. Her death is the end of her own life, not the end of a chapter in it. The use of the word *chapter* here is, I believe, a sign of someone writing from the outside-in, not from the inside.

Even the proposition that the writer is hurting does not seem real. 'I wouldn't be hurting the way I am now' does not really commit to a state of hurting now, it only asserts that if the person had done something different then they would not be hurting the *way* 'I am now'. But we do not know how the person is hurting now: *way* is manner not degree. *Way* collocates much more frequently with *feel* than with *hurt*. According to my search engine, *way* and *feel* are about 5,000 times more common than *way* and *hurt*.

Moreover, to be 'hurting' is not the same as to 'hurt' or to be 'in pain' or to be 'suffering'. There seems to be something wrong with the tense of this sentence as applied to *hurt* (see *continuing* in Forensic Text 10.3) though the continuous does work with *suffer* in this context. Again, I would suggest that 'hurting' is a verb from the outside, particularly with the addition of the word 'now'. Once Paula dies, it would seem, then Eddie (believes) that he will stop hurting: because he is hurting *now*. There is the perception that the hurting is temporary.

Finally, I doubt very much that the writer is having a baby: 'I don't want to have this baby that I'm carrying'. Allegedly, the writer is writing to her husband. The husband works in a hospital, he has accompanied his wife to the ante-natal clinic on several occasions (according to another letter). Therefore it is clear that *he* (as the supposed addressee of the 'suicide' letter) knows she is expecting a baby. Why then '*this* baby *that* I'm carrying'? The husband knows she is carrying a baby. There is no need to specify which baby: 'I don't want to have the baby' would be sufficient. The *over*-supply of information in a suicide letter is almost as much a symptom of simulated text as the *under*-supply of information in an emergency call in that both violate Grice's maxim of quantity. In my view the writer wants to emphasize the baby as the cause for the mother's 'suicide', and so overstates *baby* by preceding it with a demonstrative determiner, and by then appending a dependent clause after *baby*, i.e. that I'm carrying. Note also that the situation of context is very obvious in the Gilfoyle text. We know 'why' the writer is (allegedly) committing suicide, and we are given all the necessary 'facts' about the context. In genuine suicide notes this is rarely the case: you often have to 'read between the lines', because in most suicide notes that I have seen, there is very little that is obvious. Add this to the very indirect phrasing of the proposition in the Gilfoyle text – if it is a proposition – and its unnecessary complexity. 'I have decided to . . . put an end to . . . and in doing so . . .'. All in all, then, the Gilfoyle 'suicide' note is not, in my view, like any other suicide note that I have encountered.

FINAL DEATH ROW STATEMENTS

Final death row statements (also just called 'final' or 'last' statements) are a relatively recent addition to text types in forensic linguistics, and stem from the longstanding American tradition of allowing the condemned person to say a few words immediately prior to execution. This practice was not, to my knowledge, carried out in the UK, Australia or elsewhere in the English-speaking world.

Even though final death row statements represent a fairly small corpus overall, yet there is a surprising degree of variety among them. The following is a fairly typical *tacit* admission of a crime:

> **Text 10.5   Dennis Dowthitt (Texas death row prisoner)**
>
> I am so sorry for what y'all had to go through. I am so sorry for what all of you had to go through. I can't imagine losing two children. If I was y'all, I would have killed me. You know? I am really so sorry about it, I really am.
>
> I got to go sister, I love you. Y'all take care and God bless you.
>
> Gracie was beautiful and Tiffany was beautiful. You had some lovely girls and I am sorry. I don't know what to say.
>
> All right, Warden, let's do it.

In this statement Dowthitt does not admit the crime directly, but by saying that had he been the family of the victims then he would have had himself killed he effectively appears to be making an admission. Even though his admission is indirect, the statement itself is very direct, brutally so: 'I would have killed me'.

By contrast Mitchell, also a Texas death row prisoner makes a more direct admission in his final statement. He also asks for forgiveness from the victim's family:

> **Text 10.6   Texas death row prisoner Gerald Mitchell's last statement (killed 20-year-old Charles Marino)**
>
> Yes, sir. Where's Mr. Marino's mother? Did you get my letter? Just wanted to let you know, I sincerely meant everything I wrote. I am sorry for the pain. I am sorry for the life I took from you. I ask God for forgiveness and I ask you for the same. I know it maybe hard, but I'm sorry for what I did. To my family I love each and every one of you. Be strong. Know my love is always with you . . . always. I know I am going home to be with the Lord. Shed tears of happiness for me. I love each and everyone of you. Keep on living.
>
> Betty, you have been wonderful. You guided me to the Lord. You have been like a mother to me. Sean, Rusty, Jenny, Marsha, God Bless each and every one of y'all.
>
> Jesus, I confess you as my Lord and Savior. I know when I die, I'll have life in heaven and life eternal everlasting. I am ready for that mansion that you promised me.
>
> Take care.
>
> It's alright Sean, it's alright. I'm going to a better place.

Mitchell's 'I am sorry for the life I took from you' is also very direct. Unlike the previous statement, however, in Mitchell's text the mention of religion is significant. In the next statement Doughtie barely makes even an indirect admission:

Text 10.7   Jeffrey Carlton Doughtie (murdered elderly couple aged 80 and 76)

For almost nine years I have thought about the death penalty, whether it is right or wrong and I don't have any answers. But I don't think the world will be a better or safer place without me. If you had wanted to punish me you would have killed me the day after, instead of killing me now. You are not hurting me now. I have had time to get ready, to tell my family goodbye, to get my life where it needed to be.

It started with a needle and it is ending with a needle.

Carl, you have been a good friend, man. I am going to look for you. You go back and tell your daughter I love her. Tell her I came in here like a man and I will leave like a man. It's been good, dude. Thank you, Shorty. I appreciate you. I came in like a man and I will leave like a man. I will be with you. I will be with you every time you take a shower. If you leave crying you don't do me justice. If you don't see peace in my eyes you don't see me. I will be the first one you see when you cross over.

They got these numbers that I called today. Calling my family.

That is it. Ready, Warden.

Rather, Doughtie makes the death penalty the issue, about how – in his view – it is wrong and ineffective as a punishment. Others, by contrast, refer to the conditions of death row inmates, and specifically condemn either the death penalty process itself or the way in which prisoners are kept. For example, Jose Jesus Ceja wrote:

> Arizona's death row has become a swamp of inhumane treatment with men driven to various degrees of madness and suicide. Isolation, noise, mistreatment by guards and public indifference take a terrible toll on the human psyche.

Still others deny to the end the crimes of which they were accused:

Text 10.8   Last statement of Basil McFarland

I owe no apologies for a crime I did not commit. Those who lied and fabricated evidence against me will have to answer for what they have done. I know in my heart what I did and I call upon the spirit of my ancestors and all of my people and I swear to them and now I am coming home.

What do these texts have in common? Can we sensibly group them into one category, not just because of the circumstances in which they were produced, but also because of their linguistic structure?

At first sight it would seem not: death row final statements do not initially seem to represent a single genre – despite the circumstances of their production – but rather appear to form several genres, including very particular types of admission, denial, public condemnation, appeals for forgiveness, etc.

However, all of the statements have two particular features in common, which override any of their differences. The first is that these speakers share something crucial, regardless of innocence or guilt, admission or denial, condemnation or contrition: they are all about to die, they know it, and they are not (apparently) resisting it. They also have something else in common: they all seem to want to die with dignity or virtue of some kind. It is perhaps all they have left. This is why, I believe, they generally either:

- admit the crime – and so perhaps attempt to leave the witnesses with an impression of 'honesty', 'forthrightness', etc.;
- deny the crime – and thus attempt to leave at least some witnesses with an impression of innocence;
- condemn the death row process as inhumane or ineffective – and in this way take attention away from the crime and/or any part they may have played in it, or distract from the painfulness of the moment;
- or denounce witnesses as dishonest, law enforcement as corrupt, etc., and so portray themselves as innocent victims, or extract some small measure of revenge in their last moments.

Note that the above points are purely issues of linguistic content and structure: from the linguistic point of view the actual innocence or guilt of the speakers is immaterial, as is the question of whether the system which operates the death penalty is corrupt or not. Rather, what is of importance is how these various speakers respond linguistically to the moment of execution and whether, in doing so, they exhibit some kind of unified linguistic behaviour which may have resulted not just from their common fate as people about to be executed, but also from the entire death row process through which they have lived, some for many years.

American executions have to be viewed as public acts. Even though the general public is not invited to them and they take place behind closed doors, there are always witnesses, perhaps as many as twenty or thirty in some cases. This means that anything the condemned person says at such a time is also public. Condemned speakers need to create or make an impression, to be seen to be standing up for their corner. The context is not only public, but is – specifically – set within the judicial framework: the language used – e.g. 'a better or safer place', 'inhumane treatment', 'public indifference', 'crime I did not commit', 'fabricated evidence' – is articulate and appropriate, with just a hint of legalese. It too, reflects the setting. These are not simple farewell texts, but complex commentaries on society as seen from death row. They constitute a genre because only someone who has been in that situation – i.e. awaiting execution for some years and then knowingly facing the moment of death at the hands of the state – can produce such a text. Suicide notes and ransom notes also constitute genres, but they are not usually within the heavily institutionalized setting of death row prison units, whereas final statements are. It is a matter of debate as to whether final statements are of any use in determining guilt or innocence. However, of one thing we can be certain. Providing the provenance of the final statement text checks out, we are never in doubt as to the genuineness of the text.

CONFESSIONS AND DENIALS BY PUBLIC PERSONS

Previously we looked at Derek Bentley's alleged statement from an authorship point of view, while elsewhere we evaluated some aspects of veracity in Timothy John Evans's statements as part of a general investigation into statement analysis. The texts we are about to look at are different from those of the final statement variety, and those we have considered under the headings of authorship and statement analysis – they were written or spoken by public figures. Francis Bacon, for example, wrote:

> I am ready to make an OBLATION of myself to the King, in whose hands I am as Clay, to be made into a vessel of Honour or Dishonour . . . Yet with respect to this Charge of Bribery I AM INNOCENT. I never had Bribe Or Reward.
>
> (Letter to the Duke of Buckingham, 1617)

In this text Bacon offers a sacrifice of himself to save the king's 'honour', while maintaining his own innocence. In his statement from the gallows Henry Garnet, head of the Jesuits in England, confessed to his part in the Gunpowder plot as follows:

> Good countrymen, I am come hither this blessed day of The Invention of the Holy Cross to end all my crosses in this life. The cause of my suffering is not unknown to you. I confess I have offended the King, and am sorry for it, so far as I was guilty; which was in concealing it, and for that I ask pardon of his Majesty.
>
> (Harrison, 1941)

Finally, let us consider the closing words of Nelson Mandela's statement at his treason trial, at the end of which Mandela was sentenced to death, later commuted to life imprisonment on Robben Island.

During my lifetime I have dedicated my life to this struggle of the African people. I have fought against white domination, and I have fought against black domination. I have cherished the ideal of a democratic and free society in which all persons will live together in harmony and with equal opportunities. It is an ideal for which I hope to live for and to see realised. But, my lord, if it needs be, it is an ideal for which I am prepared to die.

(The British Library National Sound Archive)

Why are these public denials and confessions important linguistically? These are public figures responding to their accusers, sometimes in public and sometimes in private. In these texts – diverse as they are – we have prominent people, some of whom are members of the establishment, facing and responding to the establishment. Bacon is prepared to save the king's honour, because he believes that this is what a loyal subject should do, but he insists on his innocence as a matter of principle. Garnet admits to having known that the Gunpowder Plot was to take place. He is confessing for one reason only: to save people of his own religion from persecution. Finally, we have the statement of Nelson Mandela, who states that he is prepared to die for his beliefs, and in fact was originally sentenced to death. All of these individuals believed they were acting from principle. There are surprising linguistic similarities between these three excerpts. Both Garnet and Mandela specify aspects of a struggle, Garnet referring to 'crosses' and 'suffering', Mandela to 'this struggle of the African people'. Bacon states his preparedness to making a 'vessel' of himself. The idioms are different, and there are different shades of meaning, but the communicative purpose is very similar across all three texts, making them worth further study as part of a possible genre.

Phonetics

Health Warning:

Phonetics is a *highly* specialised and technical field. The information in this chapter is provided for illustrative purposes only and does **not** constitute specialist or expert training. Moreover, practising phoneticians would probably want to stress that there is no such thing as a perfect 100% accurate method of voice identification.

One of the main tasks of the (forensic) phonetician is to identify people on the basis of recorded spoken language samples. As a forensic activity, this has often been more successful than the identification of individuals through written language, probably because it relies on the distinctiveness of the human voice, whereas an exercise in authorship attribution relies on the notion of idiolect, in some ways a concept much harder to demonstrate than that of distinctiveness of voice. This chapter will consist mainly of a discussion on articulatory phonetics, interspersed with material on the art of reading a speech spectrogram, which is a particular kind of graphic representation of speech, and examples of which will appear in the course of this chapter. Before beginning the main section of the chapter there are several points the reader might like to note.

1. Although the spectrogram is important in the voice identification process, we should not imagine that phoneticians just 'read' a spectrogram in order to identify a voice. Rather, many calculations based on spectrographic data are carried out, and it is usually from a synthesis of these that identifications are made.
2. It should be realized that, to date, a completely reliable method of voice identification has not been discovered. Nevertheless, there are several excellent techniques which offer success rates of the order of 90 per cent.
3. Voice identification is an exacting, though not yet exact science. It requires considerable technical knowledge and skill, not only of linguistics in general and phonetics in particular, but also some knowledge of statistics and mathematics.
4. Although I offer a brief 'introduction' to phonetics here, the reader would be well advised to read the early chapters of one of the standard textbooks, in order to gain a general familiarity with the topic, for example Ladefoged's well-known *A Course in Phonetics* (2001). Additionally, there are many websites giving general introductory information on the topic. The same applies to the literature on voice identification itself: readers are referred to the professional literature for first-hand information, prime examples of which are Baldwin and French's *Forensic Phonetics* (1990), and Hollien's *Forensic Voice Identification* (2001).

PHONETICS: AN 'INTRODUCTION'

This section is a very brief sketch of phonetics, somewhat simplified for non-linguists. If you have progressed beyond your first semester of undergraduate linguistic studies, you do not need to read this section.

Speech consists of sounds made with our speech apparatus, i.e. lungs, vocal folds, oral and nasal cavities, lips, etc. The smallest sound unit of speech is known as the phoneme, for example /f/ in *forensic*, /l/ in *language*.[44] When we write phonemes using phonetic symbols they look not unlike the letters we use every day to write words in the language, but there are some important differences. A phonetic symbol represents one and only one phoneme in the language. Any single letter of the 'normal' alphabet, however, can represent several different sounds in the language. For example, the letter 'a' is pronounced differently in *father, ape, any, fall*. However, in phonetic script the 'a' sound in *father*, for example, is written /ɒ/, whereas what we term the 'a' sound in *ape* is transcribed /ɛɪ/. Although the letter 'a' is used for both of these words in ordinary writing, it bears no relationship to the real-world pronunciation of these vowels in their respective words, which is the reality that phonetic symbols attempt to represent.

The same applies to a number of other vowel sounds in English. In fact English has a very complicated vowel structure, so that, although we have only five letters to represent our vowel sounds, there are in fact about twenty actual vowel sounds and diphthongs in the language (depending on which dialect you speak). Compare this with the five vowel sounds in Spanish and Italian, for example, and about seven in Welsh (again depending on the dialect spoken). Consonants, too, are not that straightforward to represent. Consider, for example, the different sounds for the letter 's' in *is, kiss, pleasure, show*. As you can see, what we think of as 's' is actually a number of different sounds, some of which are written in phonetic symbols as follows: /z/ (is), /s/ (kiss), /ʒ/ (pleasure), /ʃ/ (show). Phonetic symbols help us to record pronunciation quite precisely and are often used in dictionaries, or other learning media. Moreover, if we know phonetic symbols well we can transcribe virtually any word in almost any language, or indeed any sequence uttered with the speech apparatus even if it is not a meaningful or recognizable language string. However, phonetics is about much more than phonetic transcription. It concerns, for example, how and where speech sounds are made (articulatory phonetics); how speech sounds are perceived (auditory phonetics); and speech as wave structure (acoustic/experimental phonetics).

Another important aspect of phonetics is the classification of speech sounds. When we classify sounds we can see the relationship between – for example – /z/, /s/, /ʒ/ and /ʃ/. One of the many benefits of understanding the relationships between different speech sounds is the ability to read even quite complex spectrograms, as a result of improving our knowledge of the speech process.

THE SPEECH PROCESS

The speech process begins with air pulsing upwards from the lungs, after which it enters the larynx (wind pipe) prior to reaching the vocal folds (vocal cords). These are a pair of elastic-like muscles which are capable of being vibrated at an astonishing range of frequencies, from very low to very high. In women and children they are usually shorter than in men, and so women and children mostly have higher-pitched voices than men. When the vocal folds vibrate to produce speech the sounds so produced are called *voiced*, otherwise they are *voiceless*. There are many such oppositions in the production of speech sounds in addition to *voiced* and *voiceless* (**p** *vs.* **b**; **t** *vs.* **d**; **k** *vs.* **g**); *plosives vs. fricatives* (**p** or **b** *vs.* **f** or **v**; **t** or **d** *vs.* **th**(in) or **th**(at)) – other English fricatives include **s**, and **z**; *nasal vs. oral* (**m** *vs.* **b**, **n** *vs.* **d**), etc. However, oppositions are only one way of classifying sound, for example **l** is a *lateral* sound, i.e. one that is produced by air being forced to the sides of the mouth (hence *lateral*); *velar* sounds are made with the tongue pressing against the velum (soft palate), such as **k**, **g** and **ng**; *palatal* sounds are sounds that are produced by approximating the tongue to the roof of the mouth (the hard palate), as in **y**ear or **y**es. Genius, **sh**op, and **ch**ew – these latter sounds measure *alveolar* (called *post–alveolar*), because they are articulated behind the alveolar ridge, but in front of the hard palate.

Note that I have combined discussion of place of articulation here with manner of articulation. Thus *lateral, velar, palatal* and *palatal–alveolar* are all terms relating to place of articulation, i.e. **where** in the speech apparatus sounds are made; on the other hand when we talk about *plosives vs. fricatives* and *voiced vs. voiceless*, then these refer to manner of articulation – i.e. **how** speech sounds are made. So, for example when we talk about the affricate (which is just a plosive plus a fricative) **ch** in **ch**ew, we are referring to how the sound is produced, which is information in addition to where it is produced (i.e. palate–alveolar, referred to above).

The forensic phonetician is first a phonetician, someone who understands how speech sounds are produced and the theory and organization behind phonetics, which is known as *phonology*. The professional phonetician will be thoroughly familiar with all aspects of speech production, the structure of speech sounds in the language, accents and dialects, sounds peculiar to certain languages (e.g. the clicks found in several Bantu languages) and dialects (e.g. English-language dialects with rhotic **r**), as well as some speech and language pathologies, voice disguise, and so on.

The forensic phonetician is concerned with the structure of the individual voice, and how it differs from other voices. Some very experienced forensic phoneticians can 'hear' a word or utterance, just on the basis of seeing a **spectrogram**. Indeed, of all the tools of modern technology

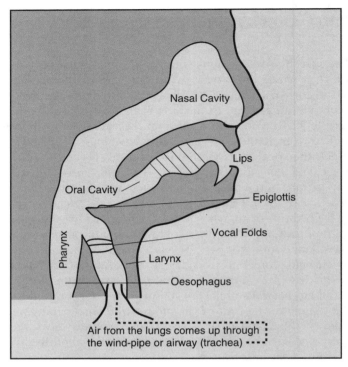

Nasal Cavity

Lips

Oral Cavity

Epiglottis

Vocal Folds

Pharynx

Larynx

Oesophagus

Air from the lungs comes up through the wind-pipe or airway (trachea)

Figure 11.1

utilized by the forensic phonetician, it is the spectrogram which has probably proved among the most useful to date.

WHAT IS A SPECTROGRAM?

A spectrogram, as applied to phonetics, is one particular way – among many – of visualizing speech. In the 'early' days the technology was referred to as 'voiceprinting', but this term was soon rejected as being too reminiscent of fingerprint technology. At a more mundane level, we should think of a spectrogram as a three-dimensional graph. Whereas most graphs can only manage to tell us about two things, a speech spectrogram analyses three dimensions simultaneously.[45]

The two things that most graphs can tell us are usually shown on the two axes of the graph: the x axis and the y axis. The x axis is the horizontal data line, as for example the value **year** in Specimen graph 1.

This graph is typical of many graphs, where **time** is shown on the **x** or horizontal axis. In this graph we also see a vertical or y axis, in this case showing an amount of money or some other numerical quantity. This

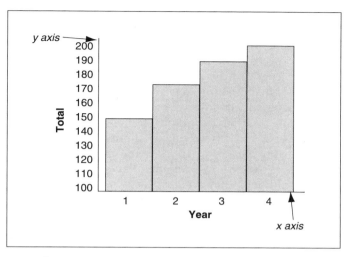

Specimen graph 1

is very common in graphs: the y or vertical axis very often records a numerical dimension to do with quantity, such as a sum of money, the number of people who took part in an experiment, etc. Put simply, the above graph might show us how many people came to visit a particular city over a period of four years, or how much money a family spent over four years, or how the average salary in a given company or industry increased over a period of four years. **Time**, in this case **years**, is given on the **x** or horizontal axis: the **amount**, or other numerical quantity, is given on the vertical or **y** axis.

In the spectrogram below we also see an x and a y axis:[46]

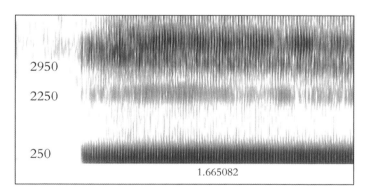

Spectrogram 1

In the above spectrogram the sound /iː/ is represented. The number, on this occasion '1.665082', represents the duration of the sound in seconds for this recording. As you can see, this value is given along the horizontal or **x** axis. The frequency of the sound (see next section) is given along the vertical or y axis. However, if you look closely at the spectrogram you will see that some areas of the spectrogram are darker than others. In this particular spectrogram these dark areas actually form fairly straight lines across the length of the picture. These lines represent intensity – the frequencies at which the sound is at its most intense. The sound /i:/ or 'ee' is very characteristic. Its lowest horizontal line is at about 250Hz (as shown by the number 250 on the graph). It then shows another horizontal line at about 2250Hz and a third one at about 2950Hz. Of course these values will vary from speaker to speaker and even occasion to occasion. These three lines are known as **formants**. Every speech sound has one or more formants, although they are not always as clear-cut as those shown here.

WHAT IS A FORMANT?

First things first. Above, I mentioned **frequency**. What is frequency? Frequency is the number of times a sound vibrates per second, usually measured in Hertz, abbreviated **Hz**. If a sound is of low frequency then its rate of vibration is relatively low. For example, a person with a deep voice will produce sounds of low frequency. On the other hand, a soprano singer will produce sounds of high frequency. This frequency, the pitch of the speaker's voice, is the fundamental frequency or F0, the rate of vocal fold vibration. Beyond fundamental frequency, each sound in the language resonates at many *different* frequencies simultaneously, as can be seen from the spectrogram above: however, the sound energy at some frequencies is more intense than at others, depending on the speaker's voice, quality of the recording, etc. Where we find a great deal of sound intensity within a narrow range of frequencies, this is described as a formant. Put simply, we can identify many speech sounds by their formants because these formants are characteristic of that sound. The lowest frequency formant is called F1, and then we have F2 and then F3. Note that 'F0' in the term 'fundamental frequency' is pronounced F-Zero (not 'O') – it is a frequency, not a formant.

Different sounds in the language resonate at different frequencies because we make our vocal tract assume a particular shape to make a particular sound. By vocal tract here we mean the entire speech apparatus – the way we shape the inside of the mouth and the lips, as well as the rate of vibration of the vocal folds. So, when we say 'ee' for example, the vocal tract is shaped differently than when we say 'aah'. For 'ee' the teeth are close together, the lips spread apart, while for 'aah' the mouth is more open and the lips are more rounded.

Spectrogram 2 depicts /i:/ followed by /a:/. Differences in the shape of the vocal tract are reflected in the spectrogram, where we see three white horizontal lines for each of the given sounds. However, in the case of 'ee' we see that the three horizontal white lines are spread quite far

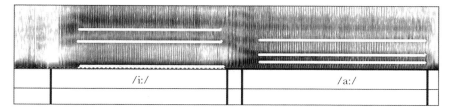

Spectrogram 2

apart, whereas for the 'aah' we see that the three horizontal white lines are closer together. I have chosen to represent the formants as white lines in this illustration, but they can be represented in many different ways. The lowest of the three white lines is known as F1, i.e. 'formant one', then F2, and then F3, as I mentioned above. For some sounds and some speakers a fourth or even fifth formant is possible, while for others it is not. Generally, if we have F1 to F3 we will be able to 'read' the sound in the spectrogram. Both 'ee' and 'aah' are vowels and it is noticeable that vowels are (relatively) long, unobstructed sounds, both in speech as we know it and in spectrograms. In Spectrogram 3 I again show these two sounds, but this time without the white lines to obscure the detail. If you compare these two pictures you should now be able to make out the formants for yourself, more or less where the white lines were in the previous illustration:

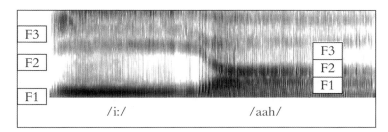

Spectrogram 3

From this illustration we can see that for 'aah' the three formants, F1, F2 and F3, have moved much closer together than they were in 'ee' (or /iː/). F1 has moved up, while F2 and F3 have moved down. As I mentioned previously, vowels are long (relatively) and continuous, and are in marked contrast to many consonants. However, vowels are not the only continuous sounds.

In Spectrogram 4 for /m/ we see that, as with the above vowels, there is little or no change in the spectrogram for the entire duration of the sound. There is, in other words, little apparent movement of the formants. This simply reflects an underlying reality: namely, the fact that you can

179

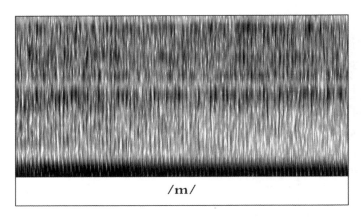

Spectrogram 4

make a prolonged /m/ sound with little or no change occurring in the speech apparatus once the sound has begun. Non-continuous sounds, on the other hand, show completely differently on the spectrogram, as might be expected.

/ba: pa: ga: ka: da: ta: /

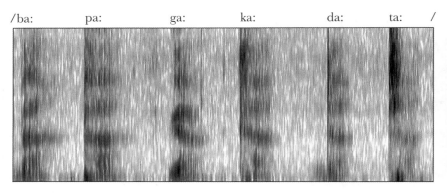

Spectrogram 5

Here we see individual sounds (all plosives) which are not continuous. Rather, each sound exhibits a brief burst of energy. Note that even though voicing totally changes the character of the sound as we *hear* it, the difference in the shape of the vocal tract between /b/ and /p/, for example, is not very significant.

In Spectrogram 6 for the repeated /b/ sound, we can appreciate the difference between a plosive and a continuous sound. The /m/ spectrogram given earlier shows an unbroken sound, but /b/ cannot be held as a continuous sound. We cannot prolong the sound, we can only repeat it.

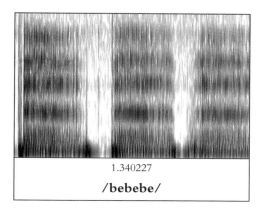

1.340227

/bebebe/

Spectrogram 6

However, in the above representation of /b/ the sound produced was very flat. If produced with the typical energy found at the beginning of a word, we see something slightly different:

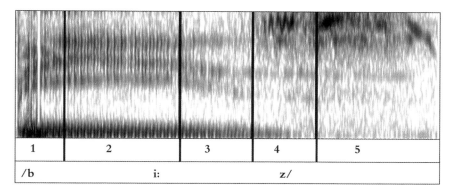

| 1 | 2 | 3 | 4 | 5 |

| /b | i: | z/ |

Spectrogram 7

In this representation of the word 'bees', rendered /bi:z/ in phonetic tran-script, I have divided the sound into five sections according to what is happening in the spectrogram. In (1) /b/ is sounded. We have the typical energy profile of a voiced plosive: there is a sudden surge of energy as evidenced by the wave-like appearance of the graph at all formants, and – in this instance – we have a fourth formant. By the time (2) starts, the energy level flattens and produces the long characteristic almost parallel 'lines' of the /i:/ sound, as previously discussed. In (3) the vowel /i:/ antici-pates the consonant /z/ and so we notice a further decline in the frequencies of the three formants, F1–F3. In (4) there is another strong burst of energy, mainly in the upper frequencies. Notice the sharpness and distinctness of the upper formants here: by the time we get to (5) it is as though this sharpness has been 'smudged' somehow. In fact this is just the de-voicing

181

of /z/ into /s/. Perhaps a better way to notice the de-voicing is in the lowest part of the spectrogram, going from left to right, i.e. at F1: there is apparently a constant F1 all the way through the sound, until – more or less – the beginning of (5), which is where the sound de-voices.

What about other sounds, similar to 'bees'? Well, let us take the invented word 'deez', identical except for the initial plosive. This is what it looks like in spectrographic form:

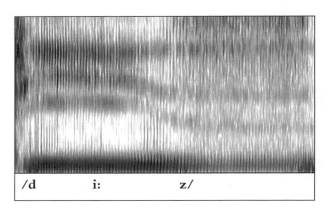

Spectrogram 8

In the previous spectrogram we spoke about the typical energy of the initial voiced plosive. But, as any phonetician will tell you, /b/ is a lot weaker as a plosive than /d/, and here we see spectrographic evidence for it. Compare the /d/ sound here with the /b/ sound in the previous example. You will see that this plosive demonstrates considerable energy right at the beginning of the sound. This energy even carries over into the /i:/ phoneme, and seems to sustain the 'voicedness' of the final phoneme for longer than in the previous example, where /z/ gave way to /s/ almost immediately. In the next example we see the invented word /giz/, the main change from the previous two words being the initial voiced plosive /g/:

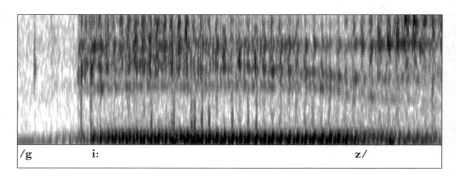

Spectrogram 9

Here we see the initial closure associated with voiced plosives, the sudden release with the typical burst of energy (where I have indicated /iː/) and the long continuous vowel subsiding at the end into a diphthong (just before the indicated /z/).

Lastly, let us look at a real word, not an invented one this time, namely 'geese'. There is little difference between this word and the previous one, the invented word 'geez'. However, the voiced /z/ is replaced by the /s/ of 'geese'.

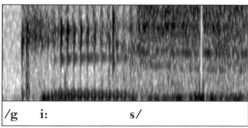

Spectrogram 10

After the long vowel /iː/, notice the sudden 'falling' away of the three formants, just before the indicated /s/. In 'bees' and 'geez' this was described as a move from a vowel into a diphthong. But in the case of 'geese' it is more a matter of loss of vocal energy. Note also, when comparing 'geese' with 'geez', that F1 (i.e. the formant at the bottom of the graph) is more or less constant with 'geez', 'deez' and 'bees'. However, with 'geese' there is a decline at the onset of the voiceless 's'. This appears to show us that F1 has something to do with the sound being voiced. If F1 is very weak, then the sound or phoneme we are studying would appear to be voiceless. For instance, if we substituted /k/ in the above spectrogram for /g/ we would find that there would be a build up of F1 prior to the voicing that comes with the vowel, /i/.

LEARNING TO READ SPECTROGRAMS

In the preceding sections you have been given some information on spectrograms. To supplement this information you need access to a computer with a good spectrogram program. There are many free and shareware programs available on the Internet. You can find these by typing in the word 'spectrogram' in any major Internet search engine. You will note that in the previous section I took a word, made a spectrogram of that word, and then altered the word one phoneme at a time. This is a simple way to proceed. It is of course, very painstaking, but it is an excellent way to teach yourself the basics of reading spectrograms.

In this section I conclude the discussion on speech spectrography by showing two spectrograms, these being representations of an attempt by a speaker to disguise his voice, his accent and his native language. One common ploy (worth briefly mentioning here) used by people who do disguise their voice, is to alter pitch. The thing about disguising pitch is that it is almost always predictable. People with naturally deep voices tend to disguise their voices by raising pitch, whereas people with high-pitched voices tend to do the opposite (Kunzel, 2000). The experienced phonetician can probably uncover most attempts at disguise and perhaps even identify the undisguised voice from several other versions.

In the following example the speaker attempts to disguise his accent, not just his voice. In the first effort he tries to sound like a Londoner, in the second effort he pretends to be someone from the south west of England.

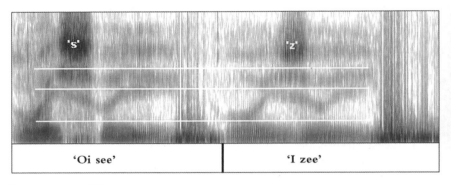

Spectrogram 11

In the left-hand example the speaker attempts to emulate his concept of how a Londoner would say 'I see', changing 'I' to 'Oi', and diphthongizing the vowel sound in *see*. In the second example the effort at sounding like a person from the west country includes voicing the 's' sound to produce 'zee' instead of *see*. Notice how 's' has much more *fortis* (i.e. strength) than 'z' (marked respectively in the illustration). Again, the formants are represented as white lines. In this case the tops of each formant on the left-hand side seem remarkably close to the tops of each formant on the right-hand side. Moreover, each side has upper formants (F4 and F5) visible at and above the 's' and 'z' respectively. A professional forensic phonetician would doubtless remark on many other similarities between the two efforts. Doubtless, also, the forensic phonetician would not be fooled for one second by these pathetic attempts at emulating these two British accents, that of London and that of the south west of England.

The two previous examples were concerned with disguise: disguise of voice in the first (high pitched and deep), and disguise of accent in the second (London *vs* west country). In the following example we take the notion of disguise a step further: here the speaker is trying to disguise the fact that his native language is English (left-hand side). In fact he is pretending to be a German-native speaker saying 'we demand a ransom'. On the right-hand side he says the same thing, but with his normal English-native-speaker accent.

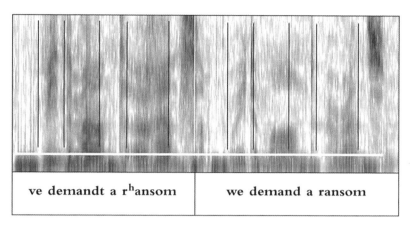

ve demandt a rʰansom   we demand a ransom

Spectrogram 12

In this disguise the give-away is in the timing. Despite the speaker's best efforts the stress in the fake 'German' attempt falls in exactly the same places as it does in the non-disguised effort. Moreover, each of the six syllables is remarkably similar in length in the disguise attempt to the length of the syllables in the native speaker attempt (note the black vertical lines I have drawn in to show this). Finally, when we look at the position of F1 on the left and right-hand sides they are almost identical.

Very often a forensic phonetician will be called upon to identify a speaker, despite the presence of disguised material. There are many ways to disguise a voice: we have mentioned only three here, to do with pitch, accent and native language (L1). Others include deliberate ageing or juvenation of the voice, the impersonation of a famous person, and even attempts to disguise gender.

What makes disguise difficult is the fact that speakers are more or less stuck with their voice as it is: you cannot alter the length of your vocal tract without fairly major surgery. You may be able to adopt a false accent, but for how long? Unless you are a trained professional, maintaining the pretended accent for any length of time, particularly under conditions of tension, is almost impossible. You could pretend that your L1 was German, English or whatever you wanted, but this too has pitfalls. Either you would give the game away by failing to keep up the pretence or, worse still, a genuine native speaker of your 'adopted' L1 might challenge you.

Voices are distinct, and distinctive. Forensic phoneticians are now developing many methodologies and strategies in their bid to document

185

individual differences between voices. The chapter concludes with a brief discussion of some of these.

VOICE IDENTIFICATION: METHODS AND PRACTICES

In this section I will look at some aspects of current voice identification practices.

Overall method – impression *vs.* machine

No method has yet been discovered which successfully distinguishes voices from each other in each and every case. Some methods rely on *impressionistic* identification – the analyst's own impressions, while others rely on *instrumental* identification – the use of various kinds of mechanical or computerized equipment (Ingram, Prandolini *et al.*, 1996). However, there is now broad agreement that the best results are obtained by combining the strength and power of computers with the judgement of specialists (Rodman, McAllister *et al.*, online).

Content

The speech content used in voice identification tasks broadly breaks down into two types, text-dependent content and text-independent content. Text-dependent content (Ingram, Prandolini *et al.*, 1996) involves having the suspect speaker and the various candidate speakers record an

---

Information Panel 1

The main voice types

Hoarse voices: there is a difference between the vocal folds and the rate at which they vibrate. This causes a different sound to be produced for each vocal fold resulting in a hoarse voice. Causes can be neurological – e.g. paralysis – or of a more temporary nature, such as some kind of respiratory tract infection (Scherer, online).

- **Diplophonic voices:** two different pitches are heard.
- **Vocal fry:** the vocal folds are constantly vibrated at a low pitch.
- **Breathy voices:** excessive aspiration (breathing) during speech production.
- **Voice pathologies:** many, including **aphonia** (lack of phonation); **dysphonia** (dysfunction of phonation).

identical 2–3 second stretch of speech as each other. Usually this text is identical to that which was uttered by the criminal in the commission of the crime. This enables a direct comparison between the criminal's voice and the voices of any suspects. Text-independent content methods do not rely on the suspect and the speakers speaking/reading the same text, but on phonetic and spectrographic similarities between the candidate voices.

There are several views regarding what exactly it is that makes an individual voice distinct from other voices. These have given rise to a number of approaches, some of which are given in the following sections.

Formant plotting

On the one hand, formant trajectories are a way of smoothing out the formant data in a spectrogram, to make it more 'readable'. There are many ways of producing the plot of a formant, but they mostly involve some kind of algorithm (i.e. mathematical formula). Some phoneticians believe that analysis of formant plots assists in the identification of speakers. Spectogram 13 is an example of a formant plot.

Fundamental frequency

The rate at which the vocal cords vibrate, i.e. the length of time they take to open and close, is known as **fundamental frequency**, abbreviated F0 (Jiang, 1996). According to Jiang, both mean (i.e. average) speaker fundamental frequency (F0) and F0 standard deviation are 'among the most frequently-used parameters' for voice identification, although they are not able to provide 'a robust index . . . for identification purposes' (Jiang, *ibid.*), which is why Jiang suggests combining these two values into a 'vector' for identification purposes. Fundamental frequency is sometimes also referred to as 'glottal pulse'. However, technically, the two are quite different, since the glottis is the space between the vocal folds, whereas fundamental frequency measures the rate at which the vocal folds themselves open and close.

The identification of a voice itself is often carried out by means of a *voice line-up*, also referred to as an *earwitness line-up*. As the name suggests it is not unlike the concept of an eyewitness line-up. First, the language of the incident is recorded by one or more witnesses, and a number of recordings of the incident language are then made by the suspect/s and other persons of the same gender, similar age, class, educational and dialect background and, crucially, with a similar type of voice to the suspect (e.g. creaky, breathy, etc. – see Information Panel 1). These recordings will be played to the witness who may or may not be able to identify the suspect's voice on the basis of this information. Generally, however, the process of the earwitness parade is little understood (Heselwood, online)

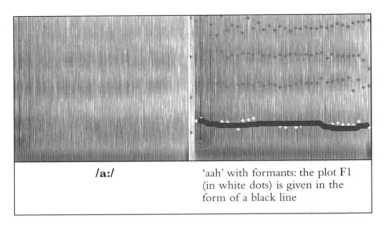

| /aː/ | 'aah' with formants: the plot F1 (in white dots) is given in the form of a black line |

Spectrogram 13

and not satisfactory: there are few cognitive similarities between the ear and eyewitness processes. Heselwood, in fact, confirms that the phonetic specialist is considerably more successful at voice identification than general members of the public. The reader will recall the Lindbergh case referred to earlier. In the trial Lindbergh claimed to have recognized Hauptmann's voice several years after first hearing it in the cemetery where he and a friend went to meet the kidnapper. However, Lindbergh was not given alternative voices to listen to, and so the process could scarcely be judged by modern standards to have been fair or impartial in that instance.

Ongoing research

The search for viable identification techniques and procedures is ongoing. Phoneticians are constantly looking to improve data capture and assessment, and continue to research into different types and milieus of voice recording, such as the telephone *vs.* the studio, different voice types, voice disguise, native speaker *vs.* non-native speaker identification, the measurement of affect, the effect of stimulants and depressants on the voice, audio accompaniment to video recording, alteration and falsification of audio recordings, etc. There is also a growing body of researchers interested in communicating with legal professionals, with a view to keeping this group up to date on new research, techniques and information related to voice identification.

CONCLUSION

As can be seen, forensic phonetics is a vast field which is growing more specialized all the time. It is a field which requires highly trained and experienced scientists with a strong background in linguistic theory and practice. In this chapter I have done no more than to sketch a broad outline of some of its more important features. I would refer the reader to the specialist forensic phonetic publications mentioned in the course of this chapter for further information. As mentioned before: this chapter is informational only and does not constitute specialist knowledge, or knowledge for training purposes.

SUGGESTIONS FOR FURTHER READING

Baldwin, J. R. and P. French (1990) *Forensic Phonetics*, London: Pinter Publishers.

CHAPTER 12

The forensic cookbook

In this chapter the intention is to present a number of skills-related topics relevant to forensic linguistics and the training of forensic linguists. These skills are intended to augment your linguistic knowledge and provide you with the forensic part of the term *forensic linguist*. Hence, they include forensic transcription, the ability to test text almost by looking at it, and several statistical formulae and concepts which are essential to the forensic linguist. This is why I have called this chapter a cookbook. It is a motley collection of bits and pieces of information and knowledge, which it may be worth your while to know and/or to develop. Also, being the simple person I am, I have included things others would consider beneath them, like simplified definitions of what a decibel is, for example, and what a Fourier transform is and – more importantly – why you need to know.

Before doing anything else, please transcribe the following paragraph. Straight off, without thinking, and – crucially – without reading it through first. Just pick up a pen and paper, or go to your word processor and do it. When you have finished, note down anything unusual or irregular:

Exercise 12.1   Transcription of an invented text

This chapter is about the improving of your foreign [*sic.*] skills. Your first and foremost important skill is the observation of text, wether written or spoken, whether text or numbers, such such as the sum of $123,453.78. What this necessitates is, in the first instance, the ability to observe what it is a text is comprised of, and secondly, the ability to transcribe text with total accurately. Your need to be very aware of any idiosyncracies the writer has, such as unconventual spellings, odd capitalizing, underlinings, *ect.* It is necessary to honour the text.

When you have finished transcribing this text and have noted down any peculiarities, check through Exercise 12.1 in Appendix A: Exercises.

TRANSCRIPTION: A DYING SKILL

The art of transcription may be a dying skill, perhaps because very few schools now practise dictation. For this reason, it is important for students of forensic linguistics to work continually on their transcription skills. The above exercise will have demonstrated the importance of this to you. For example, there are several versions of the Derek Bentley text. A and B below show two versions of the 'same' excerpt:

> A   I did not answer the door or speak to them. My mother told me that they had called and I then ran after them.
>
> B   I did not answer the door or speak to them. My mother told me that they had called and I then ran out after them.

C and D below show how two different versions end:

> C   and I heard someone call him 'Mac'. He was with us when the other policeman was killed.
>
> D   and I heard someone call him 'Mac'. He was with us when the other policeman was moved.

What possible explanation could there be for such differences? I believe we should be creatively critical about this, rather than pejorative. Of course there may be an element of carelessness in the first example, 'ran' instead of 'ran out', but the second example seems to offer at least two interpretations, depending on whether 'moved' was changed to 'killed' or vice versa. If 'killed' was the word altered, then the change may be something of a deliberate alteration – unless of course the scribe was thinking of something else while transcribing, for example, the details of how the body of the wounded officer may have been moved. That is one explanation of what may have happened here: the scribe anticipated what was being said and failed to register 'killed'. On the other hand, the police officer preparing the statement for court may have felt that 'killed' was too sensitive and changed it to 'moved'.

However, if 'moved' was the original word and this was changed to 'killed', then I believe the motivation for the change is much less benign. It would appear that, since 'killed' was the last word in the text, that the scribe wanted to leave the audience with the strongest possible impression of death and murder, whereas 'moved' on the other hand would have been much more neutral.

Bear in mind, however, our previous remarks about the Bentley text: it is not being stated here that Bentley said any of the things quoted in A–D above. What is at issue here is transcription, and learning to do it accurately. Accuracy is a complex notion: two people can produce different transcriptions, but both could still be accurate. This is because the idea of 'accuracy' includes many things – for instance, our own expectations as scribes, about what is being said, and sometimes even about what is being meant. We alter things because we want them to mean something different. And, depending on our own cultural associations, we may not even be aware of this. Moreover, sometimes it is impossible to transcribe what someone says 'accurately', either because the speaker (if live) is indistinct or the recording or recording copy (if not live) is poor. Here there is always a temptation to 'interpret'. I had exactly this problem when attempting to transcribe Susan Smith's video recording of the alleged carjacking. The text was full of pauses and hesitations, and I had to listen many times before I was reasonably confident that I had produced an accurate result. I tried to keep a flavour of the breaks and pauses in the way I presented the text:

Forensic text 12.1

all he ever told me was shutup or i'll kill you . . . (break) . . . and i just
screamed i said what are you doing he said shutup and drive and had a
gun and he was (. . .) poking it in my side you know and told me to drive
(.) and I (.) so i drove

There are many instances of inaccurate transcription of important and
historical documents. One of these concerns the speech Nelson Mandela
made at the Rivonia trial in 1964. The ANC quotes the end of that speech
as follows:[47]

Exercise 12.2

During my lifetime I have dedicated myself to this struggle of the African
people. I have fought against white domination, and I have fought against
black domination. I have cherished the ideal of a democratic and free society
in which all persons live together in harmony and with equal opportunities.
It is an ideal which I hope to live for and to achieve. But if needs be, it is an
ideal for which I am prepared to die.

However, if you listen to the speech which has been preserved for all
time by a recording, you will – I believe – hear the following:

During my lifetime I have dedicated my life to this struggle of the African
people. I have fought against white domination, and I have fought against
black domination. I have cherished the ideal of a democratic and free society
in which all persons will live together in harmony and with equal opportunities. It is an ideal for which I hope to live for and to see realised. But, my
lord, if it needs be, it is an ideal for which I am prepared to die.

There are at least four important changes. See if you can spot them, then
check Appendix A: Exercises at the end of the book.

TESTING TEXT: THE SECRET OF LEXICAL RICHNESS

What is **lexical richness**, and why is it so **important** to **forensic linguistics?**
There are at least **three aspects** to **lexical richness: lexical density, word
length** and **unique word density**. The **reader** will be **aware** that **lexical
words** are those that **have meaning** and can, at least in **English, take inflec-
tions.** In this **paragraph** I have **put** all the **lexical words** in **bold type.**

Note that some words can be lexical or non-lexical. Thus 'have' in 'have
meaning' is lexical. It is to do with possession. However, 'have' in

'have put' is not to do with possession, it is an auxiliary of the verb *to put*. As an auxiliary, it is a *non-lexical* or *functional* word.

Lexical density is the first measure of *lexical richness*. It is a simple calculation: number of lexical words in a text divided by the total number of words (length) of the text. The paragraph above in which I made the lexical words bold was 64 words long, of which 31 (by my count) were lexical. This therefore gives a lexical density of 31/64 = 0.48, or 48 per cent. Normally, however, we would be cautious about providing lexical density for a 64 word text. Short texts – as I have attempted to show in earlier chapters – cannot be guaranteed to be stable (see An experiment in measurement stability, pp. 66–8). If required to text a short text – try to supplement your result with as much other data as possible.

Word length is another important *lexical richness* measure, because it often tells us, in conjunction with lexical density, whether a text was spoken, written or even dictated.[48] Typically, speakers use longer words on average in written language than in spoken or dictated, just as they use more lexical words than when they speak or dictate. Like lexical density, word length is a measure of lexical richness.

Finally, we should consider **unique word density**, which is the density of words, lexical or not, short or long, which are unique in a given text. *Hapax legomena* as they are also called, are very important, because – like the other measures I have referred to – they also relate to lexical richness. For instance, we generally find that speech contains fewer *hapax legomena* than written language. When analysing text for its mode, i.e. whether it was written, dictated or spoken, we usually submit it to a battery of measurements which would include the above *lexical richness* tests. However, it is possible, if you have a printed copy of a text, to carry out a visual inspection of the text for lexical richness. Consider the last two paragraphs of the Gilfoyle 'suicide' text:

Forensic text 12.2

Eddie I hope that you will find it in your heart to forgive me and that one day we will meet again until that day, take care of yourself don't be afraid in life, I will watch over you and protect you from harm. I've ruined your life, its the best I can do maybe it will be the one thing I will do right in life.

I can't change or alter what I've done but if I could I would. They say time heals a broken heart. I hope your heart heals pretty quick. I don't want you to waste anymore of your life. Its time to turn the clock forward instead of backwards and go forward.

A quick visual inspection tells us that the sentences in one of the paragraphs shown here seem shorter than those in the other paragraph – but which? Perhaps you would like to take a moment to answer that question for yourself?

In fact we can confirm this just by counting the words in several sentences from each of the paragraphs: we note that the second paragraph contains what seem to be shorter sentences than the first of the two paragraphs shown. If the sentences are shorter in one excerpt, what else should be different? Recall that in a previous chapter we noted that short sentences tend to co-occur with longer words. The presence of longer words implies greater lexical richness, including – as we have noted above – unique word density and word length average. This is what our brief visual inspection leads us to:

Feature	Paragraph 1	Paragraph 2
Sentence length	33.5	10.2
Word length	3.58	3.94
Unique word density	0.4	0.63

As can be seen, the discrepancies between the two paragraphs are fairly major. The point I am making, however, is that virtually all of this information can be initially derived from a brief visual inspection. This kind of brief visual inspection is only possible if you are sensitive to text and observant of it. I believe that the practice of transcribing text is the best way of achieving this. When I began studying forensic linguistics I had a different kind of computer from the university. This meant that I could not use disks or diskettes to get the texts onto my own machine. I had to print them out at university and then key them into my own machine. At first this seemed like a ridiculous chore, very boring and time-consuming. However, I found that after some time it alerted me to what texts *actually* said, rather than what they at first *appeared* to say. Nowadays, if I am interested in a text, I will download and print it, regardless of whether I can get it straight onto my own computer. I then key in the entire text, leaving nothing unexamined. Sometimes the most important sections of a text appear to be the most insignificant when we first examine them. Consider, for example, the following two copies, A and B, of an excerpt from one of Martin Luther King's most famous speeches:

A   I have a dream that one day on the red hills of Georgia the sons of former slaves and the sons of former slaveowners will be able to sit down together at a table of brotherhood.[49]

B   I have a dream that one day on the red hills of Georgia the sons of former slaves and the sons of former slave-owners will they be able to sit down together at the table of brotherhood.

Look carefully at both these examples. Can you spot the two differences (other than the hyphen between *slave* and *owners* in B)? Here we have just two words different, yet they are very significant. The phrase '*a* table of brotherhood' is meaningless, since – I assume – *brotherhood* here is meant to indicate something universal. Therefore, I feel that in reality, '*the* table of brotherhood' is the only possible rendition of this concept. When we turn to the actual recording of Martin Luther King's voice on that memorable day in 1963, we indeed hear what we see in example B, namely '*the* table of brotherhood', not '*a* table of brotherhood'. However, note that King actually asks a question in the speech: 'will *they* be able to sit down together . . .'. The written copy of this omits the pronoun *they* altogether, thus implying that King was making a statement when in fact he was asking a question: it totally misses the point of the entire speech. The speech was not just that King had a dream, but that he had a dream in which he questioned a possibility. He was not necessarily stating it as a dream which would actually take place – I believe he was leaving this question open: perhaps in an effort to make his followers strive harder to reach the goals he was setting them. Without wishing to bore the reader, I will conclude this section by repeating what I said earlier: as forensic linguists we need to learn to transcribe accurately. You know the old joke. The musician asks the cab driver. 'Say, can you tell me how I get to Carnegie Hall?' The cab driver scratches his head, eyes him up and down and eventually says: 'Practice!'.

STATISTICAL FORMULAE

In the course of the book I have shown the importance of acquiring a basic understanding of statistics. This is really important. However, it is not necessary to become an expert in that field. In fact that could be a dangerous policy. By setting yourself up against professional statisticians, you simply prepare yourself for a fall, unless you are an exceptionally gifted mathematician. Either become a linguist or a statistician – the person who can do both is very rare. In any case, it is simply not necessary to become a statistician. Although some courts might penalize you because you used a different formula from some other expert, as long as you can give reasonable grounds for your methods, and as long as your methods are as scientific as required, that is all that really matters. In any case, if you are working on a very important case in which statistics abound – just consult with a professional. Do not try to do it yourself. It is not worth it.

In the text I have not given many statistical formulae. My reason was simple: I did not want to clutter the text. Now, however, I think it is time to provide this information. Just as in the course of the text I do not give formula, here I will not explain (in any detail) the use of the formula. What is in the body of the text itself needs supplementing with information given here, just as the information here needs that given in the text itself to make sense. One word of advice: use the spreadsheet program on your computer

– it is rich in formulae. The information provided here is just that – information only.

In Chapter 5, I discussed how to calculate a mean. I then discussed *standard deviation*: I will now show how standard deviation can be calculated.

Standard deviation measures the degree to which values disperse from the mean. Assume we have four values whose mean we have taken:

A	15
B	20
C	23
D	19
Mean	**19.25**

We now take each value, A–D, in turn and note the difference between it and the mean. We ignore whether this difference is positive or negative and get something called the absolute deviation:

	X	Absolute deviation
A	15	4.25
B	20	0.75
C	23	3.75
D	19	0.25
Average	A	A

We now take each absolute deviation, and multiply it by itself. This is known as squaring.

	X	Deviation	Squares
A	15	4.25	18.06
B	20	0.75	0.56
C	23	3.75	14.06
D	19	0.25	0.06
Average			32.74

Our next step is to add these squares together, i.e. the sum of the squares: this gives us the result of 32.74 (as can be seen from the table above).

I then divide this figure, the sum of the squares (32.74), by n (the population size). This gives us: 32.74/4 = 8.19. I take the square root of this figure, which is 2.86.

The standard deviation is 2.86. It tells me how much volatility or dispersion there is from the average. In the course of the book I discussed standard deviation, and what it was, but I would like to give you a more concrete example, to do with money.

Imagine I want to invest in the stock market but can only afford stock from one company. After looking at many companies and how they have been performing, I finally narrow my choice down to two stocks. They each have the same current value, £100, having each moved from £80 two years ago. Which should I invest in? On closer examination, I find that Stock A has a standard deviation of 3.5 and Stock B has a standard deviation of 8.7. What this means is that Stock A is much less volatile than Stock B. In that case I decide to invest in Stock A. Why? Because, over the longer term it is less of a risk – it is less volatile. Even if the market overall goes down, I am less likely to suffer than Joe who has bought Stock B. He did so because he thought the dramatic increases it periodically showed were a good sign! So, why is standard deviation important to text analysis? As we saw in Chapter 5, in the section entitled 'An experiment in measurement stability' (pp. 66–8), standard deviation is important because it shows us whether a measure is stable or not. The reader will recall that we measured a range of texts at different lengths from 200 to 1,000 words.

We noted that lexical density deviated from the mean much more in short texts than in long ones. This told us that it was not really useful to measure short texts: unless we could measure many of them we could not get accurate results from them. This is highly comparable to buying stocks and shares. Just as you wouldn't bet on a stock which showed high amounts of deviation, so too you would want to avoid attributing authorship in cases where the scores you had arrived at exhibited excessive deviation. A final example: imagine you are a doctor and you have a patient with a fever whose temperature deviates from normal body temperature excessively. You would be much more concerned about this patient than one whose temperature, though perhaps a little high, did not fluctuate so greatly. However, once the patient's temperature began to deviate less and less from the mean, you would perhaps begin to worry less than previously.

As can be seen, the standard deviation is an excellent guide to the overall picture presented by a text or set of texts. For example, you could take the average length of sentences in a text and then compute the standard deviation. You could then see not only by how much the sentences deviated, but also where in the text the greatest deviations took place. As a rule of thumb, a value in excess of two standard deviations is likely to be significant. If you wanted to find the standard deviation of the average word length, you would be advised to look at the text in sections, for example of 50 words each, or to take the average word length per sentence, and then calculate the standard deviation from that. As you can appreciate, it would not be useful to look for standard deviation of so fine a measure as word length across the entire text, without first breaking the text into manageable units.

X^2 (PRONOUNCED 'KI SQUARE', SPELLED 'CHI-SQUARE')

The X^2 is a very useful statistic for evaluating what we discover in relation to what we imagine or, put another way, what we *observe* in terms of what we *expect*. Think about it for a moment. This is exactly what judgement means, what learning to judge is all about. We expect certain things to happen based on what we have observed in the past. When we want to evaluate what we observe we simply weigh it up against what we expect. That is the basis of judging: X^2 observation and expectation.

Imagine I have two sections of text with different *sentence length* averages, as follows:

Section A	Section B
12	11
11	13
9	15
14	8
15	7

Is there a significant difference between the two samples? Our first step is to calculate E, the expected value for each section. This is done as follows. First, we add the values in the two columns together.

Observed data:

A	B	Total
12	11	23
11	13	24
9	15	24
14	8	22
15	7	22
61	54	115

We now calculate the *expected* data. We begin by taking the first set of values as a proportion of the total of the two columns. To do this take the total row value, say 23 (first row in the table), and divide it by the total columns value, 115. Now divide it by the total column value for Column

A, 61. Do the same for all the rows with respect to Column A, and then Column B. This gives us:

Expected data:
12.20   10.80
12.73   11.27
12.73   11.27
11.67   10.33
11.67   10.33

We now subtract our *expected* data from our *observed* data to obtain:

Observed – expected data:
−0.20   0.20
−1.73   1.73
−3.73   3.73
 2.33   −2.33
 3.33   −3.33

Note that column A – column B always equals zero. We now square these values and get:

(Observed – Expected)^2
0.04   0.04
2.99   2.99
13.92   13.92
5.43   5.43
11.09   11.09

We take these values and divide them by the expected data, and we obtain:

(Observed – expected)^2/Expected
0.003279   0.003704
0.235216   0.265707
1.09314   1.234843
0.465392   0.525721
0.950489   1.073701

We sum all of these values and we get **5.85**. In other words $X^2 = 5.85$.

We now check this value in a special table. If our value is greater than that for the table, it means there is a *significant difference* between the two sets of sentences. If our value is not greater than that for the table, then there is no difference. How do we look up the data in the table?

First we need to calculate something called *degrees of freedom* to read the correct data from the area. Degrees of freedom are the total number of sets of data (or columns) −1, multiplied by the total number of rows −1. Thus we have (2 columns −1) × (5 rows −1) = (1) × (4) = 4.

On looking up our table[50] we note that our value, 5.85 is higher than 0.1 but lower than 0.5. In other words, it is between 10 and 50 per cent. At worst there is a one in two probability that the two sets of sentences are from different populations, at best the probability is 1/10. These odds are not very good. It means, quite simply, that the difference is not significant. The chances of one set of sentences coming from a different author or text are extremely low. We need odds of the order of 1/20 or 1/100 or even better.

One thing you should note about X^2 – its use is limited to those instances where we have two sets of data of the same size. We couldn't use it in our tests on the Bentley text because the outer section contained fewer sentences than the inner section. If we had had a particularly long text we could have taken an equal size sample from each section. Nevertheless, the X^2 is still an extremely useful test, and where we have reasonably large sets of data to work with is very powerful.

THE *t* TEST

This section contains some very complex formulae. You can do one of two things: accept them as they are and just use computer spreadsheet programs when you want to calculate the values yourself, or you can attempt the calculations yourself.

You use the *t* test when you want to work out whether the mean of one group is different from the mean of the other group. This is just another way of looking for the difference between 'A' and 'B' – the quest of the vast majority of forensic statistical ventures. Remember that we used this test when we were comparing sentence lengths across two sections of the Bentley text. It did not matter that the two groups of sentences were of different sizes – the *t* test makes no assumptions about sample sizes being equal to each other. Below is the formula, using our previous example of the two sets of sentences.

In broad terms:

$$t = \frac{\text{The difference of the means}}{\text{The standard error of the difference}}$$

THE DIFFERENCE OF THE MEANS

First, calculate the mean for each group:

	A	B
	12	11
	11	13
	9	15
	14	8
	15	7
Mean	12.2	10.8

The mean for A is 12.2, while for B it is 10.8, and so we begin by subtracting B from A, obtaining: 1.4. This is the difference of the means.

THE STANDARD ERROR OF THE DIFFERENCE

Next, we calculate the standard deviation for each group. For A it is 2.13, while for B it is 2.99. Take the square of each of these (the square of the standard deviation is also known as the *variance*). For A this is 4.53, for B it is 8.94. Take the size of each sample and subtract 1 from it, giving you $5 - 1 = 4$ for both A and B. We divide each variance by this figure. We now add the value so obtained for A to the value so obtained for B. We take the square root of this value and this gives us the standard error of the difference. Here it is in more formal terms.

The standard error of the difference =

$$\sqrt{\frac{var_1}{(n_1 - 1)} + \frac{var_2}{(n_2 - 1)}} = \sqrt{\frac{4.53}{4} + \frac{8.94}{4}} = 1.83$$

Recall that the difference of the means was 1.4 and that t is the difference of the means divided by the standard error of the difference, in other words $1.4/1.83 = 0.76$. so, $t = 0.76$, but how do we calculate p, probability?

You may remember something called *degrees of freedom* from the last section when we were looking at X^2. We don't have columns and rows in the current example, so we have to calculate degrees of freedom in a different way. What were the sizes of the populations in group A and B? In group A it was 5, and in group B it was 5. This need not have been the case: sometimes we have populations of different sizes, such as in the Bentley text where we had 16 sentences in one group and 28 in the other.

We label the two groups 1 and 2, or A and B, or whatever we like, so long as we are consistent. When referring to the population size of each group we write it as follows: n_1 for Group 1 and n_2 for Group 2, or n_A for Group A and n_B for Group B. We noted $n_1 = 5$ and $n_2 = 5$. We add $n_1 + n_2$

and then subtract 2 (2 population sets). This gives us 8. This is the degrees of freedom (also written d.f.). We now look up t on a table known as 'The critical values of the t distribution'.[51] At 8 degrees of freedom we note that at an error rate of 0.05, and for a one-tailed test (these are the minima) the value given is 2.306. Recall that our value for t is 0.76. Actually if we use a well-known spreadsheet program and ask for t for the sets of values given above we get – not t but p, which that program indicates as 0.47. However, that aside, our t value of 0.76 is far below the required t value of 2.306: we cannot claim that the two sets are from different populations. In other words we cannot reject the null hypothesis.

ANOTHER t TEST FORMULA

We already know that t is the difference of the means ($\mu_1 - \mu_2$) or the difference of the sample means ($\overline{X}_1 - \overline{X}_2$), but as I indicated in an earlier chapter there are many different ways of calculating the standard error of the difference. The formulae appear very different, but they give very similar results, providing one feeds the right information into them (and of course the formula used will depend on the information one has). One way that I found on the Internet was this. It is not as intimidating as it looks, and so I think we should go through it just to demonstrate that t is t is t almost whatever we do:

$$t = \sqrt{\frac{N_1S_1^2 + N_2S_2^2}{N_1 + N_2 - 2}\left(\frac{N_1 + N_2}{N_1N_2}\right)}$$

Starting at the top we multiply N_1 (first group size) by the standard deviation (or its estimate) of the first group, S_1. We add this to the same calculation for the second group. We divide this by the two group sizes added together ($N_1 + N_2$) from which we subtract 2, because there are two groups. This entire equation is then multiplied by $N_1 + N_2/N_1 \times N_2$.

This gives us –

$$\sqrt{\frac{5((2.13)^2) + 5((2.99)^2)}{5 + 5 - 2}\left(\frac{5 + 5}{5 * 5}\right)}$$

– which becomes:

$$\sqrt{\frac{22.65 + 44.7}{8}\left(\frac{10}{25}\right)}$$

Finally we get: $\sqrt{3.367}$, which equals 1.83, which is the same as before, so that we divide 1.4 by 1.83 and get $t = 0.76$. There might be a difference of a few decimal places, nothing more than that.

Types of *t* test

Related samples: each member of the population contributes to two tests, for example a 'before' and 'after' scenario in which a drug is tested on a group of patients who had been previously monitored ('**before**') and were then tested following medication ('**after**'). Another example of related samples is if you compare two different phenomena on the same group of subjects. For example, comparing whether the population at large prefers X Flakes or Y Flakes: in this case we use the same group of subjects, but we give them two different tests, in this case Test 1 is their opinion of X Flakes and Test 2 is their opinion of Y Flakes. So much for the related samples test.

With independent samples, on the other hand, we have a different kind of test. We are not comparing the behaviour of a single population in regard to two different events, entities, phenomena, products, etc. Rather, we are comparing two different populations with regard to a single event, entity, product, etc. So, for example, in analysing the Bentley text we compared two different sets of sentences (populations) with regard to one phenomenon (average length). By definition, of course, in the independent *t* test we may have different population sizes (28 sentences in the inner section of the Bentley text, 16 sentences in the other section). So much for the independent *t* test.

THE FOURIER TRANSFORMATION AND SPEECH SPECTROGRAPHY

You can break down any complex sound into an infinite number of simple sounds. Open your mouth and sing top 'A'. If you have a good voice you will produce a fairly pure sound. However, even this relatively pure sound will consist of a number of frequencies. Isolate any one of these frequencies and you get a really pure sound, a sine wave. Voilà! That's what a sine wave is: a sound which cannot be further decomposed – it's pure.

This is the basis of Fourier's theorem – the essence of his discovery: no matter how complex the sound, it can be simplified into sine waves. The Fourier transformation is just the mathematics of this. It's a devilishly complicated piece of mathematical wizardry, and since we're not specialist mathematicians, but forensic linguists, we don't need to know it, only what it does.

Now the frequencies of our sound cluster together in what are called *formants*. These formants are distinctive from one human to the next.

Why? Because your collective speech apparatus, vocal tract, inside of mouth, etc., are all different from mine in shape. This means that you will produce different harmonics from mine – your voice will perhaps start deeper or higher, and the different *formants* will in all likelihood be at slightly different levels from mine.

How does all this relate to speech spectrography? Speech spectrograms (which you saw in Chapter 11) are – broadly – just the depiction of the *formants* for any given utterance (whether for a single phoneme or a long sentence). The lowest sound is FO, it's the *fundamental frequency* of the sound. We then get F1, the first formant, F2 and so on. Very often when looking at a spectrogram, we can tell which phoneme is being uttered by the positions of the formants, and whether they are in straight lines, curved, rising, falling, etc.

This is all we need to know for the moment about Fourier and speech spectrography.

WHAT IS A DECIBEL?

A *decibel* is a term which is used to talk about the 'loudness' of a sound. The human ear can hear very faint sounds and very *very* loud sounds. The range of our hearing is so great in fact that it was quite difficult for scientists to come up with a sensible scale which could measure the softest sounds we can hear and the loudest sounds we can hear. Finally they produced what is known as a logarithmic scale. In simple terms, for every 10 times that something increases by, instead of multiplying by 10, they just *add* 10 on the scale. This is because if they multiplied by 10 each time they would eventually end up with absolutely huge numbers.

The faintest sound we can hear is called the threshold of hearing. It's very soft, so soft we can barely hear it. On the decibel scale we say it is 0, 0 decibels (dB). If we produce a sound 10 times as intense as this pin-dropping sound we would get 10 decibels. If we produce one a 100 times more intense we get not 100 decibels (which would be 10×10), but 20 decibels $(10 + 10)$. A sound 1,000 times more intense is, you've guessed it, $10 + 10 + 10$ decibels, in other words 30 decibels, and *not* 1,000 (i.e. $10 \times 10 \times 10$).

So, if 0 decibels is the minimum sound, what's the maximum? The maximum we can hear before the pain becomes unbearable and the eardrum shatters is calculated to be 130 decibels. This is 10^{12} times louder than the faintest sound we can hear.

Incidentally, the faintest sound we can hear is calculated to have a very minute amount of energy: 10^{-12} w/m^2, in other words 10 to the power of -12 watts per metre squared.

So, you can see why decibels are useful. Instead of having units running into the zillions, we have a simple scale from 0 to 130. By the way, I'm sure you will have gathered that it is more professional to talk about *intensity* of sound rather than *loudness*. Loudness is a subjective measure, and relates to how sensitive a given individual is to sounds.

Appendix A: Exercises

Exercise 1.1

You were asked to show whether it is true that there is a correspondence between the mean sentence length of a text and the average number of short (i.e. two- and three-letter) words per sentence in that text. This kind of correspondence is a very specific mathematical relationship known as a *correlation*. I will first describe how I tried to answer this point and then I will very briefly go into the statistics of it. You will probably need to look up several of the terms I am going to use first, such as probability, two-tail test, degrees of freedom, correlation and (statistically) *significant*. These terms are to be found in the Index at the back of the book, but you will get more precise descriptions from statistics publications, as well as statistics sites on the Internet.

I took ten excerpts of between 2,000 and 3,000 words in length from authors Jane Austen and Anthony Trollope, measured them for sentence length and short words, and found the following:

Text	Mean sentence length (MSL)	No. of short words (SW) per sentence
1	25.45	11.40
2	18.94	7.73
3	22.84	9.76
4	22.07	9.45
5	23.95	10.98
6	26.35	11.35
7	15.20	6.71
8	23.41	10.56
9	25.81	11.37
10	37.90	16.10

Correlation ~ mean sentence length and no. of short words per sentence	**0.99**

As can be seen, there is a very high correlation between MSL and number of SW per sentence. Now here comes the key question: we see that the correlation between these two entities is high, but is it statistically *significant*, i.e. important, interesting, worth noting, of value, and so on – *in the context of statistics.* To discover whether this correlation is *significant* we look up the value (in this case 0.99 – see above) in a table known as the 'Critical values of the Pearson r correlation coefficient' table, and we take the number of texts we tested (10 in this case) and subtract 2 (because you need at least two points to make a correlation). This gives us 8. The significance of 8 is that this is the *degrees of freedom* (look up the index – you'll find several references to *degrees of freedom*, abbreviated d.f.). When we look down the d.f. column and find 8, and we look across to 0.05 (i.e. a probability of 0.05 or less that the value we found occurred by chance) for a two-tailed test, we see that the table reads '0.6319' for this value. Our value is 0.99, which is higher than the table value. Therefore the correlation is significant. In other words, in plain English, what this means is that we have demonstrated a relationship between sentence length and number of short words per sentence. It seems to be the case that the number of short words in a sentence is dependent on sentence length: short sentences will have proportionately fewer short words than long sentences. Going back to Morton's implicit claim that the proportion of short words in a sentence in relation to sentence length is indicative of individual style, we can see that since there is already a demonstrable (we never say 'proven') relationship between these two metaphenomena, there is absolutely no point in relating this to individual style – it is generally observable in the language anyway. It would be rather like saying the relationship between the size of a person's hands and the size of their feet is idiosyncratic. It is well known that these two measurements are related in the case of most human beings, and therefore it has nothing to do with (individual) idiosyncrasy.

Exercise 4.1

You were asked to compare, qualitatively, the styles of two different text excerpts and say whether in your subjective view these were the work of the same author or not. The text excerpts are reproduced here for convenience:

1   Dear Louisa, Thank you for your call this past Sunday night. I am so glad you would check up on such a rumor before you would believe it. There is no one on the Brown side of the family who would believe such a rumor nor obviously spread a rumor that you were getting a divorce since you have always been loud and clear about that. I appreciate your confronting me about it so that we could clear it – and many other things – up.

2   Fred sees only one way of dealing with things – his way – and criticizes anyone who tries to do differently. Bert and I are firm believers that there is more than one way to resolve problems and that we can indeed go beyond violence and heartlessness to do so. Bert and I choose to be an example by the lives we live, the way we raise our children, by our farming techniques, by making inroads in the public education system, etc. Constant criticism is not part of our philosophy and we choose not to be around such negativity. Bert was coming to

tell you these things the other night when you were not home. Maybe that is just as well. Bert and I are as different as day and night from you and Fred. I do wish you the very best and you have no idea how much I wish things were different but, Louisa, they are not and never will be. Fred has made that very clear. I have always been very concerned for you and for Sam and now for a new baby. You are always in my thoughts.

Text 1 above seems to have several instances of antithesis, that curious literary device whereby opposite ideas are juxtaposed in the same clause, or sentence, or even just nearby. The first of these is '. . . I am so glad you would check up on such a rumor before you would believe it'. This is a bit like 'thank you for knocking me on the head'. No one (in my experience) is grateful for being 'checked up on', and in fact most people would consider it something of an insult. There is a certain crassness about antithesis when used in earnest, and in fact we can argue would only be real antithesis if it were in a literary context. The fact that it occurs in a mundane context simply means that the writer is insensitive to the language and unaware of the effect of her words.

Consider also, 'There is no one . . . who would . . . spread a rumor that you were getting a divorce since you have always been loud and clear about that'. This is tantamount to saying: 'I have to believe you because you are being insistent about it', it is not a case of 'I believe you because I trust you'. Nor is it a case of 'no one . . . would spread' such a rumour. In other words, this writer is not denying that she (and others) would spread a rumour – just so long as the rumour were true! Again, a strong indication that the writer does not really assess what she means. There is almost a dichotomy between the first half of the sentence and the second, a kind of sentential schizosis.

In Text 2, the writer is very critical of the addressee's husband, Fred. Fred is apparently very stubborn and she, the writer, is glad that she and Bert are not like Louisa and Fred. Then she says: 'I wish things were very different, but they . . . never will be. Fred has made that very clear. I have always been very concerned for you and . . . [the] . . . baby'. Here the writer juxtaposes a mention of Fred with her concern for the addressee. She does not state the cause of her anxiety relative to the addressee and baby, but the proximity of 'Fred' and her concern leave the reader to believe that there is something dangerous or bad about Fred. This is another case of antithetic writing. Earlier she says that she and Bert choose their lifestyle to be an example to others, implying their own virtuousness. Then she says that 'constant criticism is not part of our philosophy' totally unaware of the fact that by implying she and Bert lead superior lives she *is* being critical. This is yet another example of her insensitivity to the effect of what she says.

On the above basis, there do seem to be some critical similarities between the style of the two texts. However, two points are worth making.

1. I have presented no more than the broadest outline, and in any case this is a very subjective analysis.

2. This kind of analysis would not be suitable as legal evidence, though it might be useful in an inquiry.

Exercise 6.1

You were asked whether in your view the writers of each of the following sentences were native or non-native speakers of English.

1. I decided to dig down into my memory and extricate a few anecdotes.

2. If you have any questions or comments, feel free to write it down in the following box.

3. All types of accommodation are located on good pitches and are provided with garden furniture and a full inventory.

4. Israel has used the weapon before in the conflict with the Palestinians.

5. Does Europe not run the risk of falling apart if it enlarges to the borders of the continent?

This question of native *vs.* non-native speaker English is a far more difficult question to answer than one would imagine. It is rarely straightforward. This is because in reality there is no such thing as an innate 'native-speaker*ness*'. I am inclined to think there is something of a continuum between the two poles. The next point I would make is this. If looking at native *vs* non-native speaker (NS *vs.* NNS) like features, do not concentrate on what you see as 'grammar' or 'grammatical errors' (whatever they are): rather, look at idiom.

1. Thus in sentence one we have a British native speaker of English who has lived in France, by his own admission, for more than 20 years. This is why I think he uses the word *extricate* in relation to *anecdote*. There's nothing wrong with it even at the level of idiom, but it just rings a little differently from what we might expect from a NS.

2. In sentence 2, we might imagine that the failure to provide grammatical agreement between the plural nouns in 'questions or comments' and 'write it' (as opposed to 'write **them**') indicates a NNS. However, this kind of 'error' is perfectly possible whether you are a NS or a NNS. The more significant point to note is the phrase 'the following box'. I think a NS would write, 'in the box below', rather than 'in the following box'. Otherwise the sentence looks very NS like, especially the use of 'feel free'.

3. This seems a bit cumbersome and long-winded but I think is probably NS.

4. Seems like straightforward NS.

5. This is a bit like the first example, not quite native like, but not especially NNS either. The phrase 'enlarge to the borders of the continent' is
very descriptive, precise etc. However, it seems to be a bit too precise. In
fact the sentence is a translation from the French, and although I would
guess from a British English NS, one who has perhaps lived in France a
long time or who has had a very close relationship with the French
language, at times perhaps to the exclusion of English. Note also 'Does
Europe not . . .?' as opposed to 'Doesn't Europe . . .?'.

My motivation in giving this exercise was not to trick or deceive the reader
in any way. Rather, I wanted to show that this question of NS *vs* NNS can
be very difficult. The two 'states' should not be seen as mutually exclusive.
Indeed as NSs read more and more text by NNSs on the Internet and
elsewhere, the delineation between the two groups will probably become
less and less evident. In the Lindbergh inquiry there was a lengthy debate
between experts as to whether the writer of the kidnap note really was
German or was just trying to write in the way he imagined a German
would write.

Exercise 7.1

You were asked to consider what the excerpt below was trying to get the
reader to believe, how it was attempting to do this, and whether – in your
view it was successful or not:

> DEAR BILL,
>   I SUPPOSE YOU THOUGHT I WOULD FORGET BUT YOU ARE
> WRONG HOW COULD I FORGET A RAT LIKE YOU. I HAVE SENT A
> LETTER WITH ALL YOUR PAST DETAILS TO THE PRESIDENT.
> ALL YOUR DEBTS AND PAST MISSDEMEANORS. IF YOU DON'T
> RESIGN FROM THE COUNCIL IMMEDIATELY THE PRESS WILL
> PRINT A LIST OF ALL YOUR DEBTS BOTH LOCALLY AND NATION-
> ALLY . . . YOU MIGHT BE ABLE TO FOOL SOME PEOPLE BUT NOT
> ME. YOU FORGET I HAVE KNOWN YOU FOR ALL OF YOUR LIFE.

The opening sentence attempts to persuade the addressee that the writer
knows him, which probably indicates that he/she does not. The second
sentence is easily verifiable, and is probably true because there is little
point in making a false verifiable claim. The assertion that the press would
print a list of 'your debts both locally and nationally' either shows that the
writer does not understand anything about the laws of libel and/or what
interests (or does not interest) the press. Finally, there is the claim that 'I
have known you for all of your life'. Again, this is a claim that cannot be
verified without the addressee knowing who the writer is.

   With this kind of text, do not get bogged down in pseudo-psychological
questions. It is of no concern to us as forensic linguists why – in general
terms – the writer is motivated to write to Bill (e.g. revenge, anger,
rejection) or what kind of person the writer is (lonely, depressed, sad,

bitter). What we are solely interested in is the discourse, the discourse goals and the degree to which they are successful. The discourse goal seems to be to make Bill uneasy, to try to get him to be afraid that something from his past is about to be revealed. Bill may be a totally innocent person, he probably is – it doesn't mean that he can't be made to feel nervous. The point about whether the writer has known Bill all his life could also make him feel anxious, though to you and me as outsiders, we can apparently 'see' right through it. It's worth remembering, though, that anonymous letters can cause horrendous consequences in people's lives. Suicide is not unknown among recipients. Writers of these notes often claim to have some kind of invincibility or omniscience 'I will find you wherever you go' is a frequent claim, comparable with 'I have known you for all of your life' in this instance. Incidentally, what about the phrase 'for all of your life'? Did you notice it? Does it sound NNS to you? It could be, or it could be that the writer was going to type 'known you . . . *for years . . .*' or something similar, got as far as 'known you for' and changed the planned ending of the sentence to '(for) all of your life'.

Exercise 8.1

You were asked to look at two texts, one of which had been plagiarized from the other:

1. 'Such "story myths" are not told for their entertainment value. They provide answers to questions people ask about life, about society and about the world in which they live.'

2. Specifically, story myths are not for entertainment purposes rather they serve as answers to questions people ask about life, about society and about the world in which they live.

First, you were asked which of these two was likely to be the original and which the plagiarized version. Recall that in the chapter the comment is made that plagiarists always seem to feel they have to improve what they are copying. This often results in text which is cumbersome and almost always longer than the original. In the present case the two excerpts are the same length, so that provides little help. However, Excerpt 1 consists of two grammatical sentences while Excerpt 2 is only one sentence. Moreover, Excerpt 2 is rather poorly punctuated – no comma or semi-colon before the word 'rather'. We somehow also feel that Excerpt 2 does not flow as well as Excerpt 1. Like many plagiarisms we notice that this one is of the 'shop window' variety. That is to say the dressing is all at the front, or beginning of the sentence. This is where the differences are: the last 17 words of the examples are identical with each other.

You were also asked how to assess the degree of copying involved. The easiest way to do this is to count the lexical words in each excerpt and then see how many of them are identical across the two examples.

The second (plagiarizing) example has 13 lexical items, as follows:

story myths entertainment purposes serve **answers questions people ask life society world live**

Of these 13 items, 11 are identical to that of the original text. Add to the fact that a writer is unlikely to be able to reproduce – independently – the same string of 17 words (or 80 characters) as another writer we now have 11/13 identical lexical items. 11/13 = 85 per cent, which is one way of measuring the degree of copying involved. However, put in the context of the entire paper, this is no more than 1 per cent. Some universities will expel even for this amount of plagiarism, which seems a little draconian.

Exercise 9.1

You were asked to mark-up the most important veracity features of Susan Smith's appeal for the return of her children. According to the recording she said: 'I have been to the Lord in prayers every day with my family and by myself with my husband it just seems so unfair that somebody could take such two beautiful children'. Recall that this is supposed to be an appeal for the return of children supposedly kidnapped by a stranger who also, allegedly, carjacked Ms Smith. Yet the speaker makes no appeal, just works on the sympathy of her audience and attempts to appeal to their religious feelings by mentioning prayers. This shows a loss of focus, one of the categories mentioned. She almost forgets to mention her husband (who is standing next to her in the course of the appeal). Note that she refers to the 'kidnapper' as 'somebody'. Yet she allegedly sat next to him in her car. He cannot be just 'somebody'. He has a face, and she knows what he looks like. He is a real person not 'somebody'. This is to do with *referents* or *participants*. Why does she suddenly become vague about this individual? Finally, she mixes up her word order by saying 'such two beautiful' rather than 'two such beautiful' children. This could indicate the lack of veracity relative to the taking of the children. Nobody took the children. Rather, as we know, she killed them herself. It is possible that because nobody took the children, she was unable to say 'two such beautiful children'. Note that even the claim that somebody took the children seems ill-formed: 'it just seems so unfair that somebody could take . . .' she says. She does not actually say that somebody took the children. The actual proposition, namely that 'somebody took the children', is itself a projection of 'it seems'. Moreover, this projection 'it seems' is further qualified as 'it *just* seems'. Therefore the information she is giving is of very poor quality, and we are probably justified in giving her zero credibility.

Exercise 9.2

You were asked to give your view on whether Wendy Mullins's sexual assault allegation was credible, and to give your reasons for your view.

This is quite a lengthy text, so I propose to look only at the opening sentences. The reader can then (if desired) do the same with the rest of the text:

> Upon arrival at Joe's Club, (date April Xth, 200- ⟨. . . day⟩) I had entered the lounge area to have a drink and dinner. I was approached verbally by a man (mid 30's) as walking to a seat just 2 away from him. The words I remember most from any conversation that may have taken place that evening were 'where you been? What took you so long?' I do no recall if/what I responded with in turn.

The mix of aspect 'I had entered' with 'I was approached', coincides with a change of voice from active to passive. The construction 'had entered' prevents us from knowing (in relation to the rest of the text) when the writer actually entered the lounge. This mixing of aspect and voice together and the (apparently) deliberate non-information of arrival time reduces our confidence in this witness. When did the witness arrive? Did the witness arrive at all?

The sentence 'The words I remember most' begins well – except for the word 'remember' which is almost always a give away in witness veracity tests because it takes away from the mental focus of the narrative – but then we find that 'the words I remembered' are qualified because there is no certainty that they *did* take place, only 'that [they] may have taken place'. Additionally, the writer claims she does not recall how she responded. When we add these various lacunae together, I am sure most readers will find this witness entirely without credit (in fact it gets worse if you read and analyse the whole text).

Exercise 10.1

You were asked to write down the first thing you would say to the emergency operator on evacuating a car which had caught fire. In this case I am sure most readers will agree that 'my car is on fire' is what we would normally say in that situation, rather than 'there is a fire in the car' or 'the car is on fire'. The latter would only be possible if we were driving someone else's car.

Exercise 12.1

You were asked to transcribe an invented text. Did you observe the following?

> *foreign* (sic.) for *forensic*;
> *first and foremost important skill* instead of *first and most important skill*;
> *wether* instead of *whether*;
> *such* twice in succession;
> *is comprised of*, for *comprises*;
> *accurately* for *accuracy*;

your for *you*;
unconventual for *unconventional*;
inconsistency: *capitalizing* for *capitalising* – the 'z' indicates an American
spelling;
ect. for *etc.*;
inconsistency: *honour* for *honor*; the 'u' indicates a British spelling

If you failed to observe any of the above, do not worry. It does not
mean you are not a good English scholar, or that you lack potential as a
forensic linguist. I did this not to trick you or catch you out, but for a
very sound reason: transcribing text is a totally different cognitive function from reading it or writing it. Certain very odd things can happen
when we transcribe text and we need to be aware of them. Just as when
we are listening to someone speaking we often anticipate what they are
going to say, so it is with text – we anticipate what comes next and we
do not see or hear what is really there. So, for instance, we are all familiar with
the phrase *first and foremost*, just as we are with the phrase *first and
most important*. However, the phrase *first and foremost* ends at the end
of a line. By the time we begin transcribing the next line we encounter a
new phrase *important skill*. In the back of our mind somewhere there
might be an echo of the word *most*, so we can usually be relied on to
transcribe *foremost important skill* instead of *most important skill*. The
string *such (line break) such as* operates a slightly different set of cognitive buttons: we ignore function words such as *such* and so often do not
notice repetitions in text. The word *wether* for *whether* is an old trick,
but several of my students have missed it in the past. 'Is comprised of'
for 'comprises' is much beloved of estate agents (realtors) for some
reason. *Accurately* for *accuracy* is another instance of attention transfer,
i.e. what happens when we move to a new line. The ploy of *ect.* for *etc.*
relies on the habit some speakers have of saying 'ec cetera' instead of the
more conventional '*et* cetera'. Finally, be on the look-out for possible
dialect inconsistencies, in this case American for British and/or vice
versa. I know I have the habit of sometimes using American spellings
and sometimes British. This is probably because I read a great deal of
technical literature from both countries (as well as other English-
speaking countries, notably Australia). There is bound to be some cross-
over between these different dialects. However, many people do not read
books or articles from different English-speaking countries, and so perhaps this habit of mixing spelling styles is not that common. As I noted
above, do not worry if you did not observe all of these peculiarities.
What is more important is that you realize the kinds of transcription
error which can be made. Remember, in forensics the rule is that if you
'correct' anything from the original text, it is you who are in error, not
the writer of the text. Forensic texts must be treated like all other evidence,
and not be tampered with in any way.

Exercise 12.2

You were asked to compare two versions of the closing sentence of Nelson Mandela's Rivonia trial speech. The physical recording differed in a number of important respects, as the underlined text here shows:

> During my lifetime I have dedicated my <u>life</u> to this struggle of the African people. I have fought against white domination, and I have fought against black domination. I have cherished the ideal of a democratic and free society in which all persons <u>will</u> live together in harmony and with equal opportunities. It is an ideal <u>for</u> which I hope to live for and to <u>see realised</u>. But, <u>my lord</u>, if <u>it</u> needs be, it is an ideal for which I am prepared to die.

The ANC version has it that Mandela said he had dedicated <u>himself</u> to the struggle, but the recording shows that he said he had dedicated his <u>life</u> to the struggle. Given that Mandela was facing a capital charge at the time, the implication from *life* is much stronger than from *self*. Later he talks about the <u>free society</u> in which all persons <u>will</u> live together – the paper version has Mandela referring to the present, not the future. In other words, the idea of a dream or a goal for the future is absent. Finally (aside from the 'My Lord' which shows that Mandela was addressing the judge at the time) the paper version has Mandela saying 'I hope to live for and achieve'. Mandela, however, did not see this as a personal achievement. Rather, he actually said: 'I hope to live for and to <u>see realised</u>'. These differences may appear small to some people at this remove of time. However, there are two points we can make in this connection. First, who are we to judge that these points are small? Second, whatever our view, we must remember the underlying forensic principle here: *nobody* has the right to alter the record, the body of evidence.

Appendix B: Texts

Alphabetical list of referents in the forensic texts

Bentley, Derek
Carlos the Jackal (Sanchez)
Dillingham, Jeffery
Doughtie, Geoffrey Carlton
Dowthitt, Dennis
Dyfed Powys Fire Service, Wales
Enigma Machine
Evans, Timothy John
Fawkes, Guy
Ferrie, David
Flores, Miguel
Foster, Anne
Frank Kuecken
Gilfoyle, Eddie
Hague War Crimes Tribunal (Serbia)
Hauptmann, Bruno
Helder, Luke John
Hill, Mack
Hinckley, John
Jackson, Shoeless Joe
Jonathan Kaled
Kacnler, Dennis
Lamar, Chuck
Leslie, Senator Tim
Lindbergh, Charles
Marino, Achim Joseph
McBride, Michael
McFarland, Basil
Mitchell, Alexander Hutton Johnston (Sandy)
Mitchell, Gerald
New Baltimore Police
Ocalan Abdullah
Putnam, Ann
Ramsey JonBenet
Renouf, A. T.
Rose, Joel
Salem

Sampson, William James
Sams, Michael
Sanchez, Ilich Ramirez (*see* Carlos the Jackal)
Sheldon, Sheriff
Shipman, Harold
Skevins Ralph Carl Marya
Smith, Susan
Tucker, Karla Faye
Unabomber
Woolf, Virginia

Use the texts in this Appendix to learn more about forensic linguistics. Ask yourself such questions as: what gives a forged text away as forged? How would you gauge a sexual assault report? Above all, look closely at questions of witness veracity. Also, you should practise transcribing some of these texts. This will give you a very close insight into what the texts are about, and how they are structured. Often you will find your opinion of a text changing over a period of time if you analyse and examine it often enough.

Text B.1 Forgery by Dr Harold Shipman of Mrs Kathleen Grundy's will

I GIVE ALL MY ESTATE, MONEY AND HOUSE TO MY DOCTOR. MY FAMILY ARE NOT IN NEED AND I WANT TO REWARD HIM FOR ALL THE CARE HE HAS GIVEN TO ME AND THE PEOPLE OF HYDE. HE IS SENSIBLE ENOUGH TO HANDLE ANY PROBLEMS THIS MAY GIVE HIM.

MY DOCTOR IS DrH.F.SHIPMAN 21 MARKET ST HYDE CHESHIRE SL14 2AF
   9th JUNE 1998
   SIGNED K. Grundy
   SIGNED P Spencer
   SIGNED Claire Hutchinson
                    (Author thanks the family of the late Mrs K. Grundy
                    for permission to print this text.)

Text B.2 Statement alleging sexual assault

Upon arrival at Joe's Club, (date April Xth, 200- ⟨. . . day⟩) I had entered the lounge area to have a drink and dinner. I was approached verbally by a man (mid 30's) as walking to a seat just 2 away from him. The words I remember most from any conversation that may have taken place that evening were "where you been? What took you so long?" I do no recall if/what I responded with in turn.

I then ordered a bourbon and coke while waiting for my order of "crab rolls." I wish I had more recolection of people or words exchanged, as this is where my mind is having trouble remembering. My food had arrived, enjoyed it with a glass of water topped with a lemon, finished my dinner and ordered 1 last drink, with all intentions of leaving at that point. if my memory is treating me well I had been offered another drink – hesitated but accepted offer. At this time I remember clearly going to the rest room. Upon my return, I casually had my 3rd bourbon and Coke, while conversation was minimal and do remember paying most of my attention to the television directly in front of me.

Some time in the evening I do receall speaking to, one which was a bartender, James Smith & younger brother, Ben ?? These 2 are childhood – neiborhood acquaintances – I wish I could recall any of which conversations in the evening but unfortunatelly cannot as of today.

From this point, honestly things are neither here nor there in my head. Can not seem to decifer any actual instances.

I can say that approx. times were last recolection of 8pm or 9pm roughly. I woke with my alarm clock staring the time of 10:03 am. I frantically went to check on my son, he was not there. After becoming somewhat aware of my surroundings I then realized the only clothing I had on was my sleevless dress, sweater, which was worn the day of April Xth under my blue dress jacket, which all clothing now in pocession/ evidence. No under clothing as well. My sheets were soiled in what appeared, to me, as to be a mixture of slight blood and my own urine. In discust and pure confusion I stripped the fitted sheet from my bed and replaced it with a fresh one . . . first phone call was to my mother, with my little knowledge at that time our conversation was brief, just enough to know my son, Hugh, was safe and at daycare . . . (this info as of 4–12, mom stated it was 10 or 15 min after 10 am when she received my phone call.)

She was angry and we ended the phone call. Various phone calls including Mary Williams and Sam Walker, 2 close personal friends . . . after a few conversations and tears shed with them, I then decided to call the local police to report this incedent.

(rewind: first call after mom was to close friend Darleen Brown → she gave me a number to the crisis line. moments later I discussed the situation "BRIEFLY" with a lady there . . . She (not purposely) gave me the intention if I were to report, nothing could be done on the little info I had.) So back to the police call I got disconnected, strangly, as another call was coming in. I had called my neighbor in # 94 a sally Edwards to see if she had heard or seen any thing → she came home and stated times home and awake 8:30 pm to 11pm → nothing. Sally stayed w/ me and that's when (all within moments) the 2 police officers arrived. Spoke to Ofcr. Macnamara.

All of stated information IS true & correct to the best of my knowledge.
4/12/02
Wendy M. Mullins

(Author acknowledges the co-operation of a mid-western
police department in the publication of this text.)

Text B.3   Pipe bomber's text (Luke John Helder, 21-year-old college student)

(Text of note left in mailboxes in the Midwest of America where pipe bombs were found.)

Mailboxes are exploding! Why, you ask?

Attention people.

You do things because you can and want (desire) to

If the government controls what you want to do, they control what you can do.

If you are under the impression that death exists, and you fear it, you do anything to avoid it. (This is the same way pain operates. Naturally we strive to avoid negative emotion/pain.)

You allow yourself to fear death!

World authorities allowed, and still allow you to fear death!

In avoiding death you are forced to conform, if you fail to conform, you suffer mentally and physically. (Are world powers utilizing the natural survival instinct in a way that allows them to capitalize on the people?)

To "live" (avoid death) in this society you are forced to conform/slave away.

I'm here to help you realize/ understand that you will live no matter what! It is up to you people to open your hearts and minds. There is no such thing as death. The people I've dismissed from this reality are not at all dead.

Conforming to the boundaries, and restrictions imposed by the government only reduces the substance in your lives. When 1 per cent of the nation controls 99 per cent of the nations total wealth, is it a wonder why there are control problems?

The United States strives to provide freedom for their people. Do we really have personal freedom? I've lived here for many years, and I see much limitation. Does the definition of freedom include limitation? I've learned about the history of various civilizations in history, and I see more and more limitation. Do you people enjoy this trend of limitation? If not, change it!

As long as you are uninformed about death you will continue to say "how high", when the government tells you to "jump". As long as the government is uninformed about death they will continue tell you to "jump". Is the government uninformed about death, or are they pretending?

You have been missing how things are, for very long. I'm obtaining your attention in the only way I can. More info is on its way. More "attention getters" are on the way. If I could, I would change only one person, unfortunately the resources are not accessible. It seems killing a single famous person would get the same media attention as killing numerous un-famous humans. There is less risk of being detained, associated with dismissing certain people.

Sincerely,

Someone Who Cares

PS. More info. will be delivered to various locations around the country.

(Public domain by virtue of having been publicized
by the perpetrator of a crime.)

Text B.4 Complaint by an Australian aboriginal person about verballing

Yeh – well what happens is that the police – they make the statement out and they make you sign it. They write the statement out themselves Then all you do is sign it. Oh yeh they ask you questions but they just do the writing or the typing themselves. I mean in actual fact the true statement should be in writing in the hand of the person himself but of course it's not. It's accepted as long as he's got his signatutre there. And maybe nine times out of ten he couldn't read that bloke's writing anyway. He's probably never said half those things. Or the police says Sign this here now and you can go'. Of course he wants to go so he signs it. Many's the time I've come across statements that have been different from anything that could have been said. Many's the time, yes. Then the prosecuting sergeant gets up there in court and says this is the statement he's given'. He'll read it out to the judge and that's it and that's the weakest thing and yet it's the vital thing. And it's very rarely thrown out – very rarely. Video or tape-recording should happen. It should be a right of every individual. But they don't want Aboriginal people to have rights.

(Found at: http://wwwmcc.murdoch.edu.au/ReadingRoom/Ashforth/
Terthes6.html on Saturday, March 30, 2002. Author is grateful to
Dr Teresa Ashforth for permission to publish this text.)

Text B.5   Susan Smith's admission of having killed her children

When I left my home on Tuesday, October 25, I was very emotionally distraught. I didn't want to live anymore! I felt like things could never get any worse. When I left home, I was going to ride around a little while and then go to my mom's. As I rode and rode and rode, I felt even more anxiety coming upon me about not wanting to live. I felt I couldn't be a good mom anymore, but I didn't want my children to grow up without a mom. I felt I had to end our lives to protect us from any grief or harm. I had never felt so lonely and so sad in my entire life. I was in love with someone. very much, but he didn't love me and never would. I had a very difficult time accepting that. But I had hurt him very much, and I could see why he could never love me. When I was @ John D. Long Lake, I had never felt so scared and unsure as I did then. I wanted to end my life so bad and was in my car ready to go down that ramp into the water, and I did go part way, but I stopped. I went again and stopped. I then got out of the car and stood by the car a nervous wreck. Why was I feeling this way? Why was everything so bad in my life? I had no answers to these questions. I dropped to the lowest when I allowed my children to go down that ramp into the water without me. I took off running and screaming "Oh God! Oh God, no!" What have I done? Why did you let this happen? I wanted to turn around so bad and go back, but I knew it was too late. I was an absolute mental case! I couldn't believe what I had done. I love my children with all my [a picture of a heart]. That will never change. I have prayed to them for forgiveness and hope that they will find it in their [a picture of a heart] to forgive me. I never meant to hurt them!! I am sorry for what has happened and I know that I need some help. I don't think I will ever be able to forgive myself for what I have done. My children, Michael and Alex, are with our Heavenly Father now, and I know that they will never be hurt again. As a mom, that means more than words could ever say. I knew from day one, the truth would prevail, but I was so scared I didn't know what to do. It was very tough emotionally to sit and watch my family hurt like they did. It was time to bring a piece of mind to everyone, including myself. My children deserve to have the best, and now they will. I broke down on Thursday, Nov. 3, and told Sheriff Howard Wells the truth.

It wasn't easy, but after the truth was out, I felt like the world was lifted off my shoulders. I know now that it is going to be a tough and long road ahead of me. At this very moment, I don't feel I will be able to handle what's coming, but I have prayed to God that he gave me the strength to survive each day and to face those times and situations in my life that will be extremely painful. I have put my total faith in God, and he will take care of me. [Signed]Susan V. Smith [Dated]11/3/94 5:05 p.m.

(Public domain by virtue of having been used in court proceedings.)

Text B.6 Before Susan Smith confessed, she had claimed a black man had carjacked her and driven away with her children

First video

all he ever told me was shutup or i'll kill you . . . (break) . . . and i just screamed i said what are you doing he said shutup and drive and had a gun and he was (. . .) poking it in my side you know and told me to drive (.) and I (.) so I drove

(Public domain by virtue of having been used in court proceedings.)

Text B.7 Appeal by Susan Smith at a press conference

Second video

SUSAN: I have been to the Lord in prayers every day with my family and by myself with my husband it just seems so unfair that somebody could take such two beautiful children

HUSBAND: please do not give up on these two little boys and the search for their return safe home to us

(Public domain by virtue of having been used in court proceedings.)

Text B.8 One of John Hinckley's many letters to Jodie Foster

12:45 P.M.

Dear Jodie,

There is a definite possibility that I will be killed in my attempt to get Reagan. It is for this very reason that I am writing you this letter now.

As you well know by now I love you very much. Over the past seven months I've left you dozens of poems, letters and love messages in the faint hope that you could develop an interest in me. Although we talked on the phone a couple of times I never had the nerve to simply approach you and introduce myself. Besides my shyness, I honestly did not wish to bother you with my constant presence. I know the many messages left at your door and in your mailbox were a nuisance, but I felt that it was the most painless way for me to express my love for you.

I feel very good about the fact that you at least know my name and know how I feel about you. And by hanging around your dormitory, I've come to realize that I'm the topic of more than a little conversation, however full of ridicule it may be. At least you know that I'll always love you.

Jodie, I would abandon this idea of getting Reagan in a second if I could only win your heart and live out the rest of my life with you, whether it be in total obscurity or whatever.

I will admit to you that the reason I'm going ahead with this attempt now is because I just cannot wait any longer to impress you. I've got to do something now to make you understand, in no uncertain terms, that I am doing all of this for your sake! By sacrificing my freedom and possibly my life, I hope to change your mind about me. This letter is being written only an hour before I leave for the Hilton Hotel. Jodie, I'm asking you to please look into your heart and at least give me the chance, with this historical deed, to gain your respect and love.

I love you forever,

John Hinckley

(Public domain by virtue of having been used in court proceedings.)

Text B.9   Statement allegedly made by Derek Bentley

Bentley statement

I have known Craig since I went to school. We were stopped by our parents going out together, but we still continued going out with each other – I mean we have not gone out together until tonight. I was watching television tonight (2 November 1952) and between 8pm and 9pm Craig called for me. My mother answered the door and I heard her say I was out. I had been out earlier to the pictures and got home just after 7pm. A little later Norman Parsley and Frank Fasey called. I did not answer the door or speak to them. My mother told me that they had called and I then ran after them. I walked up the road with them to the paper shop where I saw Craig standing. We all talked together and then Norman Parsley and Frank Fazey left. Chris Craig and I then caught a bus to Croydon. We got off at West Croydon and then walked down the road where the toilets are – I think it is Tamworth Road. When we came to the place where you found me, Chris looked in the window. There was a little iron gate at the side. Chris then jumped over and I followed. Chris then climbed up to the drainpipe and I followed. Up to then Chris had not said anything. We both got out on to the flat roof at the top. Then someone in a garden on the opposite side shone a torch up towards us. Chris said: 'It's a copper, hide behind here'. We hid behind a shelter arrangement on the roof. We were there waiting for about ten minutes. I did not know he was going to use the gun. A plain clothes man climbed up the drainpipe and on to the roof. The man said: 'I am a police officer – the place is surrounded.' He caught hold of me and as we walked away Chris fired. There was nobody else there at the time. The policeman and I then went round a corner by a door. A little later the door opened and a policeman in uniform came out. Chris fired again then and this policeman fell down. I could see he was hurt as a lot of blood came from his forehead just above his nose. The policeman dragged him round the corner behind the brickwork entrance to the door. I remember I shouted something but I forget what it was. I could not see Chris when I shouted to him – he was behind a wall. I heard some more policemen behind the door and the policeman with me said: 'I don't think he has many more bullets left.' Chris shouted 'Oh yes I have' and he fired again. I think I heard him fire three times altogether. The policeman then pushed me down the stairs and I did not see any more. I knew we were going to break into the place. I did not know what we were going to get – just anything that was going. I did not have a gun and I did not know Chris had one until he shot. I now know that the policeman in uniform is dead. I should have mentioned that after the plain clothes policeman got up the drainpipe and arrested me, another policeman in uniform followed and I heard someone call him 'Mac'. He was with us when the other policeman was killed.

(Public domain by virtue of having been used in court proceedings.)

Text B.10   Carlos the Jackal ransom note

(http://www.crimelibrary.com/terrorists/carlos/text/12.htm   23/12/01; reportedly dictated to British secretary Griselda Carey by Carlos the Jackal, born Ilich Ramirez Sanchez.)

To the Austrian Authorities
We are holding hostage the delegations to the OPEC conference.
We demand the lecture of our communiqué on the Austrian radio and television network every two hours, starting two hours from now.
A large bus with windows covered by curtains must be prepared to carry us to the airport Of Vienna tomorrow at 7.00, where a full- tanked DC9 with a crew of three must be ready to take us and our hostages to our destination.
Any delay, provocation or unauthorized approach under any guise will endanger the life of our hostages.
The Arm of the Arab Revolution
Vienna 21/XII/75

(Public domain by virtue of having been publicized across media worldwide.)

Text B.11   Gilfoyle 'suicide' note (referred to in the book as S1)

Dear Eddie,
I've decided to put an end to everything and in doing so ended a chapter in my life that I can't face up to any longer. I don't want to have this baby that I'm carrying. I wish now that I had got rid of it. When I was thinking about it I wouldn't be hurting the way I am now.
Don't blame yourself Eddie it's not your fault, I've caused all your pain and heartache. I've destroyed you and your life. I just hope you can rebuild everything and realize your goals and dreams.
I'm sorry for hurting my family, your family and my friends but most of all hurting you. I never meant to. Don't be afraid to tell people the truth, they can't hurt me because I'm not there to face up to them all. I loved you in my own way but I destroyed it all through my own stupidity. All my moaning and nagging at you wouldn't have helped us to rebuild things between us.
Eddie, I've done some things in my life that I'm not proud of but I got through somehow but this is just too much. I can't face up to my problems anymore, I had packed a bag and even moved some of my chothes already but I can't run anymore, it's the end of the line for me on this earth.
Give my Mum and Dad a keepsake for me, explain things as best as you can tell them I love them and that I'm sorry for everything.
Eddie I hope that you will find it in your heart to forgive me and that one

day we will meet again until that day, take care of yourself don't be afraid in life, I will watch over you and protect you from harm. I've ruined your life, its thebest I can do maybe it will be the one thing I will do right in life.

I can't change or alter what I've done but if I could I would. They say time heals a broken heart. I hope your heart heals pretty quick. I don't want you to waste anymore of your life. Its time to turn the clock forward instead of backwards and go forward.

Goodnight and God Bless

Love

Paula

I apologise for all the pain and suffering I have caused by taking my own life I don't mean to cause any problems for anyone, no-one is to blame except myself.

(Public domain by virtue of having been used in court proceedings.)

Text B.12   Gilfoyle 'confession' note (referred to in the book as S2)

Dear Eddie

I am sorry for what I am about to write, but I can't go on living a lie anymore. I've cheated & lied to you. I just can't carry on anymore. I am having to write it down on paper as I can't tell you face to face.

The baby I'm carrying is not yours. I have been having an affair for the last 14 months with a guy called Nigel, the baby is his. If you work it out the baby could not possibly be yours. I was living at Mums at the time, we hardly seen each other, never mind sleeping together. I tricked you into thinking the baby was yours by the dates I gave you, in fact the baby is due 3/4 weeks before that.

I know I have messed your life up I can't apologise enough, what you could have had as well. No one knows, not even Julie about Nigel but they will soon. Nigel has asked me to go and live with him abroad. I have said yes. You can have the house and the furniture. I will only be taking a few small items. You can divorce me on adultery, send the papers to Mum & Dad for me to sign as when I have told them what is really going on, I will give them my forwarding address.

I would like you to try and pick up the pieces with Sandra as I know she really loves you, you deserve better than me. Don't do anything stupid I'm not worth it. Hopefully by the weekend I'll be out of your life for good and I'll be starting my new life with Nigel. I suppose you feel like hitting me, you never have but I bet you feel like it now. You'll hate me, think I'm selfish. I did love you in my own way, its just that Nigel came along and my life changed. You probably wondering where did I find time, well you know that computer course I said I was on, I only went twice. I used it as an excuse to get out.

I can't imagine how you must feel, about the baby especially. Coming with me to Ante Natal, feeling it kick inside. How could I lie to you, it would have to be a lie forever. I know you would like a family but Sandra or whoever will provide you with that. I think in my own way I knew the marriage was nearly over as you hardly ever touch me unless I touch you, we never really kiss we were just like good friends in a way. Everyone will be shocked but its what I wanted all along I've destroyed you in every way that

I could and saying sorry wont help you but if I could turn the clock back I would.

You must go on and forget me and my family its all down to you now. You have been great with me over the whole situation. I couldn't have been so calm about it as you have been. But as you said you only stayed because of the baby it was not for me. I wonder what my family and friends will say, it's going to be interesting. I hope they don't blame you, I will tell them everything once I'm gone. You don't have to worry. They will all have to accept it as I am not changing my mind. Just as you won't ever let me back into your life. I've got to choose now but at least you know we are parting as friends not enemies like in your previous marriage. Take good care of yourself. Good luck for you future. Love from Paula X

(Public domain – see previous text.)

Text B.13   Anonymous letter: smear mail

To Whom it May Concern: (and I hope that's ALL of you!)
I am a true lover of Green Yellow Falls and the Green Yellow Falls area and that is why I am writing to you. I have been very, very disturbed about something for a long time but waited to see if perhaps you would become aware of the problem and take care of it without my needing to write to you. This has not happened so I feel it my civil duty to write this letter. Please understand that I would not normally do this but I am extremely fond of Green Yellow Falls and hate to see things happen that reflect so badly on the area.

I am referring to the Green Yellow Falls Inn which is promoted by your Chamber. What IS the criteria you follow for recommending lodging in the Green Yellow Falls area? Do you screen these places in any way? Are you aware of the things that go on at this Inn? The woman who runs it – Louise – has been extremely rude to customers. The conversations that take place are very inappropriate for a public place or, as a matter of fact, for just about any place! There is talk of racism, violence, radical political topics, Nazis, etc. there is talk of many weapons owned by the proprietors. There is negative talk about the Green Yellow Falls area. The children are often treated badly by their parents (The Browns). These are not isolated incidences either but have occurred many times for many years and talked about by several patrons (now former patrons) of the Inn. I just hope the people who go there do not become former patrons of the Green Yellow Falls area!

I thought that you might have become awareof these things but apparently not since this Inn is not only still on your web site but even promoted this year in the Fall Art Tour brochure!!!! This does not reflect in any way positively on the Green Yellow Falls area. Why is this allowed to go on? Does anyone care? Haven't you gotten other complaints about this? I hope others have written so that this will not seem like one person complaining about some single unimportant incident. Believe me, that is not what this is. This is VERY important and should be taken seriously.

I hope that my letter will fall into the hands of someone who will take this seriously and realize what a mistake it is to promote this Inn. Green Yellow Falls is much too nice a place to be dragged down like this.

(Author's collection.)

Text B.14 root@primenet.com (found on Internet – this was written by a 19-year-old student who was later arrested for having incited terrorism)

Instead of huntng Lions in California, let us declare open season on State SEN TIM LESLIE, his family, everyone he holds near and dear, the Cattlemen's association and anyone else who feels that LIONS in California should be killed.

I think it would be great to see ths slimeball, asshole, conservative moron hunted down and skinned and mounted for our viewing pleasure. I would rather see every right-wing nut like scumface Leslie destroyed in the name of politicl sport, then lose one mountain lion whose only fault is havng to live in a state with a fuck-ed up jerk like this shit-faced republican and his supporters. Pray for his death. Pray for all their deaths.

(Public domain by virtue of having been the subject of criminal investigation.)

Text B.15 Nikola's confession (a Serbian driver confesses to the Hague – translated from Serbian)

Because I had been a driver in the army, when I arrived I immediately got a freezer truck, empty, with the order to drive it to Kosovo, to a concentration camp east of Pristina. As soon as I arrived, a general began to interrogate me. For an hour, he asked me about my past, my political orientations, if I had ever traveled abroad and so on – was I a patriot, did I want to defend my country and things like that. Since I had already served my army term, I knew the answers to all the questions.

As we were talking, the freezer truck was loaded and sealed somewhere – I don't know where, they never allowed me to come close – and then it was brought back. My job was only to drive, without asking any questions.

I made ten of those trips. It was strange for a big truck to be traveling back and forth while fighting was going on in Kosovo – at a time when there were no people, no vehicles, no food reserves, I was driving an empty freezer truck back. It did not take me long to realize that something was not right.

I would drive the empty truck from Bor to the military camp [in Kosovo], which was filled with army, police and various paramilitary units I did not recognize. A policeman would take over from me and drive the truck away. He would return the truck fully loaded and sealed, and on the travel documents – breaking all the rules – he would write only 'Confidential!' I always drove from Kazoo to Bor at night; I would give the truck to a policeman at the entrance of the copper works in the Bor Mining and Smelting complex, then I would wait at the entrance for the truck to be brought back.

It didn't take long for me to realize that I had been transporting corpses; you don't need much wisdom for that . . .

It was clear to me where the corpses came from, but I did not understand where they ended up once I delivered the freezer truck in Bor. I assumed that they were burned in the copper melting furnaces. Perhaps not. . . Perhaps they were buried somewhere near the copper mine. There were many mining surface fields around, much accumulation of mining waste, many places one can dig a mass grave.

I don't know what happened to the corpses. The only thing I know is that I could not stand it anymore. I began to have nightmares of driving the truck and someone inside who is not dead chasing me with a gun and trying to kill me.

I could not take it anymore. And I was also afraid that I would be killed once the job was completed – as a witness, sooner or later. It is nothing for them to kill a human being. When I had made my decision, I asked two of my hometown friends whom I trusted to help me. We agreed that they would wait for me at a secret place close to Bor. Because I had to report to the police at the entrance of the smelting works by a specific time, I drove faster than I usually did so I could save half an hour for us to carry out our plan and still avoid suspicion. Like we had agreed, my friends were waiting for me. As I was changing into civilian clothes, they opened the freezer truck. It was full of corpses, almost touching the roof. My friends photographed the inside of the freezer truck, and then I ran away. They drove the truck to a hidden place where they counted the corpses. There were 78: mostly civilians, among them one woman and three soldiers from the Yugoslavian Army. They recognized one of them – it was a kid from our town.

(Public domain by virtue of having been used in court proceedings.)

Text B.16 Plagiarized text (with next text)

D.S: It is important to note that there are many other things that can be done in addition to these options. For instance, T.S. may be enrolled in a sexual education class to enhance both options, or if the mother is to be told she may be given help to understand her daughter's condition. For the sake of argument on an ethical basis, however, the two courses of action listed above are what concern the problem of confidentiality. In this case there are many different principles that need to be discussed. Both T.S. and her mother are affected by these options therefore distinguishing them as two different parties with their own interests. This makes beneficence/malificence particularly important because one option may benefit one individual while maligning the other. It is necessary to also evaluate the importance of autonomy and justice in this case. As T.S. is only 13 years old, it is very important to evaluate if she is capable of making sound decisions. Though it may violate her autonomy to disclose the infection to her mother, it needs to be determined whether autonomy at her age trumps the other principles involved. As far as T.S.'s mother is concerned, one must also question if she is being discriminated against based on her social status. What if she was a doctor who was consistently on-call? If we are to avoid violating the principle of justice, then it must be determined that the decision to withhold information from the mother has nothing to do with the fact she is a waitress and not something else. Another thing that makes this case unique is that it affects more than just T.S. and her mother. In evaluating these principles it is important to look not only at what is best for those directly involved, but also those indirectly involved. If doctors do violate confidentiality in minors, then many adolescents that need help may be swayed to not seek it for fear of their parents finding out. Even if T.S. were ultimately benefited from her mother knowing, it must be determined if that is worth the consequences of numerous other girls her age that would not seek treatment for their conditions. When establishing policies based on these matters it is important to have the foresight to analyse the actions people may take. If patients know their doctor may violate confidentiality then it is very likely that they will seek medical help less often.

Text B.17 (plagiarized text – see previous text)

V.L: In this case there are many different principles that need to be discussed. Both T.S. and her mother are affected by these options distinguishing them as two different parties with their own interests. This makes beneficence/ non-malificence particularly important because one option may benefit one individual while harming the other. However, since TS is our patient we should apply the ethical principles to TS only. It is necessary to also evaluate the importance of autonomy and justice in this case. As TS is only 13 years old, it is very important to evaluate if she is mature enough to make sound decisions. Though it may violate her autonomy to disclose her sexual activity to her mother, it needs to be determined whether she is an autonomous individual at the age of 13. As far as TS's mother is concerned, one must also question if she is being discriminated against based on her social status. What if she was a doctor who was consistently on-call? If we are to avoid violating the principle of justice, then it must be determined that the decision to withhold information from the mother has nothing to do with the fact she is a waitress and not something else. Another thing that makes this case unique is that it affects more than just T.S. and her mother. In evaluating these principles it is important to look not only at what is best for those directly involved, but also those indirectly involved. If doctor's do violate confidentiality in minors than many adolescents requiring help may be swayed to not seek it for the fear of their parents finding out. Even if T.S. were ultimately benefitted from her mother knowing it must be determined if that is worth the numerous other girls her age that would not seek treatment for their conditions.

(Above two texts: author's collection.)

Text B.18 Engima Machine, ransom demand

I have been asked by the current owner the above Enigma machine, who purchased it in good faith to say and tell you now today, the unwitting person has no ultimate desire of depraving (sic) your august self or anyone the pleasure to see it again. It is though also not his position to freely give the possession for nothing either as the large sum is not to be lost that has been paid (here the police have blanked out the sum) but only on your full acceptance which are to be published nationally, with no conditions of escape on your part or any other person or official body involved in this matter.

[blanked out paragraph]

A guarantee as said before in this letter that no pursuit of the unwitting now owner shall be made, this to get had by published notice in television and newspaper. This condition is of utmost desire to him and must be done for any further word can be exchanged to you on this matter. It is also of utmost importance also in this matter the person who will be as the negotiating medium will be afforded the same freedom of entanglement in this matter as they are not involved only on my insistence that they contact you to make this offer and for no other reason.

If no notice is to be seen by the day of Monday as the 18th day in September then nothing else is to be said again.

(Public domain by virtue of having been publicized
in the commission of a crime.)

Text B.19 Enigma Machine, second note

I have been instructed to inform you that negotiations for the return of the G312 are hereby terminated, and further, that the machine will now be destroyed.

(Public domain: see previous text.)

Text B.20 Timothy Evans, first statement made at Notting Hill police station

She was incurring one debt after another and I could not stand it any longer so I strangled her with a piece of rope and took her down to the flat below the same night whilst the old man was in hospital. I waited till the Christies downstairs had gone to bed, then took her to the wash house after midnight. This was on the Tuesday 8th November. On Thursday evening after I came home from work I strangled my baby in our bedroom with my tie and later that night I took her down into the wash house after Christies had gone to bed.

Signed T.J. Evans 9.55 pm 2/12/49

(Public domain by virtue of having been used in court proceedings.)

Text B.21 Timothy Evans, second statement made at Notting Hill police station

I was working for the Lancaster Food Products of Lancaster Road, W.11. My wife was always moaning about me working long hours so I left there and went to work for the Continental Wine Stores of Edgware Road. I started at 8 a.m. and finished at 2 p.m. and the job was very nice there. In the meanwhile my wife got herself into £20 debt so I borrowed £20 off the Guvnor under false pretences, so he give me the £20 which I took home and gave it to my wife. I asked her who she owed the money to but she would not tell me, so a week later I got sacked. I was out of work then for two or three weeks. In the meanwhile I had been driving for two or three days a week. I was earning 25/- to 30/- a day. This was for the Lancaster Food Products I used to give her this money and she was moaning she wasn't getting enough wages, so one of the regular drivers at the Lancaster Food Products left so the Guvnor asked me if I would like my regular job back at a wage of £5 15s. 0d. a week. I was doing quite a lot of overtime for the firm working late, which I used to earn altogether £6 to £7 a week. Out of that my wife used to go to the firm on a Friday and my Guvnor used to pay her £5 what she used to sign for. Perhaps through the week I would have to give her more money off different people from which I used to borrow it. I used to pay them back on a Friday out of my own pocket. I had to rely on my overtime to pay my debts and then I had a letter from J. Brodericks telling me I was behind in my payments for my furniture on the hire purchase. I asked her if she had been paying for the furniture and she said she had, then I showed her the letter I had received from Brodericks then she admitted she hadn't been paying it.

I went down to see Brodericks myself to pay them my £1 a week and ten shillings off the arrears so then I left the furniture business to my wife. I then found she was in debt with the rent. I accused her of squandering the money so that started a terrific argument in my house. I told her if she didn't pull herself together I would have to leave her, so she said "You can leave any time you like," so I told her she would be surprised one day if I walked out on her. One Sunday, early in November, I had a terrific row with her at home so I washed and changed and went to the pub dinner time. I stopped there till two o'clock. I came home, had my lunch, left again to go out, leaving my wife and baby at home, because I didn't want any more arguments. I went to the pictures – A.B.C. Lancaster Road, known as Royalty, at 4.30 p.m. I came out when the film was finished, I think about 7.15 p.m. I went home sat down and switched the wireless on. I made a cup of tea. My wife was nagging till I went to bed at 10 p.m. I got up at 6 a.m. next day, made a cup of tea, My wife got up to make a feed for the baby at 6.15 a.m. She gets up and starts an argument straight away. I took no notice of her and went into the bedroom to see my baby before going to work. My wife told me she was going to pack up and go down to her father in Brighton. I asked her what she was going to do with the baby, so she said she was going to take the baby down to Brighton with her so I said it would be a good job and a load of worry off my mind, so I went to work as usual so when I came home at night I just put the kettle on, I sat down, my wife walked in so I said, "I thought you was going to Brighton?" She said, "What for you to have a good time?" I took no notice of her. I went downstairs and fetched the pushchair up. I come upstairs she started an argument again. I told her if she didn't pack it up I'd slap her face. With that she picked up a milk bottle to throw at me. I grabbed the bottle out of her hand, I pushed her, she fell in a chair in the kitchen, so I washed and changed and went out. I went to the pub and had a few drinks. I got home about 10.30 p.m. I walked in she started to row again so I went straight to bed. I got up Tuesday morning and went straight to work. I come home at night about 6.30 p.m. my wife started to argue again, so I hit her across the face with my flat hand. She then hit me back with her hand. In a fit of temper I grabbed a piece of rope from a chair which I had brought home off my van and strangled her with it. I then took her into the bedroom and laid her on the bed with the rope still tied round her neck. Before 10 p.m. that night I carried my wife's body downstairs to the kitchen of Mr Kitchener's flat as I knew he was away in hospital. I then came back upstairs. I then made my baby some food and fed it, then I sat with the baby by the fire for a while in the kitchen. I put the baby to bed later on. I then went back to the kitchen and smoked a cigarette. I then went downstairs when I knew everything was quiet, to Mr Kitchener's kitchen. I wrapped my wife's body up in a blanket and a green table cloth from off my kitchen table. I then tied it up with a piece of cord from out of my kitchen cupboard. I then slipped downstairs and opened the back door, then went up and carried my wife's body down to the wash house and placed it under the sink. I then blocked the front of the sink up with pieces of wood so that the body wouldn't be seen. I locked the wash house door, I come in and shut the back door behind me. I then slipped back upstairs. The Christies who live on the ground floor were in bed. I went into the bedroom to see if my daughter was asleep. When I looked in the cot she was fast asleep so I then shut the bedroom door and laid on the bed all night fully dressed until it was time to get up and go to work. I then got up, lit the gas and put the kettle on. I made my baby a feed and fed it. I then changed her and put her back into the cot wrapping her up well so that she would not get cold, then went to the kitchen and poured myself out a cup of tea. I then finished my tea and slipped back into the bedroom to see if the baby had dropped off to sleep. It was asleep so I went off to work. I done my days work and got home about 5.30 p.m. that Wednesday evening. I come in, lit the gas, put the kettle on and lit the fire. I fed the baby, had a cup of tea myself, sat in front of the fire with my baby. I made the baby a feed about 9.30 p.m. I fed her then I changed her, then I put her to bed. I come back into the kitchen sat by the fire until about twelve o'clock, then went to bed. I got up at 6 a.m. next day lit the gas put the kettle on, made the baby a feed and fed it. I then changed her and dressed her. I then poured myself out a cup of tea I had already made. I drank half and the baby drank the other half. I then put the baby back in the cot, wrapped her up well and went to work. I done my day's work and then had an argument with the Guvnor then I left the job. He give me my wages before I went home. He asked me what I wanted my wages for. I told him I wanted to post some money off to my wife first thing in the morning. He asked me where my wife was and I told him she had gone to Bristol on a holiday. He said "How do you intend to send the money to her" and I said, "In a registered envelope." He paid me the money so he said "You can call over tomorrow morning for your cards." I then went home picked up my baby from her cot in the bedroom, picked up my tie and strangled her with it. I then put the baby back in the cot and sat down in the kitchen and waited for Christies downstairs to go to bed. At about twelve o'clock that night I took the baby downstairs to the wash house and hid her body behind some wood. I then locked the wash house door behind me and came in closing the back door behind me. I then slipped back upstairs and laid on the bed all night, fully clothed. I got up the following morning, washed, shaved and changed, and went up to see a man in Portobello Road about selling my furniture. I don't know his name. During the same afternoon he came to my flat, looked at it and offered me forty quid for it. I told him I would take £40 for it and then he asked me why I wanted to sell it. I told him I was going to Bristol to live as I has a job there waiting for me. He asked me why I wasn't taking the furniture with me. I told him my wife had already gone there and had a flat with furniture in it. He then asked me if it was paid for. I said it was. He said he would call Sunday afternoon to let me know what time the driver would call on Monday for it. I said I would wait in for him. Between 3 and 4 p.m. on Monday this man took all the furniture all the lino, and he paid me £40 which I signed for in a receipt book. He handed me the money which I counted in his presence. I waited till he went then picked up my suitcase which I took to Paddington. The same night I caught the 12.55 a.m. train from Paddington to Cardiff and made my way to 93 Mount Pleasant, Merthyr Vale, where I stayed with my Uncle, Mr. Lynch. The rest I think you know. I have been asked to read this statement myself, but I cannot read. It has been read over to me and it is all the truth.

(Public domain by virtue of having been used in court proceedings.)

Text B.22   New Baltimore Police Department. Written Voluntary Statement of Jonathan Kaled, 10/27/00, 1:40 a.m.

Me, Matt Dannells, and Frank drove up to Mancinos. I went in and lock the doors and told Justin to give me the money. Then I took him in to the walk-in to lock him in there and as I was walking out the gun went off so I turned off the lights and ran out the back. Then we left and went to Matt's brothers house.

I also I'm the one who make the fake call and order a pizza and a grinder and told them it was down County Line. He told me that they can't and I said that I was a friend of Ken.

Justin's wallet was through in a dumster at Van Pamle car lot. I didn't mean for this to happen. It was an accident.

(Public domain by virtue of having been used in criminal investigation.)

Text B.23   Frank Kuecken's police statement. New Baltimore Police Department Written Voluntary Statement of Frank Kuecken, 10/27/00, 1:30 a.m.

1. Who were you with on October 21, 2000 around 10 p.m.?
F.J.
2. Were you in a vehicle and if so, who's vehicle?
Mine, "68" Ford F–100 black.
3. Did you and F.J. go to Mancino's Pizza in New Baltimore on October 21, 2000 and if so what time?
Yes. 9:50 p.m.
4. What did F.J. do at Mancino's Pizza?
Went in and ripped the kid off.
5. How do you know F.J. ripped the kid off?
He told me when he came out.
6. What was F.J. wearing when he ripped the kid off?
Olive color cargo pants, burgandy hooded sweatshirt.
7. Did you and F.J. talk about what he was going to do at Mancino's Pizza that night?
F.J. told me he was going to rip the kid off.
8. Where were you and F.J. coming from when he told you his plan?
From Matt Daniels.
9. When F.J. got out of your truck and entered Mancino's Pizza, what did you see him do?
He turned around and locked the door then turned off the lights and both of them went toward the back, then F.J. came from the back and entered my truck and said I ripped the kid off.
10. After F.J. got in your truck and told you what happened where did you go?
Went to Matt's and picked him up and went to his brother's.
11. After you left Matt's brother's house, who was with you?
Matt and F.J.
12. Where did you go?
Back to Joe Goolins.
13. Did you drop F.J. off at his house?
Yes.

14. Did F.J. say anything else to you besides what you have already said about the robbery?

No.

15. When F.J. and Justin went to the back of the pizza store did you hear a gunshot?

Yes.

16. Did F.J. tell you he shot Justin when he got into your truck after you heard the gunshot?

Yes.

17. Is the gun F.J. used to shoot Justin in Matt Daniels' closet at far as you know?

Yes.

18. After F.J. told you he shot Justin, you swore at him and did he then tell you he had to get rid of the gun?

Yes.

19. When you and F.J. got to Matt's house did F.J. tell Matt he shot Justin?

Yes.

(Public domain by virtue of having been used in court proceedings.)

Text B.24   Excerpt from Unabomber text (the chapter entitled 'Revolution is easier than Reform')

Therefore two tasks confront those who hate the servitude to which the industrial system is reducing the human race. First, we must work to heighten the social stresses within the system so as to increase the likelihood that it will break down or be weakened sufficiently so that a revolution against it becomes possible. Second, it is necessary to develop and propagate an ideology that opposes technology and the industrial society if and when the system becomes sufficiently weakened. And such an ideology will help to assure that, if and when industrial society breaks down, its remnants will be smashed beyond repair, so that the system cannot be reconstituted. The factories should be destroyed, technical books burned, etc.

(Public domain by virtue of author's publication.)

Text B.25   Mitchell's confession (Saudi Arabia)

My name is Alexander Hutton Johnston Mitchell. I am also known as Sandy.

I am of British nationality and I work at the Security Forces Hospital here in Riyadh.

I am the chief anaesthetic technician. I confirm and confess that I was ordered to carry out an explosion here in Riyadh, which took place on Friday, 17 November 2000.

The explosion was directed against Mr Christopher Rodway, who is of British nationality.

During this explosion I was assisted by Dr William Sampson, of Canadian nationality.

I placed the explosive device under the driver's seat of Christopher's car. That afternoon, Christopher came out with his wife, got into the car and drove off.

William detonated the remote control, which caused the explosion in Christopher's car.

We then turned south away from the scene of the incident. We found out later that Christopher had been killed in the explosion and his wife had been injured.

A second explosion was authorised and we carried out the order in a car which was similar to that of Christopher Rodway.

The second explosion was planned for 22 November. As Bill and I were discussing the results of the first explosion, a friend of ours, Mr Ralph Carl, a Belgian citizen, overheard our conversation.

It became necessary for us to involve Ralph in carrying out the second explosion to ensure his silence.

(Public domain by virtue of having been televised as a confession.)

Text B.26   Sampson's confession (Saudi Arabia)

My name is William James Sampson, also known as Bill. I am a Canadian national working as a marketing consultant for the Saudi Industrial Development Fund.

I admit and acknowledge that I participated with Mr Alexander Mitchell in setting up an explosive device on the vehicle belonging to Mr Christopher Rodway, a British national.

Two days later, Mr Mitchell ordered me to set up a second explosion with the participation of Mr Ralph Skevins, a Belgian national.

The date for this explosion was set at Wednesday 22 November 2000. The explosive device and the remote switch were given to me by Mr Mitchell personally.

Dummy device

Under an agreement with Mr Mitchell, I constructed a dummy device which was given to Mr Ralph Skevins, as we both felt that his correct participation in the following events was uncertain.

I phoned Mr Skevins and told him to plant the device, his device, on the GMC Blazer, parked next to his . . . I waited in my vehicle and then proceeded to the target vehicle, where I removed the dummy device and planted the real explosive device.

(Public domain: see previous text.)

Text B.27   Skevins' confession (Saudi Arabia)

My name is Ralph Carl Marya Skevins. I am of Belgian nationality. I work in King Fahd National Heart Hospital as a trauma co-ordinator.

I admit that I was in the house with Mr Alexander Mitchell, and also that I have heard a conversation between Alexander Mitchell and Dr William Sampson regarding the first car explosion where Mr Christopher Rodway died.

Later, Mr Alexander Mitchell informed me of his real involvement in the explosion. He also told me that he required me for the second explosion. My role would be to actually place the explosion under the car, which would be later appointed to me.

I received the explosive device from Dr William Sampson and I went to Al-Falah compound . . . Later on, I received a phone call from Dr William

Sampson to say that I have to place the device under the car parked on the right side of me . . .

[A short time later] I saw the car explode in front of me. I parked my car immediately behind the car and I helped the people out to extricate them.

There was one severe injury and three are light injuries. Everything I write down is in the books and is all in detail. Everything I say is a truth.

(Public domain: see previous text.)

Text B.28   JonBenet Ramsey ransom note

Mr. Ramsey,
Listen carefully! We are a group of individuals that represent a small foreign faction. We do respect your bussiness but not the country that it serves. At this time we have your daughter in our posession. She is safe and unharmed and if you want her to see 1997, you must follow our instructions to the letter.

You will withdraw $118,000.00 from your account. $100,000 will be in $100 bills and the remaining $18,000 in $20 bills. Make sure that you bring an adequate size attache to the bank When you get home you will put the money in a brown paper bag. I will call you between 8 and 10 am tomorrow to instruct you on delivery. The delivery will be exhausting so I advise you to be rested. If we monitor you getting the money early, we might call you early to arrange an earlier delivery of the money and hence a earlier pick-up of your daughter.

Any deviation of my instructions will result in the immediate execution of your daughter. You will also be denied her remains for proper burial. The two gentlemen watching over your daughter do not particularly like you so I advise you not to provoke them.

Speaking to anyone about your situation, such as Police, F.B.I., etc., will result in your daughter being beheaded. If we catch you talking to a stray dog, she dies. If you alert bank authorities, she dies.

If the money is in any way marked or tampered with, she dies. You will be scanned for electronic devices and if any are found, she dies. You can try to deceive us, but be warned that we are familiar with Law enforcement coun-termeasures and tactics. You stand a 99% chance of killing your daughter if you try to out smart us. Follow our instructions and you stand 100% chance of getting her back. You and your family are under constant scrutiny as well as the authorities. Don't try to grow a brain John. You are not the only fat cat around so don't think that killing will be difficult.

Don't underestimate us John. Use that good southern common sense of yours. It is up to you now John!
Victory!
S.B.T.C.

(Public domain by virtue of worldwide publicity.)

Text B.29   E-mail confession (excerpt) in the JonBenet Ramsey case

I feel so guilty for what I've done. I was there when the whole thing occurred. I never wanted any part in it, but they said if I didn't help I would be killed as well. I was only 14 when this took place, so I went along with the whole plan.

(Public domain: see previous text.)

Text B.30   Lindbergh ransom note (Note 1)

Dear Sir!

Have 50000$ redy with 2500$ in 20$ bills 1500$ in 10$ bills and 1000$ in 5$ bills. After 2–4 days we will inform you were to deliver the Mony.

We warn you for making anyding public or for notify the polise the child is in gute care.

Indication for all letters are singnature and 3 holes.

(Public domain by virtue of having been used in court proceedings.)

Text B.31   Lindbergh ransom note (Note 2)

Dear Sir. We have warned you note to make anything public also notify the police now you have to take consequences- means we will have to hold the baby until everything is quite. We can note make any appointments just now. We know very well what it means to us. It is realy necessary to make a world affair out of this, or to get your baby back as soon as possible to settle those affair in a quick way will be better for both- don't be afraid about the baby- keeping care of us day and night. We also will feed him acording to the diet.

We are interested to send him back in gut health. And ransom was made aus for 50000$ but now we have to take another person to it and probably have to keep the baby for a longer time as we expected. So the amound will be 70000 20000 in 50$ bills 25000$ in 20$ bill 15000$ in 10$ bills and 10000 in 5$ bills Don't mark any bills or take them from one serial nomer. We will form you latter were to deliver the mony. But we will note do so until the Police is out of the cace and the pappers are quite. The kidnapping we prepared in years so we are prepared for everyding.

(Public domain by virtue of having been used in court proceedings.)

Text B.32   Marino Achim Joseph confession

Dear Governor Bush Sir,

My name is Achim Josef Marino, #573514 and I am currently confined in the McConnell Unit of the T.D.C.J.-I.D., serving three life sentences plus three ten-year sentences for crimes committed at Austin, Texas in both 1988 and 1990. While in Austin in 1988, I also robbed, raped and shot a 20 year old woman at the Pizza Hut at Reinli Lane. This was in late October of 1988, after purchasing the murder weapon via the Austin American States-mans classified section. The womens name was Nancy Lena Dupriest, and I have not been convicted for this crime. Approximately a month after this crime, I was arrested in El Paso, Texas, where the murder weapon was confiscated by the El Paso police department, however, the federal goverment ultimately convicted me for it. At the time of my arrest, I had the keys as well as two currency bags from the Pizza Hut with the name of Pizza Huts bank on the bag, in my possession and which remained in my personal property in the county jail for approximately 14 months. My friend, Janet Vaughn of P.O. Box 4973, El Paso, Tx., 79914, picked up my personal property after I was transferred to T.D.E.J.-I.D., for parole violation. She later took these items to my parents home where they remain to this day. Included with this confession to you is a B.O.T.F. report in conection with the confiscated murder weapon, and the purchase of it in Austin, Texas, shortly before the murder. In 1990, after I was re-paroled by T.D.E.J.-I.D., I was once again arrested in Austin, Texas for robbery on approximately 5/30/90. While in the county jail, I was told by my cell mate, Raughleigh Lawson, that two men named Dansinger and Ochoa had been convicted for that crime. I told Raughleigh at that time that they had gotten the wrong people, that I knew the guy who had done it. He then told me that Dansinger and Ochoa had plead guilty to the murder. Governor Bush Sir, I do not know these men nor why they plead guilty to a crime they never committed. I can only assume that they must have been facing a capital murder trial with a poor chance of aguittal, but I tell you this sir, I did this awfull crime and I was alone.

Early last year, I wrote the Editor of the Austin American-Statesman, Chief Elizabeth Watson of the O.P.D., and Ms Susan Maldonado of the Austin office of the A.C.L.U. confessing to this crime because I believed that I was about to be killed here at the prison, and therefore I wanted to clear my conscience somewhat in regards to the lives of Dansinger, Ochoa and their loved ones. However, the confessions I'd made to these people was ultimately ignored. Now, I make this confession for a different reason. My life is no longer in danger, but my conscience still sickens me. I can not help Nancy Lena Dupriest or her family, but at least I can attempt to make ammends to Dansinger and Ochoa and their loved ones by doing my Christian duty and come clean about this terrible crime, a crime which has been enlarged and magnified by the arrest and conviction of two innocent men. Additionally, I have had a spiritual awakening and conversion, resulting in me becoming a Christian. This is a direct result of joining the Alcoholics Anonymous/Narcotics Anonymous Twelve Step Program, some 21 months ago and whose 12 steps and guiding principles caused me to have a spiritual awakening which ultimately lead me to the answer, Jesus Christ, His Father our Creator, the Holy Spirit, and ofcourse, this confession. The Christian lifestyle and value system demands that I do this, even at the loss of my life, which I am fully pre-pared to lose and expect to loose. I 'am deeply sickened, disgusted and mortified for the crime I have committed, as well as my entire past life. I grieve for Nancy Lena Dupriest, her loved ones, as well as those of Dansinger and Ochoa, and also my familly. Prior to my Christian conversion and healing, I was insane. Never the less, there can be no excuses for my crime, because I knew exactly what I was doing. I am pre-pared to pay the prise for my actions. Governor Bush Sir, a copy of this letter/confession to you will also be sent to Ronny Earle of the Travis County District Attorney's Office. I wish to respectfully remind you, that in the event that you all decide to once again ignore this confession that you all are legally and morally obligated to contact Dansinger and Ochoa's attorneys and families concerning this confession. Thank you. God bless you and your family,

Yours in Jesus Christ,
Achim J. Marino
#573514
McConnell Unit
3001 S. Emilly Dr.
Beeville, Texas 78102

      (Public domain by virtue of having been used in court proceedings.)

Text B.33 Confession of Anne Foster at Salem (1692)

The Devil appeared to her in the shape of a bird at several times, such a bird as she never saw the like before; and she had had this gift (viz., of striking the afflicted down with her eye) ever since. Being asked why she thought that bird was the Devil, she answered, because he came white and vanished away black; and that the Devil told her she should have this gift, and that she must believe him, and told her she should have prosperity: and she said that he had appeared to her three times, and always as a bird, and the last time about half a year since, and sat upon a table, had two legs and great eyes, and that it was the second time of his appearance that he promised her prosperity. She further stated, that it was Goody Carrier that made her a witch. She told her, that, if she would not be a witch, the Devil would tear her to pieces, and carry her away, at which time she promised to serve the Devil; that she was at the meeting of the witches at Salem Village; that Goody Carrier came, and told her of the meeting, and would have her go: so they got upon sticks, and went said journey, and, being there, did see Mr. Burroughs, the minis- ter, who spake to them all; that there were then twenty-five persons met together; that she tied a knot in a rag, and threw it into the fire to hurt Timothy Swan and that she did hurt the rest that complained of her by squeezing puppets like them, and so almost choked them; that she and Martha Carrier did both ride on a stick or pole when they went to the witch-meeting at Salem Village, and that the stick broke as they were carried in the air above the tops of the trees, and they fell: but she did hang fast about the neck of Goody Carrier, and they were presently at the village; that she had heard some of the witches say that there were three hundred and five in the whole country, and that they would ruin that place, the village; that there were also present at that meeting two men besides Mr. Burroughs, the minister, and one of them had gray hair; and that the discourse among the witches at the meeting in Salem Village was, that they would afflict there to set up the Devil's kingdom'.

(Public domain by virtue of absence of copyright.)

Text B.34 Ann Putnam, Salem (New England Historical and Genealogical Register, Volume XII, July 1858, p. 245)

The deposition of Ann Putnam Junr who testifieth and saith some time in April 1692 there appeared to me the Apparition of an old short woman that told me her name was Martin and that she came from Amesbury who did immediately afflict me, urging me to write in her book, but on the 2 May 1692 being the day of her examination Susanna Martin did most grievously afflict me during the time of her examination for when she did but look personally upon she would strike me down or almost choke and several times since the Apparition of Susanna Martin has most grievously afflicted me by pinching me and almost choking me urging me vehemently to write in her book. Also on the day of her Examination I saw the Apparition of Susanna Martin go and afflict the bodies of Mary Walcott, Mercy Lewis, Elizabeth Hubbard and Abigial Williams.

(Public domain by virtue of absence of copyright.)

Text B.35   Fake suicide note from www.onion.com

I know you must be very angerey with me now but it had to be This way. Dont you see that now my pain is finnelley over forevr. My soul is set free. Tell Brittany I loved her truely. I just want something I can never have – Trent Reznor KIN 4Ever

I apologilze to all whom I have brought sadness too.

love, ethan

(Copyright onion.com 2001 – a text produced for its satirical value, accompanied by a humorous article criticizing educational standards in modern schools.)

Text B.36   From David Ferrie (1) (suspect in JFK assassination)

Dear Al: When you read this I will be quite dead and no answer will be possible. I wonder how you are going to justify things.

Tell me you treated me as you did because I was the one who always got you in trouble. The police arrest. The strip car charge. The deal at Kohn School. Flying Barragona in the Beech.

Well, I guess that helps ease your conscience, even if it is not the truth. All I can say is that I offered you love, and the best I could. All I got in return in the end was a kick in the teeth. Thus I die alone and unloved.

You would not even straighten out Carol about me, though this started when you were going steady.

I wonder what your last days and hours are going to be like. As you sowed, so shall you reap.

(Public domain by virtue of absence of copyright.)

Text B.37   Virginia Woolf

Dearest, I feel certain I am going mad again. I feel we can't go through another of those terrible times. And I shan't recover this time. I begin to hear voices, and I can't concentrate. So I am doing what seems the best thing to do. You have given me the greatest possible happiness. You have been in every way all that anyone could be. I don't think two people could have been happier till this terrible disease came. I can't fight any longer. I know that I am spoiling your life, that without me you could work. And you will I know. You see I can't even write this properly. I can't read. What I want to say is I owe all the happiness of my life to you. You have been entirely patient with me and incredibly good. I want to say that – everybody knows it. If anybody could have saved me it would have been you. Everything has gone from me but the certainty of your goodness. I can't go on spoiling your life any longer.

I don't think two people could have been happier than we have been.

V.

(Public domain.)

Text B.38   Guy Fawkes (was he framed by Sir Robert Cecil or did he do it?) (Excerpt)

I confesse that a practise in general was first broken unto me against his Majesty for reliefe of the Catholique cause, and not invented or propounded by myself. And this was first propounded unto me about Easter last was

twelve month, beyond the Seas, in the Low Countries of the Archduke's obeyance, by Thomas Wintour, who came thereupon with me into England
(Crown copyright.)

Text B.39   Shoeless Joe Jackson (baseball player)

Q   You played in the World Series between the Chicago Americans Baseball Club and the Cincinatti Baseball club, did you?

A   I did.

Q   What position did you play in that series?

A   Left field.

Q   Were you present at a meeting at the Ansonia Hotel in New York about two or three weeks before – a conference there with a number of ball players?

A   I was not, no, sir.

Q   Did anybody pay you any money to help throw that series in favor of Cincinatti?

A   They did.

Q   How much did they pay?

A   They promised me $20,000 and paid me five.

Q   Who promised you the twenty thousand?

A   "Chick" Gandil.

Q   Who is Chick Gandil?

A   He was their first baseman on the White Sox Club.

Q   Who paid you the $5,000?

A   Lefty Williams brought it in my room and threw it down.

Q   Who is Lefty Williams?

A   The pitcher on the White Sox Club

Q   Where did he bring it? Where is your room?

A   At that time I was staying at the Lexington Hotel, I believe it is.

Q   On 21st and Michigan?

A   22nd and Michigan, yes.

(Copyright, Chicago Historical Society. Permission
gratefully acknowledged.)

Text B.40   Dennis Dowthitt (Texas death row prisoner)

I am so sorry for what y'all had to go through. I am so sorry for what all of you had to go through. I can't imagine losing two children. If I was y'all, I would have killed me. You know? I am really so sorry about it, I really am. I got to go sister, I love you. Y'all take care and God bless you.

Gracie was beautiful and Tiffany was beautiful. You had some lovely girls and I am sorry. I don't know what to say.

All right, Warden, let's do it.

(Death row final statements do not carry copyright in
the USA; Texts 40– 8.)

243

Text B.41   Texas Death Row Penpal Request:

My name is Dennis and I have been incarcerated since my birthday on June 20, 1990. I do not have any penpals and would like to start writing to a few people who are truly interested in a close relationship on paper.

Although I am where I am, I am an honest straightforward person with needs just like anyone else and the main need like most is companionship. I have a sister who has stuck by me through the entire ordeal of my trial and incarceration and is now having many problems of her own, including not being able to walk, and can no longer come to visit. I really don't want to burden her any longer and try to make things easier on her by not telling her many of my problems. Truth is, I need a friend and someone to talk to and share with. However, I am one who likes to listen more than talk and need someone who would share their life and be honest with me.

I would really enjoy a family who would let me live the rest of my life with them.

I love kids and enjoy answering their questions and trying to help them. If there is anyone who would be interested in writing and sharing with me, please don't hesitate to write and we can take it slow and easy and get to know each other. Thank you.

Text B.42   Last statement of Basil McFarland

I owe no apologies for a crime I did not commit. Those who lied and fabricated evidence against me will have to answer for what they have done. I know in my heart what I did and I call upon the spirit of my ancestors and all of my people and I swear to them and now I am coming home.

Text B.43   Gerald Mitchell (Texas death row prisoner). His last statement (robbed and slayed 20-year-old Charles Marino)

Yes, sir. Where's Mr. Marino's mother? Did you get my letter? Just wanted to let you know, I sincerely meant everything I wrote. I am sorry for the pain. I am sorry for the life I took from you. I ask God for forgiveness and I ask you for the same. I know it maybe hard, but I'm sorry for what I did. To my family I love each and every one of you. Be strong. Know my love is always with you . . . always. I know I am going home to be with the Lord. Shed tears of happiness for me. I love each and everyone of you. Keep on living.

Betty, you have been wonderful. You guided me to the Lord. You have been like a mother to me. Sean, Rusty, Jenny, Marsha, God Bless each and every one of y'all.

Jesus, I confess you as my Lord and Savior. I know when I die, I'll have life in heaven and life eternal everlasting. I am ready for that mansion that you promised me.

Take care.

It's alright Sean, it's alright. I'm going to a better place.

Text B.44 Jeffrey Carlton Doughtie (murdered elderly couple aged 80 and 76)

For almost nine years I have thought about the death penalty, whether it is right or wrong and I don't have any answers. But I don't think the world will be a better or safer place without me. If you had wanted to punish me you would have killed me the day after, instead of killing me now. You are not hurting me now. I have had time to get ready, to tell my family goodbye, to get my life where it needed to be.

It started with a needle and it is ending with a needle.

Carl, you have been a good friend, man. I am going to look for you. You go back and tell your daughter I love her. Tell her I came in here like a man and I will leave like a man. It's been good, dude. Thank you, Shorty. I appreciate you. I came in like a man and I will leave like a man. I will be with you. I will be with you every time you take a shower. If you leave crying you don't do me justice. If you don't see peace in my eyes you don't see me. I will be the first one you see when you cross over.

They got these numbers that I called today. Calling my family.

That is it. Ready, Warden.

Text B.45 Mack Hill (admitted to nothing but convicted of murdering a friend)

First, I would like to tell my family that I love them. I will be waiting on them. I am fine. I hope that everyone gets some closure from this. I am innocent. Lubbock County officials believe I am guilty. I am not. Travis Ware has the burden on him to prove that he did not commit felonies. He needs to be stopped or he is going to do it time and time again. The power is invested in you as a public official to do your job.

That's all Warden. I love y'all.

Text B.46 Miguel Flores (Convicted of capital murder for kidnapping, sexually assaulting and murdering a 20-year-old female)

I want to thank my attorneys, Father Walsh . . . Sylvia, te quiero mucho y a Consulado, te quiero decir muchas gracias por todo. I want to say I am sorry and I say a prayer today for you so you can have peace and I hope that you can forgive me. God is waiting and God is waiting now.

Text B.47 Last statement: Jeffery Dillingham (contract-killed 40-year-old Caren Koslow)

I would just like to apologize to the victim's family for what I did. I take full responsibility for that poor woman's death, for the pain and suffering inflicted on Mr. Koslow.

Father, I want to thank you for all of the beautiful people you put in my life. I could not have asked for two greater parents than you gave me. I could just ask for two greater people in their life now. It is a blessing that there are people that they love so much but even more so, people that I love so much. I thank you for all the things you have done in my life, for the ways that you have opened my eyes, softened my heart.

The ways that you have taught me. For teaching me how to love, for all of the bad things you have taken out of my life. For all the good things you have added to it.

I thank you for all of the beautiful promises that you make us in your word, and I graciously received every one of them. Thank you Heavenly Father for getting me off of death row and for bringing me home out of prison.

I love you Heavenly Father, I love you Jesus. Thank you both for loving me. Amen.

Text B.48   Karla Faye Tucker (last statement) slayed 27-year-old Jerry Dean with a pickax.

Yes sir, I would like to say to all of you – the Thornton family and Jerry Dean's family that I am so sorry. I hope God will give you peace with this.

Baby, I love you. Ron, give Peggy a hug for me. Everybody has been so good to me.

I love all of you very much. I am going to be face to face with Jesus now. Warden Baggett, thank all of you so much. You have been so good to me. I love all of you very much. I will see you all when you get there. I will wait for you.

Text B.49   Hoax ransom note to Sheriff Sheldon. (The following note was received 28 November via US Mail at the Yoknapatawpha County Sheriff's Department. The postmark was dated 25 November from Jackson, MS. The note arrived in a plain white envelope with no return address)

"SHERIFF" SHELDON
Bust another card room and we will bust her head!
Leave it alone like all the others
Busting card rooms won't help make you a real sheriff.
Busting card rooms won't help her at all.
If you want her back, BACK OFF!

Text B.50   Chuck Lamar's 'suicide note'. The following note was found on the desk in Lamar's study at his home. The note was left on the centre of the deskblotter and was the only item on the desktop, aside from a family photograph

ITS THE COWARDS ROAD BUT IT SUITS ME. I'VE SACRIFICED TOO MUCH TO LIVE AS AN HONORABLE MAN. I'D BE LYING TO CONTINUE.

I'VE CHOSEN THIS ROAD MYSELF. NO ONE HAS FORCED ME TO DO IT. ITS ALL MY OWN DOING AND I HAVE NO ELSE ONE TO BLAME.

MY FAMILY, MY PRECIOUS MACY- I LOVE YOU, I KNOW I'VE HURT YOU, BUT ITS THE ONLY WAY I COULD CHOOSE. ITS NOT ABOUT YOU, ITS ME AND MY CONSCIENCE AND ITS A STRUGGLE I HAVE TO END.

Charles

(Public domain.)

Text B.51   Excerpt: elderly male, 82, Allegheny County, Pennsylvania

I am at a situation where I cannot bear the future and subject you to the many months or years of trying to take care of an invalid who is suffering from emphysema and senility, and possibility of worse

(Public domain.)

Text B.52   Excerpt: elderly male, 73, Allegheny County, Pennsylvania

"It's time for my exit," his note said. "I can't breathe, I can't sleep, my legs are swollen and can't walk. My back has been killing me . . . I'm trying to eliminate costly hospitals that will cut into finances"

(Public domain.)

Text B.53   Joel Rose (excerpt)

"I am so sad – I have ruined your life – but it will be proved, I didn't do these awful things, I hope the DNA test helps show that," Joel Rose wrote in a hastily composed suicide note to his wife Lois.
"Those men who invaded our house killed me, and those awful people bringing these bogus charges . . .
"When your integrity has been destroyed you have nothing . . ."

(Public domain.)

Text B.54   A.T. Renouf's suicide note

To Whom It May Concern
Last friday (13–October) my bank account was garnisheed. I was left with a total of $00.43 in the bank.
At this time I have rent and bill's to pay which would come to somewhere approaching $1500.00 to $1800.00.
Since my last pay was also direct deposited on friday I now have no way of supporting myself. I have no money for food or for gas for my car to enable me to work. My employer also tells me that they will only pay me by direct deposit. I therefore no longer have a job, since the money would not reach me. I have tried talking to the Family Support people at 1916 Dundas St. E. their answer was:- "we have a court order." repeated several times.
I have tried talking to the welfare people in Markham. Since I earned over $520.00 last month I am not eligible for assistance.
I have had no contact with my daughter in approx. 4 year's. I do not even know if she is alive and well. I have tried to keep her informed of my current telephone number but she has never bothered to call.
I have no family and no friend's, very little food, no viable job and very poor future prospects. I have therefore decided that there is no further point in continuing my life. It is my intention to drive to a secluded area, near my home, feed the car exhaust into the car, take some sleeping pills and use the remaining gas in the car to end my life.
I would have prefered to die with more dignity.
It is my last will and testament that this letter be published for all to see and read.
Signed
A.T. Renouf

(Public domain.)

Text B.55   Ocalan's Final Statement

(Text of Abdullah Ocalan's Statement just before the verdict was handed down at his trial. Copyright the Associated Press.)

I reject the accusation of treason. I believe that I am struggling for the unity of the country and freedom. I believe that my struggle was for a democratic republic not against the republic.

I hope that the problem which has grown as a result of historic mistakes will reach a solution. I want this trial to contribute to that. I am repeating my call, the determined promise I made at the onset, for a fair and honorable peace and brotherhood in line with the democratic republic.

I call on humanity, the state and all societal forces to fulfill their duty. The future of the country lies with peace not war.

I greet you all.

(Public domain.)

Text B.56   Michael McBride's Final statement (after receiving the lethal injection)

Thank you um I anticipated that I would try to memorize and recite beatitudes New Testament more or less Luke's beatitudes I should say and ah a chapter.on love in first Corinthians chapter 13, ah I pretty much knew that I would not be able to memorize so much there was also a poem that went along with it and in anticipation of not being able to um fulfill that desire I provided a written statement that will be made available to anybody that will be made available to anybody that wants it I believe, isn't that correct? So uh I wanted you to hear me say that and I apologize and for any other grief I have caused you know, including that a what your about to witness now. It won't be very long as soon as you realize that appear I am falling asleep I would leave because I won't be here after that point I will be dead at that point. It's irreversible. God Bless all of you thank you.

(Public domain.)

Text B.57   Joel Rose – sent from David Morton, the news editor at the Cleveland Free Times, Colorado USA in Jan 2002. Joel Rose committed suicide after being accused of sending women innuendoes through the mail. Dennis Kacnler was his boss

To Dennis Kacnler
Chief – check that garbage theft thing – I'm sure this was connected – I remember seeing one BUC pickup truck with cab picking it up one morning it was stolen – a CIZ employee was driving – I don't know who –
Chief, I did not do this but I cannot face anyone again –
There is a DNA test outstanding that was done Wed at Parma hosp, – I am sure the results will clear me but no one will believe it –
Bless you
JR

(Public domain.)

Text B.58   Michael Sams – one of several ransom demands

Your employee has been kidnapped and will be released for a ransome of
£175,000. With a little luck he should be still O.K. and unharmed, to prove
this fact to you will in in the next day or so receive a recorded message from
him. He will be released on Friday 31 January 1992, provided:
On Wednesday 29 January a ransome of £175,000 is paid, and no extension
to this date will be granted.
The police are not informed in any way until he has been released.
On Wednesday 29th at 4pm (on line 021 358 2281) you will receive a short
recorded message from the hostage. To prove he is still alive and O.K. he will
repeat the first news item that was on the 10am, Radio 2 news. He will then
give further instructions. A second and more detailed message will be given
at 5.05 pm the same day. Your watch must be synchronized with the 5pm
pips on Radio 2. The location of the second call will be given at 4pm, so
transport with a radio must be available.
The money must be carried in a holdall and made up as folows, precisely;
£75,000 in used £50. £75,000 in used £20. £25,000 in used £10 packed in
31 bundles, 250 notes in each.
Kevin Watts (if not the hostage) mst be the person to receive all messages and
carry the money to the appointed place.
However, please note that all messages will be pre-recorded, so no communication or negotiations can be made.
YOU HAVE BEEN WARNED. HIS LIFE IS IN YOUR HANDS.
(Public domain by virtue of having been used in criminal and court
proceedings.)

Text B.59   Michael Sams – another ransom demand

A young prostitute has been kidnapped from the Chapeltown area last night
and will only be released unharmed if the conditions below are met if they
are not met then the hostage will never be seen again also a major ciy centre
store (not necessary in Leeds) will have a fire bomb explode at 5am 17 July.
A payment of £140,000 is paid in cash (one hundred & fourty thousand)
£5,000 is put in two bank accounts, 2 cash cards and P.I.N. issued, those two
bank accounts to allow
(Public domain by virtue of having been used in criminal and court
proceedings.)

Text B.60   Dyfed-Powys Fire Service, emergency call

Hello can I help you?
Yes security guard here XYZ Electronics at the ABC canal.
Yes?
I've just been walking on the back well there's smoke coming out of one of
our roofs. So, could you tell the fire service our curtain shop there's a lot
of chemicals and what have you in there.
Right. Is it XYZ Electronics.
Yeah.
ABC Industrial Estate.
That's right.

By the ABC Canal?
Yeah. What I'll do I'll make my way round the back and I'll leave the gates open for them.
Right and it's smoke is it?
Yeah. Smoke coming out of the roof.
From the roof?
I haven't been there to investigate but I'll –
Right – are you . . . any of the chemicals that are kept there?
I couldn't really tell you.
Are they just –
chemicals from the –
So –
phuric acid is in there.
It's what sorry?
Sulphuric acid is in there.
Okay, don't worry now, we're on our way there.
Okay.
Thank you. Bye.

(Grateful acknowledgements to the Dyfed-Powys Fire Service.)

ENDNOTES

1. Verballing is the process whereby police officers alter the statements of suspects and witnesses.
2. This is because many of these texts are themselves the subject of investigation. We cannot therefore propose them as a standard against which to take measurements for the purpose of discovering norms.
3. Assume for the sake of argument that the test in this hypothetical example has a reputation for reliability and usefulness in the field of authorship attribution.
4. Assume that this is a closed inquiry, i.e. the author can only be A, B or C.
5. Names changed for the usual reasons.
6. An important point – as discussed elsewhere.
7. This section is largely adapted from a review article I wrote in the *Forensic Linguistics Journal* VIII (1) (Olsson, 2001).
8. 'Ramus reduced his definition of rhetoric in *Rhetorica* to mere ornamentation and appropriacy. This interpretation demanded that rhetoric only dealt with form and not with content.' Author's (somewhat loose) translation.
9. The astute reader will have perceived that we are back to questions of what is *appropriate* in a given context, i.e. *ars rhetorica*. This shows us, perhaps, that there is a very fine dividing line between *individual style* and *genre*.
10. These remarks are made only with reference to the English language; see Barton, 1994: 124–5.
11. At the beginning of 2001 there were an estimated one billion pages on the Internet, six months later this figure had increased by 50 per cent. In other words it took six months to achieve what had previously taken three years. In mid-2002 there are 2.01 billion pages on Google alone.
12. Information for this section has largely been taken from websites discussing the Daubert tests, notably: *http://faculty.ncwc.edu/toconnor/daubert.htm* (as at 22/02/02 (acknowledgements to Dr T O'Connor).
13. *Kelliher (Village of) V. Smith*, ([1931] SCR 672) (see: *http://www.economica.ca/ew42p2.htm* (as at 23/02/02).
14. *R. V. Mohan*, ([1994] 2 SCR 9, at 23).
15. This valuable *insight* into Canadian forensic expertise may be found at: *http://www.economica.ca/ew42p2.htm* (as at 23/02/02).
16. More information can be found at: *http://www.umanitoba.ca/faculties/law/Courses/esau/legal_systems/outline20–99.html*
17. Careful examination of the features show that almost all of them involve some kind of confusion between categories, e.g. a noun for a

verb (apologies for apologize); past participle for present participle (been for being); particle for adverb (to for too); possible confusion between end of a sentence and end of a clause (stop + comma for comma); because of capitalization, a possible confusion of the status of such words as *Check* and *Rang* with those 'club-centred' expressions like 'Show President' which could be capitalized by people within the context of club correspondence); preceding the date with the word 'Date', etc. Because of this confusion of categories, it may be that the writer has some kind of aphasic problem or other similar neurolinguistic difficulty.

18. It may not be a misspelling, but a miscategorization of the noun for the verb.

19. i.e. the 'qualitative' vs. 'quantitative' debate.

20. Many suppositions can be made about this note, but as linguists we should always refrain from speculation, and confine ourselves to a disciplined observation and analysis of the text, even if this leads to a very limited result.

21. Note that, as with Bentley, the Gilfoyle text shows two styles of word length average and sentence length average. This suggests that this tests may be generally applicable.

22. See the NIDCD website on aphasia at: *http://www.nidcd.nih.gov/health/pubs_vsl/aphasia.htm*

23. This press comment was recorded and is available in full at: *http://www.historybuff.com/realaudio/hauptm.ram*

24. Neurolinguists might find this particular inquiry of some interest.

25. A WWW search using Google.com reveals 11 instances of 'penacilin' as opposed to 'penicillin' with AltaVista.com showing a similar quantity. The main instances are in pop, hip hop music, rap and other emblems of 1980s and 1990s youth culture including a reference to LSD.

26. *www.extension.harvard.edu/2001–02/policy/honesty.shtml* at 00.17 on 27 June 2002.

27. *http://www.bhsu.edu/artssciences/asfaculty/dsalomon/plag/plag.html* at 00.20 on 27 June 2002.

28. *http://www.cob.sjsu.edu/dept/acct&fin/syllabi/01spring/feakins129A-sp01.doc*

29. Experiment carried out at 02.21 on 27 June 2002 on Google, set for searching the Internet.

30. As found at *http://www.depauw.edu/admin/arc/plag.html* on 29 June 2002 at 01.15.

31. Generally, only experienced editors are able to reduce the length of a text as they work: mosaic plagiarists always seem to lengthen it, and try to 'improve' it.

32. Many other categories are possible, including the following (some of which will be explained at the end of the chapter): character naming – should be consistent; register – should either be formal,

informal or neutral; pronouns – subject pronouns should not be omitted before important clauses; participants – should be introduced as they appear; absence of private verbs – e.g. 'I think'; Gricean maxims, especially of quantity – as you read the text ask yourself whether excessive detail is being given; nicknames – if people are given nicknames after being introduced with their 'usual' name, this may be suspicious, could indicate a 'padding' of the text with 'realistic' details; negatives are much rarer than positives – also, look out for spontaneous, i.e. unforced denials; watch out for ascriptive adjectives, especially if they are 'stacked'.

33. See end of chapter for discussion on statement analysis of *reports*.

34. My suspicion about the word *copper* – unconfirmed at this time – is that it is a word police officers use to refer to themselves, not a word in common use by members of the public.

35. Names and other information changed to protect the identities of parties involved.

36. The reader will appreciate that very few contexts in forensic linguistics are 'typical'.

37. Note this is not a full conversation analysis (CA), but the author's own modified version.

38. I am indebted to the Dyfed-Powys Fire Service, Wales, for their kind provision of this corpus of genuine and simulated taped calls.

39. In each case the text of the complete call is given here even though not all of it is analysed.

40. Note that the operator, the security guard, the householder and the police officer are all native-English speakers, and drawn from similar social backgrounds. Major social and linguistic differences, however, might place tensions on the model proposed here.

41. As a matter of fact this is exactly what happened. The recipient did resign, but several years later received further letters threatening 'exposure' of 'misdemeanours'.

42. As found in Schneidman and Farberow (1957) who founded the science of suicidology. Even today their work on this subject is a classic.

43. Note that under no circumstances should you ask people to create simulated suicide notes. This is not only ethically very suspect, it could also be very dangerous.

44. In line with convention, transcriptions will be written between forward slashes, e.g. /ˈfɒðə/

45. In Chapter 12, I discuss a number of statistical and other methods, shortcuts and general 'handy hints'. Among these I outline how a spectrogram is arrived at, through a mathematical process known as the Fourier transformation. This is not something you have to know, but it is there if you want it.

46. My thanks to the producers of **Praat**, a phonetics program downloadable from *www.praat.org*

47. African National Congress website at *http://www.anc.org.za/ ancdocs/history/mandela/1960s/rivonia.html*

48. Evidence from experiments I have undertaken suggests that speakers inexperienced at dictating ('naïf dictators') produce texts of low lexical richness – lower even than those of their 'normal' speech. However, more experienced 'dictators' can produce levels of lexical richness not much less than that which they usually produce in written language.

49. From *http://web66.coled.umn.edu/new/MLK/MLK.html* at 01:37 28/08/2002.

50. There are several on the Internet, one of which is at: *http://bmj.com/ collections/statsbk/apptabc.shtml* as at 28/08/2002.

51. If you can't find a book with such a table just type the words 'the critical values of the *t* distribution' into your search engine, placing them between double quotation marks. There are several such tables on the Internet.

BIBLIOGRAPHY

Ashforth, T. *Silence in Court*. *http://wwwmcc.murdoch.edu.au/ ReadingRoom/Ashforth/Terthes6.html* 30 June 2002 at 16:18.

Baldwin, J. R. and P. French (1990) *Forensic Phonetics*. London: Pinter Publishers.

Barton, D. (1994) *Literacy: An introduction to the Ecology of Written Language*. Oxford: Blackwell.

Bax, R. *http://www.let.leidenuniv.nl/English/studiepad/SHT/ corpus_ linguistics. htm* 30 May 2002 15:39h UTC

Biber, D. (1988) *Variation across speech and writing*. Cambridge: Cambridge University Press.

Bilgrami, A. (1993) *Belief and Meaning*. Oxford: Blackwell.

Binongo, J. N. and M. W. A. Smith (1999) 'The application of principal component analysis to stylometry', *Literary and Linguistic Computing*.

Bower, K. M. Using CUSUM Charts to Detect Small Process Shifts [online].

Burrows, J. F. (1987) *Computation into Criticism*. Oxford: Clarendon.

Canter, D. and J. Chester (1997) 'Investigation into the claim of weighted Cusum in authorship attribution studies', *Forensic Linguistics* 4(2): 252–61.

Charteris-Black, J. (1997) 'A Study of Arabic, Chinese and Malay First and Second Language Punctuation', in A. Ryan and A. Wray (eds) *Evolving Models of Language*. Clevedon, Philadelphia, Toronto, Sydney, Johannesburg: BAAL and Multilingual Matters, pp. 23–40.

Chaski, C. (2001) 'Language based author identification techniques'. *Forensic Linguistics* VIII(1): 1–65.

Computer-Based Authorship Attribution Without Lexical Measures at http://www.google.co.uk/search?q=cache:Xo-Vm1WNa9wC: slt.wcl.ee. upatras.gr/papers/stamatatos6.pdf+%22computational+ linguistics%22 +%22authorship+attribution%22+ %22short+texts%22&hl=en

Coulthard, M. (1994) 'On the use of corpora in the analysis of forensic texts'. *Forensic Linguistics* I(1): 27–43.

Coulthard, M. (1994b) 'Forensic discourse analysis', in *Advances in Written Text Analysis*, M. Coulthard (ed.). London: Routledge, pp. 242–58.

Coulthard, M. (1994c) 'Powerful evidence for the defence: an exercise in forensic discourse analysis', in J. Gibbons (ed.), *Language and the Law*. London: Longman, pp. 414–27.

Craig, H. 'Authorial Attribution and Computational Stylistics: if you can tell authors apart, have you learned anything about them?' Centre for Literary and Linguistic Computing, University of Newcastle, NSW, Australia online at *http://lingua.arts.klte.hu/allcach98/abst/abs7.htm* on 02 April 2002.

Crystal, D. (1991) 'Stylistic Profiling' in Aijmer, Karin and Bengt Altenberg (eds) pp. 221–38 (cited in Hänlein (31)).

Crystal, D. 'Vanishing languages' (online) *http://www.farsarotul.org/nl21_4.htm* 30 May 2002 17:42h UTC.

de Morgan, S. (1882) *Memoir of Augustus De Morgan*. London.

De Vito, J. A. (1965) 'Comprehension Factors in Oral and Written Discourse of Skilled Communicators'. Speech Monographs, 32, 124–8.

Eichhorn, J. G. (1812) *Historische-kritische Einleitung in das Testament*. Jena.

Ephratt, M. 'Authorship attribution – the case of lexical innovations' (online at *http://www.cs.queensu.ca/achallc97/papers/p006.html* at 02 April 2002).

Farringdon, J. M. (1996) with contributions by A. Q. Morton, M. G. Farringdon and M. D. Baker, *Analysing for Authorship. A Guide to the Cusum Technique*. Cardiff: University of Wales Press.

Goffman, E. (1981) *Forms of Talk*. Philadelphia: University of Pennsylvania Press.

Goutsos, D. (1995) Review article: 'Forensic stylistics', review of McMenamin, G. (1993) *Forensic Stylistics*, *Forensic Linguistics* 2(1): 99–113.

Grant, T. and K. Baker. (2001) 'Reliable, valid markers of authorship', *Forensic Linguistics* VIII(1): 66–79.

Hänlein, H. (1998) *Studies in Authorship Recognition – A Corpus- based Approach*. Frankfurt: Peter Lang.

Harrison, G. B. (1941) *A Jacobean Journal 1603–06*. London: George Routledge & Sons.

Heselwood, B. *Speaker Identification by Earwitness: A Bigger Picture*, online at *http://www.ling.ed.ac.uk/~anthonyb/undergrad_diss.pdf*, found on 05/08/2002 at 02:56 UTC.

Hill, O. (online) *Who Wrote Shakespeare? The Authorship Controversy* at *http://www.urbana.k12.oh.us/699/oh/authorship%20controversy.html* on 06/04/2002.

Hollien, H. (2001) *Forensic Voice Identification*. New York: Harcourt.

Holmes, N. (1887) *The Authorship of Shakespeare*. Boston and New York: Houghton, Mifflin and Company.

Hoover, D. L. (2001) 'Statistical stylistics and authorship attribution: an empirical investigation,' *Literary and Linguistic Computing* 16(4): 421–44.

http://lcg-www.uia.ac.be/conll98/pdf/131139so.pdf [30 December 2001].

http://www.minitab.com/company/VirtualPressRoom/Articles/Using CUSUMChartsForSmallShifts.pdf [1 1 2002].

Ingram, J. C. L., R. Prandolini and S. Ong. (1996) 'Formant trajectories as indices of phonetic variation for speaker identification', *Forensic Linguistics* 3(1): 129–45.

Jiang, M. (1996) Fundamental frequency vector for a speaker identification system.

Johnson, D. E. Online Phonetics course. *http://www.unil.ch/ling/ phonetique/api1-eng.html* on 04 07 2002 at 03.45 (online).

Joseph, A. (1995) *We Get Confessions*. New York: AJ Books.

Kenny, A. (1982) *The Computation of Style: An Introduction to Statistics for Students of Literature and Humanities*. Pergamon Press, Inc.

Kerlinger, F. (1973) *Foundations of Behavioral Research*. New York: Holt, Reinhart & Winston.

King, G., R. Keohane and S. Verba (1994) *Designing Social Inquiry*. Princeton: Princeton University Press.

Kunzel, H. J. (2000) 'Effects of voice disguise on speaking fundamental frequency', *Forensic Linguistics* 7(2): 149–79.

Ladefoged, P. (2001) *A Course in Phonetics*, 4th edn, New York: Harcourt Brace.

Lancashire, I. (online) *http://www2.arts.ubc.ca/fhis/winder/cochcosh/ abs_1997.htm#Tirvengadum* 30 May 2002 15:39h UTC.

Leech, G. and M. H. Short (1981) *Style in Fiction. A Linguistic Introduction to English Fictional Prose*. London, New York: Longman (cited in Hänlein (30)).

Lewin, B. A., J. Fine and L. Young (2001) *Expository discourse*. London and New York: Continuum.

Lightfoot, D. (1979) *Principles of Diachronic Syntax*. Cambridge: Cambridge University Press.

McMenamin, G. (1993) *Forensic Stylistics*. Amsterdam: Elsevier.

McMenamin, G. (2002) *Forensic Linguistics: Advances in Forensic Stylistics*, Boca Raton and New York: CRC Press.

Mendenhall, T. C. (1887) 'The Characteristic Curves of Composition', *Science*, IX, 237–49.

Michaelson, S. and A. Q. Morton (1990). *The Qsum Plot*. Internal Report CSR-3–90, Department of Computer Science, University of Edinburgh.

Mosteller, F. and D. Wallace (1964) *Inference and Disputed Authorship: The Federalist*. Reading, MA: Addison-Wesley.

Nilo, J., G. Binongo and M. W. A. Smith (1999) 'The application of principal component analysis to stylometry', *Literary and Linguistic Computing* 14(4): 445–65.

Olsson, J. G. (1997) 'The alteration and dictation of text', *Forensic Linguistics* IV(2): 226–51.

Olsson, J. G. (2000) 'Some aspects of dictation and text analysis: A study of language configuration and the structure and proportionality of text', unpublished M.Phil. dissertation. University of Birmingham, England.

Owen, C. (1995) Review article: 'Language and the law', *Forensic Linguistics* II(2): 168–87.

Pappas, T. (1998) *Plagiarism and the Culture War: The Writings of Martin Luther King Jr. and Other Prominent Americans*. Hallberg.

Pennebaker, J. W. (1999) 'Psychological factors influencing the reporting of physical symptoms', in A. A. Stone, J. S. Turkkan, C. A. Bachrach, J. B. Jobe, H. S. Kurtzman and V. S. Cain (eds) *The Science of Self-report: Implications for Research and Practice*. Mahwah, NJ: Erlbaum Publishers, pp. 299–316.

Pennebaker, J. (online) *http://www.psy.utexas.edu/psy/undergrad/courses/ fall01/pennebaker2.html* 30 May 2002 15:39h UTC.

Radford, A. (1990) *Syntactic Theory and the Acquisition of English Syntax*, Oxford: Blackwell.

R. Rodman, D. McAllister, D. Bitzer, L. Cepeda and P. Abbitt. 'Speaker identification based on spectral moments', online at: *http:// www.csc.ncsu.edu/faculty/rodman/Speaker%20identification%20 using%isophonemic%20sequences.pdf* on 04/08/2002 at 18:06 UTC.

Rogers, M. L. 'Coping with alleged false sexual molestation: examination and statement procedures', *IPT Online Journal*, 2(2) 1990 (online at *http://www.ipt-forensics.com/journal/volume2/j2_2_1.htm* on 24/03/ 2002).

Sandblom, G. *Peter Ramus, I Serien Om Historiska Retoriker*, online at *http://www.utv.mh.se/~gorans/ramus.html* on 04 01 2002.

Sanford, T., J. Aked, L. Moxey and J. Mullin (1994) 'A critical examination of assumptions underlying the Cusum technique of forensic linguistics', *Forensic Linguistics* 1(2): 151–67.

Scherer, R. 'A basic overview of voice production', online at *http:// www.voicefoundation.org/VFScherervoiceprod.html* found on 25/08/ 2002 at 15:04 UTC.

Schils, E. and P. de Haan (1995) *Mortons Qsum plot Exposed*, available at *http://lands.let.kun.nl/literature/dehaan.1995.2.html* as at 30 December 2001.

Schneidman, E. S. and N. L. Farberow (1957) *Clues to Suicide*. New York: Mcgraw-Hill.

Shuy, R. W. (1997) 'Ten unanswered language questions about Miranda', *Forensic Linguistics* 4(2): 175–96.

Somers, H. 'An Attempt to Use Weighted Cusums to Identify Sublanguages'. [online].

Stamatos, E., N. Fakotakis and G. Kokkinakis [online].

Steller, M. and G. Koehnken (1989) 'Criteria-based statement analysis', in D. C. Raskin (ed.), *Psychological Methods in Criminal Investigation and Evidence*. New York: Springer, pp. 217–46.

Svartvik, J. *The Evans Statements*. Gothenburg Studies in English no. 20.

Theobald, R. (1901) *Shakespeare Studies in Baconian Light*. London: Sampson Low & Marston.

Trankell, A. (1958) 'Was Lars sexually assaulted? A study in the reliability of witnesses and of experts', *Journal of Abnormal and Social Psychology* 56: 385–95.

Triandafilou, R., M. McCullough and M. Eslea (1998) 'Using criteria-based content analysis to identify true and false allegations of bullying', symposium paper, British Psychological Society Developmental Section, Annual Conference 1998, University of Lancaster, online at *http://www.uclan.ac.uk/facs/science/psychol/bully/triand.htm* as at 25/03/2002.

Yule, G. Udney (1938) 'On sentence-length as a statistical characteristic of style in prose, with application to two cases of disputed authorship', _Biometrika_XXX (1938–39): 363–90.

Yule, G. Udney (1944) *The Statistical Study of Literary Vocabulary*. Cambridge: Cambridge University Press.

Undeutsch, U. (1967) *Beurteilung der Glaubhaftigkeit von Aussagen*, in U. Undeutsch (Hrsg.), Handbuch Forensische Psychologie. Göttingen: Hogrefe, pp. 26–181.

Williams, P. J. [online review] Riad Aziz Kassis: *The Book of Proverbs and Arabic Proverbial Works*.

Wright, L. (ed.) (2000) *The Development of Standard English, 1300–1800: Theories, Descriptions, Conflicts*. Cambridge: Cambridge University Press.

Yegnanarayana, K. S. Reddy and S. P. Kishore. 'Source and system features for speaker recognition using AANN Models', online at http://www.ee.columbia.edu/~dpwe/papers/YegRK01-aannspkrid.pdf on 08 07 2002 at 05.15.

INDEX